SOCIOLOGICAL ECONOMICS

Published in collaboration with the Maison des Sciences de l'Homme and the Centre National de la Recherche Scientifique.

For information address:

SAGE Publications Ltd
28 Banner Street
London EC1Y 8QE

SAGE Publications Inc
275 South Beverly Drive
Beverly Hills
California 90212
USA

First Printing

International Standard Book Number:
0 8039 9894 5 cloth
0 8039 9895 3 paper

Library of Congress Number: 78-055255

Printed in Great Britain by
Biddles Ltd., Guildford, Surrey

SOCIOLOGICAL ECONOMICS

Edited by
Louis Lévy-Garboua

University of Paris XIII and Centre de Recherche pour l'Etude et l'Observation des Conditions de Vie (CREDOC), France

SAGE Publications Ltd · London and Beverly Hills

CONTENTS

Part III ORGANIZATIONS

INTRODUCTION

This volume contains the papers presented at an international and interdisciplinary seminar on Sociological Economics held in Paris on 28-30 September 1977, and sponsored by the Centre National de la Recherche Scientifique and Maison des Sciences de l'Homme and by the National Science Foundation.

The papers were revised after the discussion took place with the editorial assistance of some of the English-speaking discussants. We owe our thanks especially to David Marsden.

The idea of this seminar grew out of the recognition that an increasing number of economists are interested in topics that tradition attributes to the domain of sociology, and that some of them at least are trying to incorporate into economic theory concepts borrowed from sociology and other social sciences. In the last decades, many new fields have been opened to economic analysis, such as education, the family, social interaction, irrational and deviant behavior, organizations and collective choice; this list is neither complete nor exhaustive. The explanatory power of the economic approach to social phenomena is now arousing a growing interest among sociologists and other social scientists. Economists and sociologists have therefore begun to ask themselves whether or not a bridge can be built between their two disciplines. Trying to answer this question has led them to re-examine the relevance of the economic and the sociological approaches to human behavior.

As a result the boundaries of economics and sociology are becoming blurred and a new relation of substitution is emerging. Thus, different schools of thought are more adequately distinguished by the model of human behavior to which they refer than by which domain they investigate. It can be increasingly argued that there is as much variation in the models currently in use within a given discipline as there was between disciplines. The choice of contributors to this Conference and the organization of formal discussions are intended, as far as possible, to reflect this diversity.

The first three papers are essays on *paradigms.* Sociological Economics owes a great deal to the pioneering work of Gary Becker. In his paper he characterizes the 'economic' approach by three assumptions – those of maximizing behavior, the existence of markets, and the stability of preferences – and he contends that *all* kinds of behavior can be explained within the same framework. In contrast with this comprehensive view, Jacques Lesourne offers an eclectic view. Instead of broadening the scope of economics without altering the set of concepts, as Becker does, he seeks to integrate sociological, psychological and political notions into economic theory in order to increase its relevance. He argues here that the individual behaves as a unique system constantly searching for information and allocating his efforts between and within roles, and he outlines the implications of his theory for economic dynamics. In spite of their differences, both of these views rest heavily on the assumption of rational behavior. However, Jon Elster, a philosopher of science, questions the scope and power of the rational choice model. It is not very relevant if various constraints restrict the set of possibilities too much, or if the rational solution is non-existent or unstable, and this theory should in fact be rejected if causality dominates intentionality. Elster reviews a number of anomalies of rationality which he discusses at length. His final impression is that rational behavior is certainly the best and most general assumption to be made although it is often hard to discard irrationality at some point in the interpretation of human actions.

Next come three papers on *preferences and choices.* In the first place, Louis Lévy-Garboua uses the economic approach to understand the formation of choice, a process currently overlooked by the assumption of given preferences. He argues that individuals are ignorant of their own intrinsic preferences. Since they make their decisions on the basis of the perceived characteristics of the objects of choice, that is, with less than full information, they are willing to search in order to increase their confidence in their present choice. The elaboration of this concept of confidence helps to explain many phenomena pertaining to the stability or instability of choice, such as habits, impulses, addictions, social norms and satisficing behavior. In addition, it provides a simple way in which to analyse a variety of market (eg advertising) and nonmarket (influence) mechanisms which economize on perception costs. The paper by Philippe d'Iribarne emphasizes the impossibility of using the classical choice-theoretic approach to draw normative implications on welfare. The problem arises because the conditions under which the measured consumption of goods of two individuals chosen at random can be compared in terms of welfare are so restrictive that they will never be met in practice. Thus, d'Iribarne argues that individuals' knowledge of goods from past consumption and their social environment should not be overlooked by the policy-analyst, as is often the case, and that economists should accept the need to go one step beyond the obvious and to go deeper into understanding human feelings, the true determinants of welfare. The title of Gordon Tullock's paper may seem misleading because it does not introduce any careful study of income redistribution. It is, however, another paper on choice, namely how public choices are to be implemented by an appropriate political process. In Tullock's mind, the latter should be based on the demand-revealing process (which he has described in a recent article with Tideman) as it permits much more precise adjustment of governmental behavior to people's preferences than does democracy. The trouble is that preferences with respect to redistribution do not seem to be clear at all . . . Behind the witty style of the paper lies a serious question: do we really know what we want?

The last three papers deal with *organizations.* The first two are concerned with the family while the third is about firms. Bertrand Lemennicier and Robert Michael present two studies on marital dissolution. In the former an index of the frequency of quarrels between spouses and the wife's own evaluation of her probability of divorce are inversely related to the gains from specialization within marriage. The mediating factor is the wife's decision to work in the market in view of her own earning power relative to that of her husband. The model is tested on French cross-sectional data. The second article is a concise review of recent US divorce behavior using several sets of cross-sectional data. The empirical findings are interpreted in the light of an economic theory of divorce which predicts the different factors which may, over the life-cycle, reduce the gains of marriage and the costs of divorce so that previously stable marriages are dissolved. The influence of unexpected events, decisions made after marriage, and institutional barriers to divorce, is examined in detail. While Lemennicier investigates some of the reasons why the gains from marriage are small at the outset, Michael tends to place emphasis on the reasons why they may diminish over the life cycle. Finally, the paper by Herbert Gintis and Donald Katzner looks at the production process within the firms as not purely technical. Work contracts are not totally binding so that each worker is left some freedom to act as he wants subject to the rules constituting the authority structure of the organization. It is argued that worker's preferences depend both on the decisions he may take with respect to himself and his subordinates and on a number of parameters which reflect the major lines of influence of other members of the firm (incentives, goals and premises, value orientations and information). Under these assumptions, it is shown that in most cases profit-maximizing firms tend to be inefficient with the consequence that authority relations, worker sovereignty and wage differentials cannot be said to be socially neutral.

Louis Lévy-Garboua

Part I

PARADIGMS

1

Economic Analysis and Human Behavior

Gary Becker

University of Chicago, USA

'Economy is the art of making the most of life.'
George Bernard Shaw, *Maxims for Revolutionaries*

Although few persons would dispute the distinctiveness of an 'economic' approach to human behavior, it is not easy to state exactly what distinguishes the economic approach from social, psychological, anthropological, political or even genetical approaches. In this essay I attempt to spell out the principal attributes of the economic approach.

Let us turn for guidance first to the definitions of different fields. At least three conflicting definitions of economics are still common. Economics is said to be the study of (1) the allocation of material

For valuable comments I am indebted to Joseph Ben-David, Milton Friedman, Victor Fuchs, Robert T. Michael, Jacob Mincer, Richard Posner, and T. W. Schultz. I am especially indebted to George J. Stigler for many discussions, comments, and much needed encouragement, and to Robert K. Merton for a helpful and lengthy response to an earlier draft that provided a sociologist's perspective on the issues covered in this essay. The usual disclaimer to the effect that none of these persons should be held responsible for the arguments made in this essay is especially appropriate since several disagreed with the central theme.

This essay is a revised version of the Introduction to Professor Becker's book, *The Economic Approach to Human Behavior*, University of Chicago Press, 1976.

goods to satisfy material wants;[1] (2) the market sector;[2] and (3) the allocation of scarce means to satisfy competing ends.[3]

The definition of economics in terms of material goods is the narrowest and the least satisfactory. It does not describe adequately either the market sector or what economists 'do'. For the production of tangible goods now provides less than half of all the market employment in the United States, and the intangible outputs of the service sector are now larger in value than the outputs of the goods sector (see Fuchs, 1968). Moreover, economists are as successful in understanding the production and demand for retail trade, films, or education as they are for autos or meat. The persistence of definitions which tie economics to material goods is perhaps due to a reluctance to submit certain kinds of human behavior to the 'frigid' calculus of economics.

The definition of economics in terms of scarce means and competing ends is the most general of all. It defines economics by the nature of the problem to be solved, and encompasses far more than the market sector or 'what economists do'.[4] Scarcity and choice characterize all resources allocated by the political process (including which industries to tax, how fast to increase the money supply, and whether to go to war); by the family (including decisions about a marriage mate, family size, the frequency of church attendance, and the allocation of time between sleeping and waking hours); by scientists (including decisions about allocating their thinking time and mental energy to different research problems); and so on in endless variety. This definition of economics is so broad that it often is a source of embarrassment rather than of pride to many economists, and usually is immediately qualified to exclude most nonmarket behavior.[5]

All of these definitions of economics simply define the scope, and none tells us one iota about what the 'economic' approach is. It could stress tradition and duty, impulsive behavior, maximizing behavior, or any other behavior in analyzing the market sector or the allocation of scarce means to competing ends.

Similarly, definitions of sociology and other social sciences are of equally little help in distinguishing their approaches from others. For example, the statement that sociology 'is the study of social aggregates and groups in their institutional organization, of institutions and their organization, and of causes and consequences of changes in institutions and social organization' (Reiss, 1968) does not distinguish the subject matter, let alone the approach, of sociology from, say, economics. Or the statement that 'comparative psychology is concerned with the behavior of different species of living organisms' (Waters and Brunnel, 1968) is as general as the definitions of economics and sociology, and as uninformative.

Let us turn away from definitions, therefore, because I believe that what most distinguishes economics as a discipline from other disciplines in the social sciences is not its subject matter but its approach. Indeed, many kinds of behavior fall within the subject matter of several disciplines: for example, fertility behavior is considered part of sociology, anthropology, economics, history, human biology and perhaps even politics. I contend that the economic approach is uniquely powerful because it can integrate a wide range of human behavior.

Everyone recognizes that the economic approach assumes maximizing behavior more explicitly and extensively than do other approaches, be it the utility or wealth function of the household, firm, union, or government bureau that is maximized. Moreover, the economic approach assumes the existence of markets that with varying degrees of efficiency coordinate the actions of different participants – individuals, firms, even nations – so that their behavior becomes mutually consistent. Preferences are assumed not to change substantially over time, nor to be very different between wealthy and poor persons, or even between persons in different societies and cultures.

Prices and other market instruments allocate the scarce resources within a society and thereby constrain the desires of participants and coordinate their actions. In the economic approach these market instruments perform most, if not all, of the functions assigned to 'structure' in sociological theories.[6]

The preferences that are assumed to be stable do not refer to market goods and services, like oranges, automobiles, or medical care, but to underlying objects of choice that are produced by each household using market goods and services, their own time, and other inputs. These underlying preferences are defined over fundamental aspects of life – such as health, prestige, sensual pleasure, benevolence, or envy – that do not always bear a stable relation to market goods and services (see Michael and Becker, 1973). The assumption of stable preferences provides a stable foundation for generating predictions about responses to various changes, and prevents the analyst from succumbing to the temptation of simply postulating the required shift in preferences to 'explain' all apparent contradictions to his predictions.

Maximizing behavior and stable preferences are not simply primitive assumptions, but can be derived from arguments about natural selection of suitable behavior as humans evolved over time (see Wilson, 1975; Dawkins, 1976; and Becker, 1976). Indeed, the economic approach and the modern biological theory of natural selection are closely related (recall that both Darwin and Wallace stated that they were greatly influenced by Malthusian population theory), and are perhaps different aspects of the same more basic theory (see the discussion in Hirshleifer, 1977; also see Tullock, 1971).

The combined assumptions of maximizing behavior, market equilibrium, and stable preferences, used relentlessly and unflinchingly, form the heart of the economic approach as I see it. They are responsible for the many theorems associated with this approach. For example, that (1) a rise in price reduces quantity demanded,[7] be it a rise in the market price of eggs reducing the demand for eggs, a rise in the 'shadow' price of children reducing the demand for children, or a rise in the office waiting time for physicians, which is one component of the full price of physician services, reducing the demand for their services; (2) a rise in price increases the quantity supplied, be it a rise in the market price of beef increasing the number of cattle raised and slaughtered, a rise in the wage rate offered to married women increasing their labor force participation, or a reduction in 'cruising' time raising the effective price received by taxicab drivers and thereby increasing the supply of taxicabs; (3) competitive markets satisfy consumer preferences more effectively than monopolistic markets, be it the market for aluminium or the market for ideas; or (4) a tax on the output of a market reduced that output, be it an excise tax on gasoline that reduces the use of gasoline, punishment of criminals (which is a 'tax' on crime) that reduces the amount of crime, or a tax on wages that reduces the labor supplied to the market sector.

The economic approach is clearly not restricted to material goods and wants, nor even to the market sector. Prices, be they the money prices of the market sector or the shadow imputed prices of the nonmarket sector, measure the opportunity cost of using scarce resources, and the economic approach predicts the same kind of response to shadow prices as to market prices. Consider, for example, a person whose only scarce resource is his limited amount of time. This time is used to produce various commodities that enter his preference function, the aim being to maximize utility. Even without a market sector, either directly or indirectly, each commodity has a relevant marginal shadow price, namely, the time required to produce a unit change in that commodity; in equilibrium, the ratio of these prices must equal the ratio of the marginal utilities.[8] Most importantly, an increase in the relative price of any commodity – i.e. an increase in the time required to produce a unit of that commodity - would tend to reduce the consumption of that commodity.

The economic approach does not assume that all participants in any market necessarily have complete information or engage in costless transactions. Incomplete information or costly transactions should not, however, be confused with irrational or volatile behavior.[9] The economic approach has developed a theory of the optimal or rational accumulation of costly information[10] that implies, for example, greater investment in information when undertaking major rather than minor decisions – the purchase of a house or entrance into marriage versus the purchase of a sofa or bread. The assumption that information is often seriously incomplete because it is costly to acquire is used in the economic approach to explain the same kind of behavior that is explained by irrational and volatile behavior, or traditional behavior, or 'nonrational' behavior in other discussions.

When an apparently profitable opportunity to a firm, worker, or household is not exploited, the economic approach does not take refuge in assertions about irrationality, contentment with wealth already acquired, or convenient ad hoc shifts in values (i.e. preferences). Rather, it postulates the existence of costs, monetary or psychic, of taking advantage of these opportunities that eliminate their profitability – costs that may not be easily 'seen' by outside observers. Of course, postulating the existence of costs closes or 'completes' the economic approach in the same, almost tautological, way that postulating the existence of (sometimes unobserved) uses of energy completes the energy system, and preserves the law of the conservation of energy. Systems of analysis in chemistry, genetics, and other fields are completed in a related manner. The critical question is whether a system is completed in a useful way; the important theorems derived from the economic approach indicate that it has been completed in a way that yields much more than a bundle of empty tautologies in good part because, as I indicated earlier, the assumption of stable preferences provides a foundation for predicting the responses to various changes.

Moreover, the economic approach does not assume that decision units are necessarily conscious of their efforts to maximize or can verbalize or otherwise describe in an informative way reasons for the systematic patterns in their behavior.[11] Thus, it is consistent with the emphasis on the subconscious in modern psychology and with the distinction between manifest and latent functions in sociology (Merton, 1968). In addition, the economic approach does not draw conceptual distinctions between major and minor decisions, such as those involving life and death[12] in contrast to the choice of a brand of coffee; or between decisions said to involve strong emotions and those with little emotional involvement,[13] such as in choosing a mate or the number of children in contrast to buying paint; or between decisions by persons with different incomes, education, or family backgrounds.

Indeed, I have come to the position that the economic approach is a comprehensive one that is applicable to all human behavior, be it behavior involving money prices or imputed shadow prices, repeated or infrequent decisions, large or minor decisions, emotional or mechanical ends, rich or poor persons, patients or therapists, businessmen or politicians, teachers or students. The applications of the economic approach so conceived are as extensive as the scope of economics in the definition given earlier that emphasizes scarce means and competing ends. It is an appropriate approach to go with such a broad and unqualified definition, and with the statement by Shaw which begins this essay.

The economic approach to human behavior is not new, even outside the market sector. Adam Smith often (but not always!) used this approach to understand political behavior. Jeremy Bentham was explicit about his belief that the pleasure-pain calculus is applicable to all human behavior: 'Nature has placed mankind under the governance of two sovereign masters, *pain and pleasure.* It is for them alone to point out what we ought to do as well as to determine what we shall do . . . They govern us in all we do, in all we say, in all we think' (1963). The pleasure-pain calculus is said to be applicable to *all* we do, say, and think, without restriction to monetary decisions, repetitive choices, unimportant decisions, etc. Bentham did apply his calculus to an extremely wide range of human behavior, including criminal sanctions, prison reform, legislation, usury laws, and jurisprudence as well as the markets for goods and services. Although Bentham explicitly states that the pleasure-pain calculus is applicable to what we 'shall' do as well as to what we 'ought' to do, he was primarily interested in 'ought' – he was first and foremost a reformer – and did not develop a theory of actual human behavior with many testable implications. He often became bogged down in tautologies because he did not maintain the assumption of stable preferences, and because he was more concerned about making his calculus consistent with all behavior than about deriving the restrictions it imposed on behavior.

Marx and his followers have applied what is usually called an 'economic' approach to politics, marriage, and other nonmarket behavior as well as to market behavior. But to the Marxist, the economic approach means that the organization of production is decisive in determining social and political structure, and he places much emphasis upon material goods, processes, and ends, conflict between capitalists and workers, and general subjugation of one class by another. What I have called the 'economic approach' has little in common with this view. Moreover, the Marxist, like the Benthamite, has concentrated on what ought to be, and has often emptied his approach of much predictive content in the effort to make it consistent with all events.

Needless to say, the economic approach has not provided equal insight into and understanding of all kinds of behavior: for example, the determinants of war and of many other political decisions have not yet been much illuminated by this approach (or by any other approach). I believe, however, that the limited success is mainly the result of limited effort and not lack of relevance. For, on the one hand, the economic approach has not been systematically applied to war, and its application to other kinds of political behavior is quite recent; on the other hand, much apparently equally intractable behavior – such as fertility, child-rearing, labor force participation, and other decisions of families – has been greatly illuminated in recent years by the systematic application of the economic approach.

Support for the wide applicability of the economic approach is provided by the extensive literature developed in the last twenty years that uses the economic approach to analyze an almost endlessly varied set of problems including the evolution of language (Marschak, 1965), church attendance (Azzi and Ehrenberg, 1975), political behavior (Buchanan and Tullock, 1962; Stigler, 1975), the legal system (Posner, 1973; Becker and Landes, 1974), the extinction of animals (Smith, 1975), the incidence of suicide (Hammermesh and Soss, 1974), altruism and social interactions (Becker 1974, 1976; Hirshleifer, 1977), and marriage, fertility, and divorce (Schultz, 1974; Becker et al., 1977). To convey dramatically the flavor of the economic approach, I briefly discuss several of the more unusual and controversial applications.

Good health and a long life are important aims of most persons, but surely no more than a moment's reflection is necessary to convince anyone that they are not the only aims: somewhat better health or a longer life may be sacrificed because they conflict with other aims. The economic approach implies that there is an 'optimal' expected length of life, where the value in utility of an additional year is less than the utility forgone by using time and other resources to obtain that year. Therefore, a person may be a heavy smoker or so committed to work as to omit all exercise, not necessarily because he is ignorant of the consequences or 'incapable' of using the information he possesses, but because the lifespan forfeited is not worth the cost to him of quitting smoking or working less intensively. These would be unwise decisions if a long life were the only aim, but as long as other aims exist, they could be informed and in this sense 'wise'.

According to the economic approach, therefore, *most* (if not all!) deaths are to some extent 'suicides' in the sense that they could have been postponed if more resources had been invested in prolonging life. This not only has implications for the analysis of what are ordinarily called suicides,[14] but also calls into question the common distinction between suicides and 'natural' deaths. Once again the economic approach and modern psychology come to similar conclusions since the latter emphasizes that a 'death wish' lies behind many 'accidental' deaths and others allegedly due to 'natural' causes.

The economic approach does not merely restate in language familiar to economists different behavior with regard to health, removing all possibility of error by a series of tautologies. The approach implies, for example, that both health and medical care would rise as a person's wage rate rose, that ageing would bring declining health although expenditures on medical care would rise, and that more education would induce an increase in health even though expenditures on medical care would fall. None of these or other implications are necessarily true, but all appear to be consistent with the available evidence.[15]

According to the economic approach, a person decides to marry when the utility expected from marriage exceeds that expected from remaining single or from additional search for a more suitable mate. Similarly, a married person terminates his (or her) marriage when the utility anticipated from becoming single or marrying someone else exceeds the loss in utility from separation, including losses due to physical separation from one's children, division of joint assets, legal fees, and so forth. Since many persons are looking for mates, a *market* in marriages can be said to exist: each person tries to do the best he can, given that everyone else in the market is trying to do the best they can. A sorting of persons into different marriages is said to be an equilibrium sorting if persons not married to each other in this sorting could not marry and make each other better off.

Again, the economic approach has numerous implications about behavior that could be falsified. For example, it implies that 'likes' tend to marry each other, when measured by intelligence, education, race, family background, height, and many other variables, and that 'unlikes' marry when measured by wage rates and some other variables. The implication that men with relatively high wage rates marry women with relatively low wage rates (other variables being held constant) surprises many, but appears consistent with the available data when they are adjusted for the large fraction of married women who do not work (see Becker, 1973). The economic approach also implies that higher-income persons marry younger and divorce less frequently than others, implications consistent with the available evidence (see Keeley, 1977) but not with common beliefs. Still another implication is that an increase in the relative earnings of wives increases the likelihood of marital dissolution, which partly explains the greater dissolution rate among black than white families.

According to the Heisenberg indeterminacy principle, the phenomena analyzed by physical scientists cannot be observed in a 'natural' state because their observations change these phenomena. An even stronger principle has been suggested for social scientists since they are participants as well as analysts and, therefore, are supposed to be incapable of objective observation. The economic approach makes a very different but distantly related point: namely that persons only choose to follow scholarly or other intellectual or artistic pursuits if they expect the benefits, both monetary and psychic, to exceed those available in alternative occupations. Since the criterion is the same as in the choice of more commonplace occupations, there is no obvious reason why intellectuals would be less concerned with personal rewards, more concerned with social well-being, or more intrinsically honest than others.[16]

It then follows from the economic approach that an increased demand by different interest groups or constituencies for particular intellectual arguments and conclusions would stimulate an increased supply of these arguments, by the theorem cited earlier on the effect of a rise in 'price' on quantity supplied. Similarly, a flow of foundation or government funds into particular research topics, even 'ill-advised' topics, would have no difficulty generating proposals for research on those topics. What the economic approach calls normal responses of supply to changes in demand, others may call intellectual or artistic 'prostitution' when applied to intellectual or artistic pursuits. Perhaps, but attempts to distinguish sharply the market for intellectual and artistic services from the market for 'ordinary' goods have been the source of confusion and inconsistency (see Director, 1964; Coase, 1974).

The economic approach assumes that crime is a part-time or full-time occupation like carpentry, engineering, or teaching. Persons choose to become criminals for the same reason that others choose to become carpenters or teachers; namely, because they expect the 'profit' from becoming a criminal – the present value of the series of differences between returns and costs, both nonmonetary and monetary returns and costs – to exceed the 'profit' from other occupations. An increase in return or a decrease in costs from criminal activity increases the number of persons becoming criminals by increasing the 'profit' from crime relative to other occupations.

Therefore, this approach implies that felonies like robbery and theft are committed mainly by poorer persons not because of anomie or alienation but because their deficiencies in education and other training reduce the 'profit' to them from legal occupations. Similarly, unemployment in the legal sector increases the number of crimes against property (see Ehrlich, 1973) not because of restlessness and bitterness, but because unemployment reduces the 'profit' from legal occupations. The number and severity of the crimes committed by women have been growing relative to those committed by men (see Bartel, 1976) because it has become more 'profitable' for women to participate in market occupations, including crime (see Mincer, 1963).

The most controversial implication of the economic approach to crime is that punishment 'works' in the sense that an increased probability of conviction of criminals or punishment when convicted reduces the amount of crime because returns from crime are reduced. If criminals correctly anticipated the probability and magnitude of punishments, a high rate of recidivism would be no more surprising and no more indicative of the failure of punishments than would the return to carpentry of a large fraction of unemployed or injured carpenters be indicative that the number of carpenters is unaffected by the frequency of their unemployment and injury. Similarly, rehabilitation programmes have generally failed (see Martinson, 1974) for the same reason that retraining persons in the legal sector has generally failed: when people have chosen their 'occupations', including crime, wisely, their choices would not be much affected by exhortation or by minor changes in their prospects in other occupations.

Punishments deter crimes of 'passion'[17] like rape or terrorism (see Landes, 1977) as much as 'economic' crimes like bank robbery (Ozenne, 1974) and embezzlement; among other things, this conclusion raises doubts about the insanity plea, premeditation, and other distinctions made in the conviction and sentencing of criminals. The economic approach implies that capital punishment would significantly deter murder and other crimes *if the alternative is the usual punishment for these crimes* in the United States and many other Western countries (see Ehrlich, 1975, 1977; National Academy of Science, 1977).

I am not suggesting that the economic approach is used by all economists for all human behavior or even by most economists for most human behavior. Indeed, many economists cannot resist the temptation to hide their own lack of understanding behind allegations of irrational behavior, unnecessary ignorance, folly, ad hoc shifts in values, and the like, which is simply acknowledging defeat in the guise of considered judgement. For example, if some Broadway theater-owners charge prices that result in long delays before seats are available, the owners are alleged to be ignorant of the profit-maximizing price structure rather than the analyst ignorant of why actual prices do maximize profits. When only a portion of the variation in earnings is explained, the unexplained portion is attributed to luck or chance,[18] not to ignorance of or inability to measure additional systematic components. The coal industry is called inefficient because certain cost and output calculations point in that direction (see Henderson, 1958), although an attractive alternative hypothesis is that the calculations are seriously in error.

War is said to be caused by madmen, and political behavior, more generally, dominated by folly and ignorance. Recall Keynes's remark about 'madmen in authority, who hear voices in the air' (1962: 383), and although Adam Smith, the principal founder of the economic approach, interpreted some laws and legislation in the same way that he interpreted market behavior, even he, without much discussion, lamely dismissed others as a result of folly and ignorance.[19]

Examples abound in the economic literature of changes in preferences conveniently introduced ad hoc to explain puzzling behavior. Education is said to change preferences – about different goods and services, political candidates, or family size – rather than real income or the relative cost of different choices.[20] Businessmen talk about the social responsibilities of business because their attitudes are said to be influenced by public discussions of this question rather than because such talk is necessary to maximize their profits, given the climate of public intervention. Or advertisers are alleged to take advantage of the fragility of consumer preferences, with little explanation of why, for example, advertising is heavier in some industries than others, changes in importance in a given industry over time, and occurs in quite competitive industries as well as in monopolistic ones.[21]

Naturally, what is tempting to economists nominally committed to the economic approach becomes irresistible to others without this commitment, and without a commitment to the scientific study of sociology, psychology, or anthropology. With an ingenuity worthy of admiration if put to better use, almost any conceivable behavior is alleged to be dominated by ignorance and irrationality, values and their frequent unexplained shifts, custom and tradition, the compliance somehow induced by social norms, or the ego and the id.

I do not mean to suggest that concepts like the ego and the id, or social norms, are without any scientific content. Only that they are tempting materials, as are concepts in the economic literature, for ad hoc and useless explanations of behavior. There is no apparent embarrassment in arguing, for example, both that the sharp rise in fertility during the late 1940s and early 1950s resulted from a renewed desire for large families, and that the prolonged decline starting just a few years later resulted from a reluctance to be tied down with many children. Or developing countries are supposed simply to copy the American's 'compulsiveness' about time, whereas the growing value of their own time is a more fruitful explanation of their increased effort to economize on their use of time (see Becker, 1965). More generally, custom and tradition are said to be abandoned in developing countries because their young people are seduced by Western ways; it is not recognized that while custom and tradition are quite useful in a relatively stationary environment, they are often a hindrance in a dynamic world, especially for young people (see Stigler and Becker, 1977).

Even those who believe that the economic approach is applicable to all human behavior recognize that many noneconomic variables also significantly effect human behavior. Obviously, the laws of mathematics, chemistry, physics, and biology have a tremendous influence on behavior through their influence on preferences and production possibilities. That the human body ages, that the rate of population growth equals the birth rate plus the migration rate minus the death rate, that children of more intelligent parents tend to be more intelligent than children of less intelligent parents, that people need to breathe to live, that a hybrid plant has a particular yield under one set of environmental conditions and a very different yield under another set, that gold and oil are located only in certain parts of the world and cannot be made from wood, or that an assembly line operates according to certain physical laws – all these and more influence choices, the production of people and goods, and the evolution of societies.

To say this, however, is not the same as saying that, for example, the rate of population growth is itself 'noneconomic' in the sense that birth, migration, and death rates cannot be illuminated by the economic approach, or that the rate of adoption of new hybrids is noneconomic because it cannot be explained by the economic approach. Indeed, useful implications about the number of children in different families have been obtained by assuming that families maximize their utility from stable preferences subject to a constraint on their resources and prices, with resources and prices partly determined by the gestation period for pregnancies, the abilities of children, and other noneconomic variables (see Becker, 1960; Becker and Lewis, 1973; Schultz, 1974). Similarly, the rate of adoption of hybrid corn in different parts of the United States has been neatly explained by assuming that farmers maximize profits: new hybrids were more profitable, and thus adopted earlier, in some parts because weather, soil, and other physical conditions were more favorable (Griliches, 1957).

Just as many noneconomic variables are necessary for understanding human behavior, so too are the contributions of sociologists, psychologists, sociobiologists, historians, anthropologists, political scientists, lawyers, and others. Although I am arguing that the economic approach provides a useful framework for understanding all human behavior, I am not trying to downgrade the contributions of other disciplines, or even to suggest that the economists' are more important. For example, the preferences that are given and stable in the economic approach, and that determine the predictions from this approach, are analyzed by sociologists, psychologists, and potentially most successfully in judgement by the sociobiologist (see Wilson, 1975). How preferences have become what they are, and their perhaps slow evolution over time, are obviously relevant in predicting and understanding behavior. The value of some other disciplines is not diminished even by an enthusiastic and complete acceptance of the economic approach.

At the same time, however, I do not want to soften the impact of what I am saying in the interest of increasing its acceptability in the short run. I am saying that the economic approach provides a valuable unified framework for understanding all human behavior, although I recognize, of course, that much behavior is not yet understood, and that non-economic variables and the techniques and findings from other fields contribute to the understanding of human behavior. A comprehensive *framework* is provided by the economic approach, although some of the important concepts and techniques are provided and will continue to be provided by other disciplines.

The heart of my argument is that human behavior is not compartmentalized, sometimes based on maximizing, sometimes not, sometimes motivated by stable preferences, sometimes by volatile ones, sometimes resulting in an optimal accumulation of information, sometimes not. Rather, all human behavior can be viewed as involving participants who maximize their utility from a stable set of preferences and accumulate an optimal amount of information and other inputs in a variety of markets.

If this argument is correct, the economic approach provides a unified framework for understanding behavior that has long been sought by and eluded Bentham, Comte, Marx, and others.

Notes

1. '[Economics] is the social science that deals with the ways in which men and societies seek to satisfy their material needs and desires', Albert Rees (1968); '[Economics is the] study of the supplying of man's physical needs and wants', art. 'Economics', *The Columbia Encyclopedia,* 3rd edn, p. 624; and see the many earlier references to Marshall, Cannan, and others in Robbins (1962).

2. Pigou (1962: 11) said '[Economic welfare is] that part of social welfare that can be brought directly or indirectly into relation with the measuring rod of money'.

3. 'Economics is the science which studies human behavior as a relationship between ends and scarce means which have alternative uses', Robbins (1962: 16); 'Economics . . . is the study of the allocation of scarce resources among unlimited and competing uses', Rees (1968) and many other references.

4. Boulding (1966) attributes this definition of economics to Jacob Viner.

5. Almost immediately after giving the broad definition of economics, Rees (1968) gives one in terms of material needs, without explaining why he so greatly reduced the scope of economics. Even Robbins, after an excellent discussion of what an economic problem is in the first chapter of his classic work on the nature and scope of economics (1962), basically restricts his analysis in later chapters to the market sector.

6. An excellent statement of structural analysis can be found in Merton (1975).

7. That maximizing behavior is not necessary to reach this conclusion is shown in Becker (1962).

8. He maximizes $U = U(Z_1 \ldots Z_m)$ subject to

$$Z_i = f_t\ (t_i)$$

and

$$\sum_{i=1}^{m} t_i = t,$$

where Z_i is the ith commodity, f_i the production function for Z_i, and t_i is the time input into Z_i. The well-known first-order equilibrium conditions for the allocation of his scarce resource, time, are

$$\frac{\partial U}{\partial Z_i} = \lambda \frac{\partial t_i}{\partial Z_i} = \frac{\lambda}{\partial Z_i / \partial t_i} = \frac{\lambda}{MP_{t_i}},$$

where λ is his marginal utility of time.

9. Schumpeter appears to confuse them, although with considerable modification (1950: ch. 21, section 'Human Nature in Politics').

10. The pioneering paper is Stigler's 'The Economics of Information' (1961).

11. This point is stressed in Milton Friedman's seminal article, 'The Methodology of Positive Economics' (1953).

12. The length of life itself is a decision variable in the important study by Grossman (1972).

13. Jeremy Bentham said 'As to the proposition that passion does not calculate, this, like most of these very general and oracular propositions is not true . . ., I would not say that even a madman does not calculate. Passion calculates, more or less, in every man' (1963). He does add, however, that 'of all passions, the most given to calculation . . . [is] the motive of pecuniary interest'.

14. Some of these implications are developed in Hammermesh and Soss (1974).

15. These implications are derived, and the evidence is examined, in Grossman (1972).

16. This example is taken from Stigler (1976). Also see the discussion of the reward system in science and of related issues in Merton (1973: esp. part 4).

17. Even passion calculates; see the quotation from Bentham in note 13.

18. An extreme example is Jencks (1972). Jencks even grossly understates the portion that can be explained because he neglects the important work by Mincer and others (see especially Mincer, 1974).

19. See Stigler (1971). Smith does not indicate why ignorance is dominant in the passage of certain laws and not others.

20. For an interpretation of the effects of education on consumption entirely in terms of income and price effects, Michael (1972).

21. For an analysis of advertising that is consistent with stable preferences and implies that advertising might even be more important in competitive than monopolistic industries, see Stigler and Becker (1977). For a good discussion of advertising that also does not rely on shifts in preferences, see Nelson (1975).

References

AZZI, C. and R. EHRENBERG (1975) 'Household Allocation of Time and Church Attendance', *Journal of Political Economy* 83 (February).

BARTEL, A. P. (1976) 'Women and Crime: An Economic Analysis', Graduate School of Business, Columbia University Research Paper No. 143.

BECKER, G. S. (1960) 'An Economic Analysis of Fertility', in: *Demographic and Economic Change in Developed Countries,* a Conference of the Universities-National Bureau Committee for Economic Research. Princetown University Press for the National Bureau of Economic Research.

-- (1962) 'Irrational Behavior and Economic Theory', *Journal of Political Economy* 70 (February).

-- (1964) (1st edn.); (1975) (2nd edn.) *Human Capital: A Theoretical and Empirical Analysis.* New York: Columbia University Press for the National Bureau of Economic Research.

-- (1965) 'A Theory of the Allocation of Time', *Economic Journal* 75 (September).

-- (1973) 'A Theory of Marriage, Part 1', *Journal of Political Economy* 81 (August).

-- (1974) 'A Theory of Social Interactions', *Journal of Political Economy* 82 (December).

-- (1976) 'Altruism, Egoism, and Genetic Fitness: Economics and Sociobiology, *Journal of Economic Literature* 14 (September).

-- and W. M. LANDES (eds.) (1974) *Essays in the Economics of Crime and Punishment.* New York: Columbia University Press for the National Bureau of Economic Research.

-- and H. G. LEWIS (1973) 'On the Interaction Between the Quantity and Quality of Children', *Journal of Political Economy* 81 (2) (April).

-- E. LANDES and R. T. MICHAEL (1977) 'An Economic Analysis of Marital Instability', *Journal of Political Economy* 85 (December).

BENTHAM, J. (1963) *An Introduction to the Principles of Morals and Legislation.* New York: Hafner.

BOULDING, K. (1966) *Economic Analysis.* New York: Harper & Row.

BUCHANAN, J. M. and G. TULLOCK (1962) *The Calculus of Consent.* Ann Arbor: University of Michigan Press.

COASE, R. H. (1974) 'The Market for Goods and the Market for Ideas', *American Economic Review* 64 (May).

DAWKINS, R. (1976) *The Selfish Gene.* New York: Oxford University Press.

DIRECTOR, A. (1964) 'The Parity of the Economic Market Place', *Journal of Law and Economics* 7 (October).

EHRLICH, I. (1973) 'Participation in Illegitimate Activities: A Theoretical and Empirical Investigation', *Journal of Political Economy* 81 (May/June).

-- (1975) 'Capital Punishment: A Case of Life or Death', *American Economic Review* 65 (June).

-- (1977) 'Capital Punishment and Deterrence: Some Further Thoughts and Additional Evidence', *Journal of Political Economy* 85 (August).

FRIEDMAN, M. (1953) 'The Methodology of Positive Economics', in: *Essays in Positive Economics.* Chicago: University of Chicago Press.

FUCHS, V. (1968) *The Service Economy.* New York: Columbia University Press for the National Bureau of Economic Research.

GRILICHES, Z. (1957) 'Hybrid Corn: A Exploration in the Economics of "Technical Change" ', *Econometrica* 25 (October).

GROSSMAN, M. (1972) *The Demand for Health: A Theoretical and Empirical Investigation.* New York: Columbia University Press for the National Bureau of Economic Research.

HAMMERMESH, D. and N. M. SOSS (1974) 'An Economic Theory of Suicide', *Journal of Political Economy* 82 (January/February).

HENDERSON, J. M. (1958) *The Efficiency of the Coal Industry: An Application of Linear Programming.* Cambridge: Harvard University Press.

HIRSHLEIFER, J. (1977) 'Economics from a Biological Viewpoint', *Journal of Law and Economics* 20 (April).

JENCKS, C. (1972) *Inequality.* New York: Basic Books.

KEELEY, M. C. (1977) 'The Economics of Family Formation', *Economic Inquiry* 15 (April).

KEYNES, J. M. (1962) *The General Theory of Employment, Interest, and Money.* New York: Harcourt, Brace and World.

LANDES, W. (1977) 'Fear of Flying: An Economic Study of U.S. Aircraft Hijacking.' Mimeographed. University of Chicago.

MARSCHAK, J. (1965) 'Economics of Language', *Behavioral Science* 10 (April).

MARTINSON, R. (1974) 'What Works? – Questions and Answers about Prison Reform', *Public Interest* no. 35 (Spring).

MERTON, R. K. (1968) *Social Theory and Social Structure.* New York: Free Press.

-- (1973) *The Sociology of Science.* University of Chicago Press.

-- (1975) 'Structural Analysis in Sociology', in: P. M. BLAU (ed.), *Approaches to the Study of Social Structure.* New York: Free Press.

MICHAEL, R. T. (1972) *The Effect of Education on Efficiency in Consumption.* New York: National Bureau of Economic Research.

-- and G. S. BECKER (1973) 'On the New Theory of Consumer Behavior', *The Swedish Journal of Economics* 75 (September).

MINCER, J. (1963) 'Labor Force Participation of Married Women', in: *Aspects of Labor Economics.* New York: National Bureau of Economic Research.

—— (1974) *Schooling, Experience, and Earnings.* New York: Columbia University Press for the National Bureau of Economic Research.

NATIONAL ACADEMY OF SCIENCE (NATIONAL RESEARCH COUNCIL) (1977) 'Report of the Panel on Research on Deterrent and Incapacitative Effects.' Mimeo.

NELSON, P. J. (1975) 'The Economic Consequence of Advertising', *Journal of Business* 48 (April).

OZENNE, T. (1974) 'The Economics of Bank Robbery', *Journal of Legal Studies* 3 (January).

PIGOU, A. (1962) *The Economics of Welfare,* 4th edn. New York: St Martin's Press.

POSNER, R. (1973) *Economic Analysis of Law.* Boston: Little, Brown.

REES, A. (1968) 'Economics', in: D. E. SILLS (ed.), *International Encyclopedia of the Social Sciences.* New York: Macmillan and Free Press.

REISS, A. J. (1968) 'Sociology', in: D. E. SILLS (ed.), *International Encyclopedia of the Social Sciences.* New York: Macmillan and Free Press.

ROBBINS, L. (1962) *The Nature and Significance of Economic Science.* London: Macmillan.

SCHULTZ, T. W. (ed.) (1974) *Economics of the Family: Marriage, Children, and Human Capital.* University of Chicago Press for the National Bureau of Economic Research.

SCHUMPETER, J. (1942) *Capitalism, Socialism, and Democracy.* Reprinted in New York: Harper, 1950.

SMITH, V. (1975) 'The Primitive Hunter Culture, Pleistocene Extinction, and the Rise of Agriculture', *Journal of Political Economy* 83 (August).

STIGLER, G. J. (1961) 'The Economics of Information', *Journal of Political Economy* 69 (June).

—— (1971) 'Smith's Travels on the Ship of State', *History of Political Economy* 69 (June).

—— (1975) *The Citizen and the State.* Chicago: University of Chicago Press.

—— (1976) 'Do Economists Matter?', *Southern Economic Journal* 42 (January)

—— and G. S. BECKER (1977) 'De Gustibus Non Est Disputandum', *American Economic Review* 67 (March).

TULLOCK, G. (1971) 'The Coal Tit as a Careful Shopper', *American Naturalist* (January-February).

WATERS, R. H. and B. N. BRUNNELL (1968) 'Comparative Psychology', in: D. E. SILLS (ed.), *International Encyclopedia of the Social Sciences.* New York: Macmillan and Free Press.

WILSON, E. O. (1975) *Sociobiology.* Cambridge: Harvard University Press.

• Comment

François Bourricaud

University of Paris V, France

As I see it my task is twofold. First I have to introduce the general discussion, but I have also to spell out my own reaction to the paper presented to our group. I must confess that I feel somewhat puzzled and uneasy. On many counts I feel myself quite near to Gary Becker's position, but on the other hand I can't subscribe to them in toto because they seem to me too dependent on a one-sided interpretation of what constitutes 'rational behaviour'.

Becker contrasts two current definitions of economics: that which seeks to define it by its scope or field and that which seeks to characterize it as a specific type of action with its own logic – the logic of exchange between two or more partners aiming to maximize their personal and collective advantage. The merit of the second definition is that it allows us to distinguish economic action from merely instrumental or technological action but it obviously raises many questions as to the nature of exchange itself, and the status of the partners.

So far so good. I am wholly in favour of this position because it forces us, when confronted with unexpected or paradoxical facts, to avoid the simplistic hypothesis that certain acts are 'irrational', that people behave 'passively', or obey by obsolete tradition, or that they can just be 'manipulated'. Sociologists, at least those who oppose the theoretical orientation that Jean Piaget calls 'réalisme totalitaire' cannot but feel in agreement with a conception of social action which gives back to the actor his resources of information, evaluation and decision. From this point of view Becker's proposals are very welcome. Finally, he offers us a theory which goes beyond normal market and monetary exchange, involving hypothesis about the capacity of actors to combine different categories of resources like time and information according to a scale of stable preferences and explicit constraints. So a bridge is built between economic analysis and the sociological theory of social structures (see note 6 where an explicit reference to the Mertonian scheme is proposed). Moreover, he seems to me to be interested in broadening the field of possible comparison to include other sociological contributions, like Parsons's view of institutions defined as a balance between constraints and preferences made compatible by more or less strictly defined conditions. (The meaning of my reference to Parsons will become clear at the end of my comment.)

Now let us turn to the difficulty and obscurities which cloud Becker's thesis. They all have to do with his uni-dimensional conception of rationality. I am ready to admit that apparently 'unselfish' activities like education, leisure, and cultural pursuits have a price or at least a shadow price. Even when we deal with an activity which, at first sight, looks a pole apart from the economic calculus, such as the decision to read a poem or listen to a symphony, the notion of opportunity cost is relevant. It recalls that reading Victor Hugo or listening to Beethoven means that in the end I shall have to incur an expense, which I could otherwise have avoided, for shining my shoes or fixing a lock. Similarly, it is quite meaningful to assess the cost the individual incurs when he studies for a university degree, or the cost for the collectivity which supports him when he is at school.

But if every benefit has a cost and consequently a price, costs and benefits are not homogeneous. Thus, an expression like 'shadow price' refers to quite distinct social situations. Let us suppose that to go down to Bordeaux I have to decide whether to travel by train or by plane. I can measure the net extra-cost I have to pay if I fly – given that by flying I pay more money – but I save time. But suppose now I have to decide in a tricky matter whether to take up the challenge and behave as an 'homme d'honneur', though it may cost me a good deal of money. In this case, I not only face the problem of comparing a cost and a benefit in the same value unit – time or money – but I have to decide which criterion or rod should be applied.

Let me resort to a tale. An old man takes his young bride on a journey around the world. The old man dies on the ship not too far off the coast of Ceylon. The young widow has to make a first choice: will she bring the corpse back to France in order to bury it there? That will cost her 10,000 francs, but if she decides to have the body thrown overboard it will only cost 5,000 francs. Moreover, the ticket that her late husband has paid for will be lost for the part of the journey which has not yet been completed. It happens that the tour operator is quite ready to substitute, for the remainder of the trip, any person that the widow will indicate. So why should not she invite her young lover who at the time is staying at Tahiti to join the party? The lady in fact carries out two sets of very distinct comparisons. On the one hand she compares various opportunities from the viewpoint of benefit: pay for sending the corpse of the poor man back home or throw it overboard; lose the last section of the ticket or take someone and enjoy the opportunity. But it happens that the corpse is not just anyone's corpse but that of the lady's husband – and the person who will take advantage of the ticket is not an indefinite X, but the widow's lover. These circumstances, which are not taken into account in a strictly economic calculation, are important from the view of the moral judgement. Finally, the lady decides to end the journey with her lover instead of remaining shrouded in sorrow and affliction. Moreover, when she decides to behave either as a widow or as a loving woman, she makes an overall choice which doesn't lend itself to a series of partial and marginal adjustments. What characterizes a moral choice or commitment is that whatever it costs it is binding on us and that it has the form of a choice between incompatible alternatives.

I agree with Becker that the concept of cost-benefit and the trade off between one and the other is of extreme importance, relevance and generality. The point which seems doubtful to me is the implicit assumption that costs and benefits may be treated as if they were homogeneous and immediately comparable quantities, and that the logic of comparison is the same whatever the nature of the values between which choice takes place. In my view a theory of rational action which rightly pretends to treat action in terms of calculus and choice must start by recognizing that the values and criteria which regulate our choice are heterogeneous. It is quite legitimate to ask when I do give priority to economic criteria, and when to moral or aesthetic criteria. However, action does not only involve comparison between homogeneous costs and benefits, it also involves the perception of dissonance or even dilemma, which put us before 'l'embarras du choix'. A politician who calculates in terms of the success or failure of a long-range national plan does not decide according to the same logic as the businessman who makes decisions on the basis of profit and liquidity. The same actor may in succession decide according to one logic and the other, but he may also at a particular moment have to choose between one or other logic.

The point which really puzzles me is how the plurality of values and criteria is dealt with in any attempt at generalization of the scheme of economic exchange and calculus to the various fields of social action. That is the real challenge that any theory of action has to meet and I am not convinced that these questions are given adequate attention in Becker's paper.

2

Economic Dynamics and Individual Behaviour

Jacques Lesourne

Conservatoire National des Arts et Métiers, Paris, France

A broadening of the economic modelling of individual behaviour is certainly, as Becker (1976) has constantly stressed, exceedingly important for the social sciences, but this broadening may be conceived with slightly different goals. While Becker's approach is, to a certain extent, concerned with sociological problems – and I am convinced of the fruitfulness of such an approach – I myself am exclusively aiming at an extension of economic theory.

Such an extension – which would be more in line with the French concept of 'Economie Politique', though keeping the rigour of present economic theory – could be built around five notions which, under various names, are gaining wider and wider recognition in economic publications.

(1) The notion of *resource*, as used by authors like Dahl in political science, includes not only the conventional public and private goods of economics, but anything through which an individual may influence the situations of others: physical strength, the right to give absolution, a vote in Parliament, etc.

(2) The notion of the *individual* – not of slices of individuals, as in usual theory, but of complete beings, eating and drinking, voting, taking decisions in their professional lives, and constantly establishing bridges between their various spheres of activity.

(3) The notion of the *organization*, an organization bringing individuals together on a permanent basis, with the purpose of putting into

operation given processes. A corporate firm, a church, a ministerial department, a public agency, a household, are all organizations of different kinds.

(4) The notion of *process* (electoral process, information process, transportation process, schooling process), a process transforming one bundle of resources into another. With such a definition, the market is a process, and so is the public distribution of food among poor individuals in times of famine.

(5) The notion of *constraint*, which includes not only physical possibilities, but also rules of any kind as they appear in various societies.

This paper is centred on the second notion (the *individual*). However, since such a subject is far too vast, we shall deal essentially with the implications for *economic dynamics* of a broadening of the representation of individual behaviour. As a prerequisite, we shall have to introduce, in the first part of the paper, the elements of the theory of the individual which is proposed when the economy lasts for only one period, and when the environment includes no uncertainty.

Of course, any attempt to broaden the concepts of a science must bring proof of its efficiency. Facts which were not consistently explained before have to enter the realm of what is deduced within the new framework, and the set of the new notions introduced has to be, in some sense, 'minimal' with respect to the enlargment of the set of interpreted facts. Owing to limitations of space, this paper will not discuss the adequacy – from this point of view – of the theory proposed.

Basic concepts for a theory of the individual

The two topics which have to be explored in order to sketch, in its simplest form, a theory of the individual, are the characteristics of individual behaviour and the nature of constraints. It is then possible to list a few of the theoretical fields in economics which may benefit from it.

Individual characteristics

In traditional theory, utility is defined as a function of the consumption bundle, leisure being one of the possible consumptions. Lancaster

(1971) has inserted, between the two, the characteristics of the goods in which the individual is interested, these characteristics being present in varying proportions in the different goods.

We have proposed a four-step formulation (see Figure 1).

(i) The state of the economy being described by the values of a set of parameters, the individual is concerned by a subset of these parameters. This subset is, of course, not necessarily limited to the individual's consumptions, and includes variables of the type commonly considered by Becker. Thus, the first element, the *individual social state* is introduced.

(ii) The individual is not directly sensitive to the individual social state, but to his *perception* of it, the *perceived individual social state.* Among the dimensions of such a state are found not only Lancaster's characteristics, but other perceived properties of the real situation. This separation of reality from perception is essential, since the purpose of many economic actions is to transform individual perceptions.

(iii) Psychological studies in market research constantly show the importance, for individuals, of underlying motivations concerned with power, prestige, comfort, curiosity, etc. An *ordinal satisfaction scale* may be associated with each of these motivations. Hence, a perceived individual social state corresponds to a point in a satisfaction space.

(iv) Finally, *utility* is defined as a function from the satisfaction space to the real-line.

The separation made between the second and the third step is operational. For instance, surveys make it possible to check whether an advertising campaign alters the perception of a product by a given individual, or modifies the motivations satisfied by the consumption of this product. Of course, it may not always be possible to identify the steps with a purely econometric analysis.

An individual acts to improve his utility through his behaviour. For the elaboration of an adequate theory of the individual, it would appear to be important to distinguish the various elements of this behaviour.

In elementary theory the problem is meaningless, since the individual directly selects the commodity bundle in which he is interested. But real behaviour is frequently much more indirect.

We propose to break down behaviour into five components (see Figure 2):

(a) the search for information about roles which could be played by the individual;

(b) the selection of roles;

(c) the search for information about allocations available within roles;
(d) the selection of the allocations which will be performed; and
(e) the amount of effort put into a given allocation.

For example, a young man may look for information about the various athletic activities available; he may decide to become a 400 m runner; he looks for information about the various races to which he may have access; he decides to take part in some of them; he puts more or less effort into the preparation and the running of a given race.

The first four components result from a double dichotomy: role – allocation; search for information – action. Like choosing an investment in a firm's theory, the choice of a role has a flavour of irreversibility. The last component corresponds to the idea that, through effort, the individual may influence the efficiency with which an allocation is performed.[1]

This leads us to the next concept, the concept of individual *capability* (or ability). If dimensions of capability are introduced, an individual may be attributed a value for each dimension, and his situation is thus characterized by a point in a capability space.

Although economic literature constantly refers to individual capability – for instance, in the theory of human capital or in the theory of optimal taxation – it does not seem to take into consideration the fact that capability may be as important in describing an individual as his utility function. In conjunction with effort, capability directly influences the consequences of acts; but it also helps the individual to relax the constraints which limit his possibilities.

The last task is to relate individual acts and individual social states. The simplest hypothesis is to assume that the individual forecasts with perfect accuracy the perceived individual social state which his acts will generate. However, weaker hypotheses may be nearer to reality.

Constraints

About 15 years ago various authors introduced, separately, time constraints on individual behaviour. This is just one example of the various constraints which should be considered if the limits imposed on individual action are to be properly represented. Here is a list of such constraints:

(i) time constraints;

(ii) health constraints (some acts by an individual may lead to his death or to a serious deterioration of his health; his survival and his health are influenced by the socio-economic and physical environment; the two main characteristics of an individual, his utility and his capability, depend upon his state of health);

(iii) constraints on the structure of roles which it is socially acceptable to play simultaneously;

(iv) capability constraints defining the set of roles which are known and, for each role, the set of allocations which are known;

(vi) income constraints;

(vii) regulation constraints (procedures to be followed within a firm, obligation to comply with the law of the country where one lives, etc.); and

(viii) technical constraints limiting the possibility of using a process.

One of the inadequacies of present economic theory is that it generally omits most of the above constraints, although their existence has an essential influence on the resulting economic states.

Applications

The model that has just been sketched may be used for broadening economic theory in various fields (Lesourne, 1977b):

(a) in demand analysis (for instance, advertising has the double effect of altering perceptions and relaxing information constraints, etc.) and in labour supply analysis (through attitudes towards search and preferences for roles);

(b) in organization theory (an important feature being the interaction between information and capability);

(c) in competition theory (for instance, the outcome of perfect competition is quite different when the managers' utilities and capabilities are reintroduced) (Lesourne, 1977a); and

(d) in equilibrium theory and in optimum theory (possibility of diverting resources to alter others' perceptions; influence of additional constraints on equilibria; profoundly changed meaning of a Paretian optimum in utilities, when the utilities include the characteristics of professional roles and allocations, etc.).

In addition, any improvement in the representation of human behaviour makes possible new developments in applied economics. This was clearly shown 15 years ago by the impact of the introduction of time constraints upon urban, transportation and regional economics.

Keeping the same basic concepts, but introducing time, we would like to examine in the second part of this paper the implications of individual behaviour for economic dynamics. We shall not try to be exhaustive or rigorous. Our purpose is rather to sketch a part of a research programme.

Implications of a theory of the individual for economic dynamics

Two different situations may be imagined. In the first, the individual is sensitive only to his present individual social state. We shall say that he has a spot utility. In the second, the individual takes into account his future individual social states until the time of his death. This is the usual case of a multiperiod utility.

Spot utility

In this section we explore the situations in which the individual maximizes a *spot utility function* by trying to manipulate his perceived individual social state. But this utility function may be altered through time by a learning process.

Let us look at Figure 3. Without defining the sets in which the various variables lie (to shorten the discussion), we have to introduce the following mappings:

α = the mapping of the individual social state e_t into the perceived social state e_t';

β = the mapping of the perceived social state e_t' into the satisfaction levels S_t;

s = the mapping of the satisfaction levels into utility U_t;

δ = the mapping of the acts a_t into the *expected* perceived social state $e_t'*$;

ϵ = the mapping of the acts a_t into the individual social state e_t which they will generate.

The individual chooses a_t so as to maximize $U_t\ [S_t(e_t'\ *)]$ and obtains only $U_t\ \{ S_t\ [e_t'(e_t)] \}$. Let us consider the various possibilities.

(1) *The mapping s may or may not be fixed through time.* When it is fixed, it means that the individual psychology is given; but, contrary to what happens in elementary theory, the theory proposed does not, in this case, rule out all dynamic processes.

(2) *The individual forecasts may or may not be perfect.* If they are, the individual correctly guesses that his acts a_t will generate an individual social state e'_t. Hence, in terms of mappings:

$\delta = \alpha \cdot \epsilon.$

(3) *The mapping β may be fixed or change as a consequence of a learning process* (the more I drive a prestigious car, the prouder I am of it).

(4) *The mapping α may be fixed or change as a consequence of a learning process* (the more I drive a car, the more comfortable I find it – though I may not be very much interested in comfort).

When mappings do change through time, this may be the outcome of the individual's history (sequences of individual social states, of satisfaction levels, etc.) or of others' actions (sequences of advertising campaigns, imitation processes, etc.). Figure 4 reproduces some of the most interesting cases. We shall discuss them briefly, starting from the lower part of the tree.

(1) *As a consequence of his own experience, the individual adapts his perception of the environment and consequently adapts his behaviour.* Example: A new washing powder is introduced. The housewife 'believes' it is better than the preceding ones and buys it. But, progressively, she becomes convinced that the difference is negligible. Hence, its sales have a regular tendency to decrease. To fight this trend the producer maintains a flow of advertising the purpose of which is to try to maintain the discrepancy between perception and reality.

(2) *The individual finds certain states more and more gratifying (or ungratifying) for given motivations.* Example: He becomes more and more accustomed to tobacco, and a cigarette helps him to have a fuller confidence in himself in tense situations. These progressive changes in the relations between consumption and satisfaction levels induce a regular increase (or decrease) in the consumption level.

The learning process of the individual can, of course, be altered by external social influences, but they have to be deeper than in the previous case, since here they must transform the extent to which a given state satisfies the various motivations. Advertising, for instance, is far less effective in this than it is in changing the image.

(3) *The individual learns to forecast more accurately the consequences of his acts.* In other words, assuming that one can define a 'distance' in the space of all mappings like δ, the distance $d(\delta, \alpha \circ \epsilon)$ decreases for the states which have been experienced. Of course, the individual capability should have an influence on the speed and on the final quality of the adjustment. Example: An individual who wants promotion tries to obtain it through a first protector. If nothing happens, he progressively realizes that this protector is less powerful than he thought, and he decides to look for the help of a different protector. The anecdote may be transposed to the case of a manager who wants to increase his share of the market through buying up a competitor. He decides to negotiate with a first firm, then realizes that he will not succeed, and tries with a second.

(4) *The utility of the individual changes.* This may be because of his age, his health, his increasing (or declining) capability, the loss of his wife, drug addiction, etc. Contrary to many superficial theories, psychosociological studies show that the relation between satisfaction levels and utility are easily influenced by the promotional actions of other economic agents. Those who condemn the 'consumer society' frequently attribute to corporate firms the ability to influence individual behaviour at this level; but the real impact concerns only the images, or sometimes their association with satisfactions.

Nevertheless, it is important, for economic theory, to be able to represent *endogenous* utility changes, since this introduces the long-term impact of economic systems on values, i.e. one of the loops through which the economic system is deeply altered (Lesourne, 1977a). For this reason, the next paragraph will be devoted to a brief discussion of this topic.

The changes in the utility function itself should normally result either from the *individual's past experience* or from *his expectations.* In the spot utility model the introduction of future expectations has little meaning. So we shall limit our comments here to the consideration of *past experience*. An assumption made by some authors (Krelle, 1970; Lluch, 1974) is that the individual retains a damped memory of his past consumptions. For instance, if $q(t) > 0$ is the consumption rate of a certain good at time t, the corresponding 'stock of habit' of the individual, $\sigma(t)$ is given by:

$$\sigma = \int_0^t \dot{q} e^{-\rho(t-\tau)} d\tau, \quad \text{which may also be written } \dot{\sigma} = \dot{q} - \rho\sigma \qquad (\rho > 0),$$

or by:

$$\sigma = \int_0^t q e^{-\rho(t-\tau)} d\tau, \quad \text{which may also be written } \dot{\sigma} = q - \rho\sigma \qquad (\rho > 0)$$

($\dot{q}$ being the derivative of $q(t)$ with respect to time), and the utility includes $q(t)$ as the level of consumption of a particular good and $\sigma(t)$ as a parameter influencing the choices. More precisely, it may be supposed that the higher the 'stock of habit', the lower the satisfaction levels $S\ [q\ (t),\sigma(t)]$ associated with a given rate of consumption $q(t)$, these levels tending towards a limit $S_0\ [q_0]$ when a consumption pattern has been maintained for a long period of time.

If there is another consumption good, like leisure, $l(t)$, for which there is no habit formation, the individual utility at time t may be written:

$$U_t = U\ \{\ l(t), S\ [q(t), \sigma(t)]\ \}\ .$$

Since, through habit formation, the marginal utility of the consumption of a particular good may tend to increase through time, the individual may be willing to decrease $l(t)$, and hence to work harder and to look for a higher income in order to increase $q(t)$. Such a model represents some commonly observed facts. This way of representing changes in the utility function is probably not the best, but what it is important to stress here is the need for economic theory to explore this topic further.

The various dynamics described till now involve only the mappings from behaviour into utility. For this reason we shall call them *internal*. But they are not the only ones appearing in the spot utility case.

A different type of dynamics results either from changes in the *constraints* or from transformations in *other characteristics of the individual.* For example:

(a) *Capability* is not constant through time, but is generally improved by individual action. The change in capability has, in its turn, an impact on the perception of reality, on the forecasts of consequences of acts, possibly on utility itself. In addition, capability constraints, and information constraints become less severe when capability increases.

(b) The state of *health* of the individual may not only, as mentioned above, influence utility, but may also modify capability or impose certain consumptions in order to avoid its deterioration.

(c) More generally, the individual's past and present acts may alter the future *constraints*. For instance, information is progressively accumulated through search.

This second series of dynamics will be called *external.*

Hence, even with the heroic assumption of a totally short-sighted individual, it is possible to show some transformation, through time, of individual behaviour which present some interest for economic theory. It should be stressed that these transformations are not necessarily induced from outside. For instance, an individual for whom curiosity is an important motivation will constantly maintain a certain level of information search, progressively altering his information constraints.

The above analysis can be applied to many fields of economic theory. For example:

(a) the study of the diffusion, through time, of the consumption of a product in a given population; the description of the progressive changes in the types of consumption of a given product;

(b) the economics of health;

(c) the economics of education and the description of the impact on behaviour of an increased capability;

(d) the economics of labour as far as the transformation of labour supply through time is concerned;

(e) the study of forecasting learning processes in organizations or on markets; and

(f) the analysis of a progressive transformation of the structure of the economic system through its impact on individual values.

Multiperiod utility

The distinction between *internal* and *external* dynamics is still valid, but the bulk of the progress made in recent years has been in the exploration of *external dynamics.* The individual is supposed to have a given utility function defined on all the possible consequences of his acts during his lifetime, and to be able to forecast the consequences of his act either perfectly, or with a probability distribution.

- An example of perfect forecasting is given, among many others, by the synthesis on 'human capital and labour supply' by Blinder and Weiss (1976). Here, the changes in individual situation are induced by (i) the change in assets resulting from savings, and (ii) the change in human capital resulting from the opposite effects of learning and depreciation.
- Other papers explore the consumption policies of an individual in an

uncertain world (Levhari and Srinivasan, 1969; Hahn, 1970; Hakanson, 1970; etc.).

But much still remains to be done if individual external dynamics are to be explored consistently. (An interesting problem is, for instance, to describe individual behaviour when the outside economy is regularly increasing or passes through expansion and recession periods; another is to characterize capability transformations or constraint alterations such that the individual's behaviour shows sudden discontinuities at certain times.)

Let us now consider *internal* dynamics, with two periods only, in order to simplify matters. Dropping the index t for time, we have:

$U = U(S_1, S_2)$,

S_1, S_2 being the vectors of satisfaction levels for the two periods. It is now necessary to introduce the two components characterizing the environment with which the individual is confronted before he acts in period 2:

f_2, the part of the environment controlled by the individual through his acts in period 1 (for instance, the assets available to the individual at the beginning of period 2 are one of the variables to be included in f_2);

g_2, the part of the environment not controlled by the individual (for instance, the price system which will prevail in period 2 is one of the variables to be included in g_2).

In the one period model these components were assumed given and known. Here, the situation is the one depicted in Figure 5.

- Mappings (1) and (2) relate, for periods 1 and 2, real individual states to satisfaction levels.
- Mapping (3) gives utility out of satisfaction levels.
- Mappings (4) and (5) describe the real outcomes of individual acts. For period 1, the acts a_1 generate a real individual state e_1 and the part f_2 controlled by the individual of the initial environment at the beginning of period 2. For period 2, the real individual state e_2 results from a_2 and from the initial environment (f_2, g_2).
- Mappings (6) and (7) describe the situation as perceived by the individual: acts a_1 generate $e_1'^*$, but also a perceived controlled environment $f_2'^*$ at the beginning of the second period and a forecast $g_2'^*$ for the non-controlled environment. As for the perceived consequences of acts a_2, they are considered in the context of $(f_2'^*, g_2'^*)$.

The individual is supposed to proceed in the following way. He determines a_2 so as to maximize U for given values of $S_1, f_2'^*$, and $g_2'^*$. U is then a function of $e_1'^*, f_2'^*$, and $g_2'^*$, and the individual chooses a_1 to maximize U in a second step.

A perfect forecast now implies three different types of forecast:

(1) $\delta_1 = \alpha_1 \circ \epsilon_1$, i.e. the individual perfectly forecasts the consequences of his acts on the individual state of the first period;

(2) the individual perfectly forecasts his initial situation at the beginning of the second period, i.e. if one assumes the real and perceived environments to be in the same space, $\mu_1 = \phi_1$ and $\nu_1 = \psi_1$, ψ_1 being the constant mapping from a_1 to g_2; and

(3) assuming (1) and (2), the individual perfectly forecasts the consequences of his acts of the second period on the individual state of this period:

$\delta_2 = \alpha_2 \circ \epsilon_2$.

Hence, we are confronted with a *double* learning process: learning about the future environment (forecast (2)) and learning about the consequences of the acts (forecasts (1) and (3)).

Rather than discuss all the dynamics embedded in the preceding model, most of which were already present in the spot utility model, we shall limit our comments here to (a) the changes in utility through time, and (b) the adaptation of forecasts.

Changes in utility through time

In the multiperiod utility model, both *past experience* and *expectations* have an influence on the utility function. *Past experience* alters not only the present satisfaction levels, but also the expected satisfaction levels associated to given individual social states in the future. As for *future expectations* in consumptions, they may appear not only as obvious arguments of the future satisfaction levels, but also, according to Krelle, in the present stock of habits:

$$\sigma = \int_0^t \dot{q} e^{-\rho(t-\tau)} d\tau + \int_t^{\infty} \dot{q}_E e^{-\upsilon(\tau - t)} d\tau \qquad (\upsilon > 0),$$

$\dot{q}_E$ being the *expected* rate of change in consumption of time τ, and υ a damping coefficient. Naturally, the roles of $\dot{q}$ and $\dot{q}_E$ are not entirely symmetrical, since the individual can influence $\dot{q}_E$, while he cannot influence $\dot{q}$ for $t < \tau$.

However, to build meaningful models with changes through time in the multiperiod utility function, one essential remark has to be made: the individual's acts must be classified with respect to the economic system. Some are 'within' the system, while others try to change it. For instance, if the system is a perfectly competitive market, any act of the individual consisting of buying or selling commodities is within the system. On the other hand, any attempt to create a coalition to influence prices is an effort to modify the system. Generally, the acts aiming to change the system have no immediate effect. Hence the possibility of building models, including a two-stage (or multi-stage) reaction of the individual to his utility changes: (i) in the short-run, he intensifies his effort within the system to improve his situation and (ii) simultaneously, he takes measures to modify the system permanently, in a way favourable to him.

The precise modelling of these ideas is beyond the scope of this paper, but their relevance to economic theory is obvious. Most of the theoretical effort has been devoted to the study of the operations within a given system, while it would be essential to examine the actions of economic agents to alter the system (creation of unions, efforts to transform a competitive market into an oligopoly, demands on the political system to impose new rules, etc.). The source of such actions must lie in individual's utilities and in their changes as a consequence of the perception, by the individuals, of their past and their future.

Adaptation of forecasts

A simple model will help us to analyze the issue. At each period t, an individual has a utility U covering two periods and which depends on

(a) the amount of leisure l_t and l_{t+1} for periods t and $t+1$;
(b) the consumption q_t and q_{t+1} for periods t and $t+1$; and
(c) the volume m_{t+2} of his assets at the end of period $t+1$.

Hence

$$U_t = U\,[l_t, q_t, l_{t+1}, q_{t+1}, m_{t+2}].$$

At each period t the individual has to guess separately

(a) the consumption price vector p_t^* and the average wage rate s_t^*, which are *the parameters describing the environment* (p_t^* and s_t^* may be different from their real values p_t and s_t); and

(b) the ratio a_t^* of his total wage to the average wage rate; this ratio depends on l_t and on the ability of the individual to position himself with respect to the average worker. *This function characterizes the effect of the individual's acts.* The individual may make the guess

$$a_t^* = a_t^* (l_t),$$

while the 'true' relation is

$$a_t = a_t (l_t).$$

Assume that there are no forecasting errors for the first period. This period's income constraint is

$$m_t + s_t a_t = p_t q_t + m_{t+1},$$

with

$$a_t = a_t (l_t).$$

For period t+1, the *forecast* income constraint is, on the contrary,

$$m_{t+1} + s_{t+1}^* a_{t+1}^* = p_{t+1}^* q_{t+1} + m_{t+2},$$

with

$$a_{t+1}^* = a_{t+1}^* (l_{t+1}).$$

Of course, in each period τ the individual is able to compare the real values p_τ, s_τ, a_τ (l_τ) and the guesses p_τ^*, s_τ^*, $a_\tau^*(l_\tau)$ made one period earlier. In the case of adaptive forecasting, if the shape of the function $a_\tau(l_\tau)$ is assumed known (for instance $a_t = \beta_t l_t$, where β_t is a positive constant), the individual will adjust his future guesses according to rules such that

$$\beta_{t+1}^* = f[(\beta_\tau)_{1 \leqslant \tau \leqslant t}, (\beta_\tau^*)_{1 \leqslant \tau \leqslant t}]$$

and

$$s_{t+1}^* = g[(s_\tau)_{1 \leqslant \tau \leqslant t}, (s_\tau^*)_{1 \leqslant \tau \leqslant t}].$$

An example of such rules is, for instance, the rule

$$\beta_{t+1}^* = \lambda\beta_t + (1-\lambda)\beta_t^* \qquad 0 < \lambda < 1.$$

Reality is more complex since β_t may depend on s_t and p_t, so that the individual has to guess simultaneously s_t and a function β_t (s_t, p_t), i.e. the effects of acts within context s_t.

Of course, a similar analysis could be formulated in terms of rational expectations. In that case the individual would, for instance, maximize an expected utility function the value of which would result from the probability distribution of the environment (p_{t+1}, s_{t+1}) and from the probability distribution of the effects β_{t+1} of the acts.

Recent research, for instance on the theory of temporary equilibrium, has emphasized how important the individual's forecasts concerning the environment are for the characteristics of economic equilibrium. The way in which these characteristics are adapted may stabilize or destabilize the economy as a whole. There is no doubt that a great amount of research will take place in this field in the coming years.

Less attention has been paid to the forecasts made by individuals about the effects of their action. However, the errors made may be important; for instance, when a monopolist guesses wrongly the elasticity of the future demand curve, or when the State forecasts wrongly the amount of tax evasion associated to different tax rates. Many fields of economic theory have to be reassessed in order to take into account the elaboration and adaptation of individual forecasts.

These comments suggest that the introduction of dynamic processes – either external or internal – into the analysis of individual behaviour should lead to valuable developments for economic dynamics as a whole. In spite of many challenging isolated papers, the field seems to have been, as yet, relatively unexplored.

Conclusion

This paper aims not to present results, but to stimulate thinking and to show how fruitful a broadened theory of individual behaviour could be for economic theory as a whole. Present economic theory is mutilated by its representation of the individual either as a profit-maximizing manager or as a passive consumer with fixed tastes simply trying to adapt his behaviour to the environment. A much more satisfactory picture emerges when:

(1) the individual has just one behaviour encompassing all his roles (since he may then use the power resulting from his professional roles for other purposes);

(2) the individual is constantly searching for information on possible courses of action;

(3) the individual may try, simultaneously, to act within the system and to find ways of changing it;

(4) the individual experiences changes of preferences as a consequence of his past history and of his expectations; and

(5) the individual behaves according to adaptive forecasts (partly influenced by others) about the future environment or the effect of his own acts within this environment.

An economic theory which included satisfactorily these new features of individual behaviour would not only propose a better interpretation of many observed facts but would also take into account many facts of a politico-economic or socio-economic nature.

Note

1. Normally, efforts are arguments of the utility function. As suggested by Becker, a separate constraint could also be added on the total amount of effort liable to be performed by an individual.

References

BECKER, G. S. (1976) *The Economic Approach to Human Behavior*. Chicago: The University of Chicago Press.

BLINDER, A. S. and WEISS, Y. (1976) 'Human Capital and Labor Supply: a Synthesis', *Journal of Political Economy* 84 (May-June).

HAHN, F. (1970) 'Savings under Uncertainty', *Review of Economic Studies* 37 (January).

HAKANSON, N. (1970) 'Optimal Investment and Consumption Strategies under Risk for a Class of Utility Function', *Econometrica* 38 (September).

KRELLE, W. (1970) *Production, Demande, Prix*, Vol. 1. Paris: Gauthier-Villars.

LANCASTER, K. J. (1971) *Consumer Demand, a New Approach*. New York: Columbia University Press.

LESOURNE, J. (1975) 'Esquisse d'une Théorie de l'individu pour la Science Economique', *Revue d'Economie Politique* 85 (May-June).

——, (1977a) 'Managers' Behaviour and Perfect Competition', *European Economic Review* 9 (January).

——, (1977b) *A Theory of the Individual for Economic Analysis,* Vol. 1. Amsterdam: North-Holland (vol. 2 forthcoming).

LEVHARI, D. and SRINIVASAN, T. (1969) 'Optimal Saving under Uncertainty', *Review of Economic Studies* 36 (April).

LLUCH, C. (1974) 'Expenditure, Savings and Habit Formation', *International Economic Review* 15 (October).

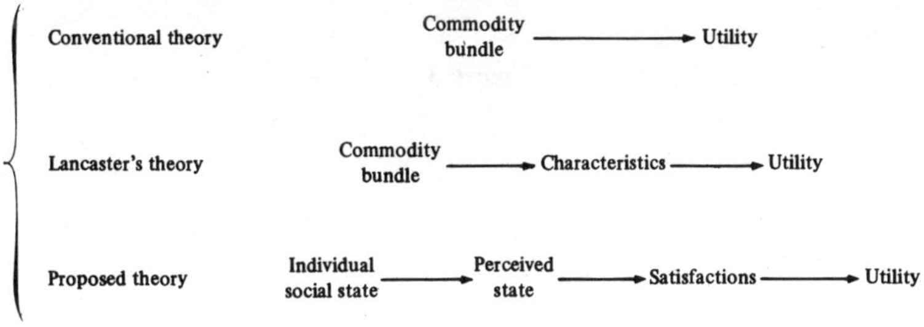

Figure 1

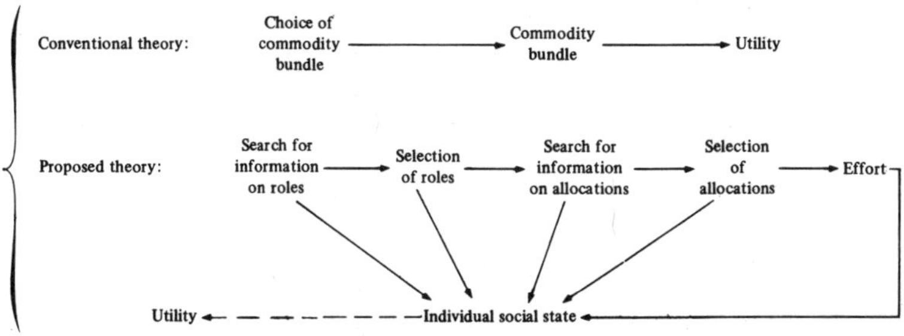

Figure 2

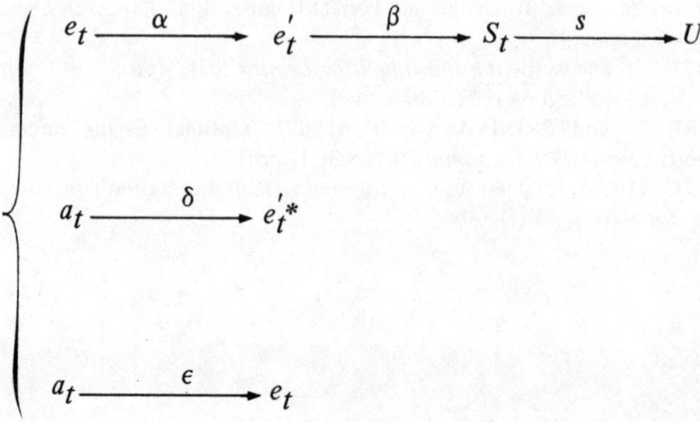

Figure 3

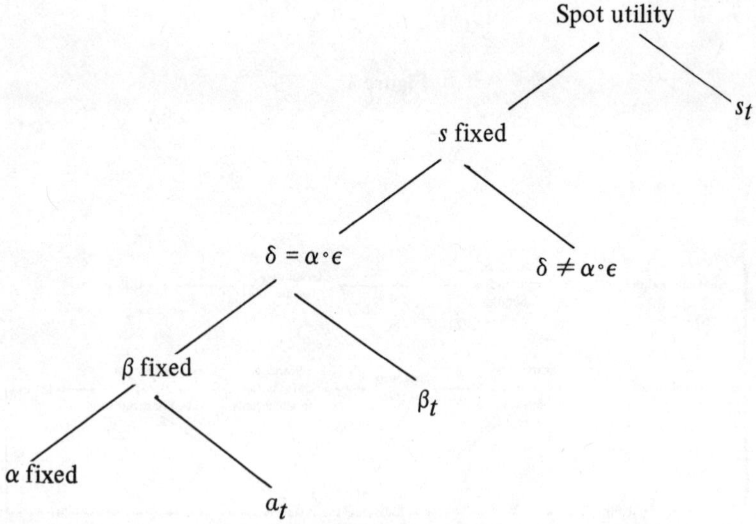

Figure 4

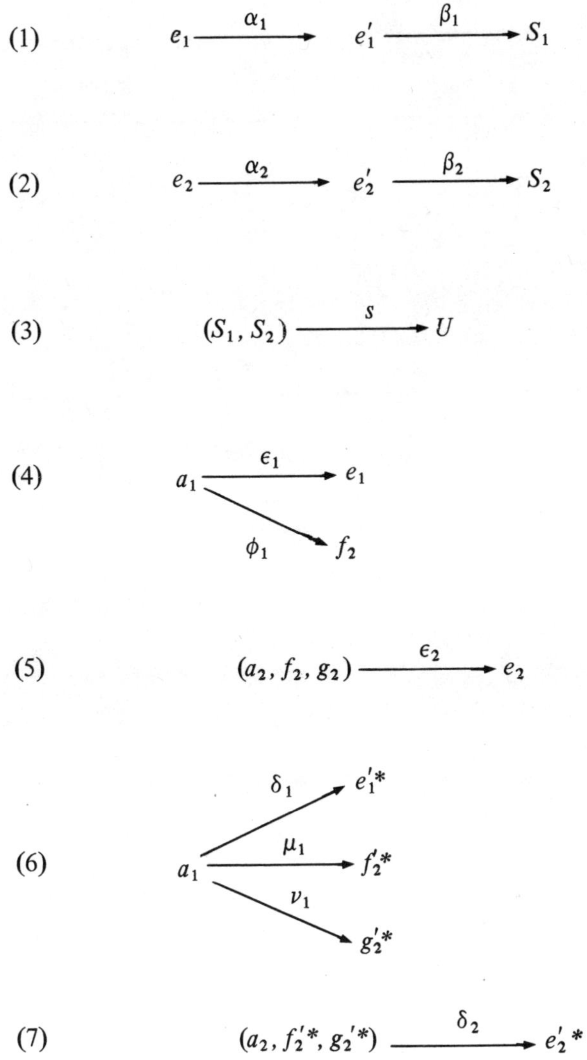
(1) e1 α1 e'1 β1 S1
(2) e2 α2 e'2 β2 S2
(3) (S1, S2) s U
(4) a1 ε1 e1 φ1 f2
(5) (a2, f2, g2) ε2 e2
(6) a1 δ1 e'1* μ1 f'2* ν1 g'2*
(7) (a2, f'2*, g2'*) δ2 e'2*

Figure 5

• Comment

David Marsden

University of Sussex, Brighton, UK

In spite of Alfred Marshall's claim that economics deals with a 'man of flesh and blood' in the ordinary business of life, the existence of the individual actor in economic theory has on the whole been somewhat truncated. For this reason the research which Professor Lesourne outlines in this paper appears very promising. Potentially, such an enriched theory of the individual economic actor could provide a focal point around which the various 'informational' theories in the sub-fields of economics, like those of 'job search' or of 'labour market signalling', might be set.

An especially interesting aspect of his paper is the way the proposed systematic introduction of information and perceptions into models of individual choice promises to bring some of the growth industries of the last two decades – those of information, marketing, and advertising – out of a theoretical no-man's land. Indeed, when we consider how long the manufacturing sector of industry in advanced capitalist countries has been taking a declining proportion of the active population, and how the proportion of non-manual occupations has been increasing, it seems surprising that the production of material goods should still hold such sway in economics.

Lesourne's paper also raises a number of interesting questions from an epistemological point of view. In recent years there has been a move away from what might be called 'mechanistic' or simple behaviourist models of explanation in the social sciences in favour of 'cybernetic' or informational models, and 'semantic', or meaning-oriented ones. The cybernetic models, which are based on a simplified form of information feedback with adapting expectations, have developed fairly rapidly in economics, no doubt because the attribution of an opportunity cost to information made its introduction into earlier mechanistic models relatively straightforward. Semantic models, on the other hand, have proved very difficult to formalize[1] in any quantifiable way, and have proved more amenable to logical than to mathematical analysis. These have on the whole remained confined to sociology, their first major development coming with Max Weber's concept of 'social action', according to which human behaviour was 'action' in so far as it had subjective meaning for the individual or group of individuals concerned, and was 'social' in so far as action took account of the behaviour of someone else. Since the late 1950s such models have of course received a great boost from advances in linguistics, anthropology, and from Wittgenstein's later philosophy.

At the outset Lesourne states that his theory of the individual is directed solely at the extension of economic theory. The problem is, however, that the theory is stated in such general terms as to cover almost everything the sociologist might want to say about individual behaviour. On the other hand, many of the basic terms used in the construction of the theory like those of 'perception', 'role', or 'social state' are drawn from the normal sociological vocabulary. For this reason, and because of the previous discussion, I propose to 'read' Lesourne's paper as an outline of a theory which aims to broaden the basis of economic theory by introducing a number of concepts which form part of the preoccupations of sociologists, rather than as an outline of a general theory of the choices and behaviour of 'the individual'. I shall take a number of concepts from Lesourne's sketch, and attempt to compare them with their sociological counterparts. To conclude, I should like to raise some questions about the problems posed by the methodological individualism of much of economic theory in this domain, and which constitutes an epistemological obstacle to this kind of theory construction.

The first major 'sociological' concept introduced is that of 'perception' as the second step in the 'four-step formulation'.

Perceptions are important in both informational and semantic models of human behaviour. In the case of theories of 'job search', for example, it is assumed that the individual worker has some fairly well informed idea of what he can achieve by remaining with his present employer, and some less well informed idea of pay and conditions with other employers. There are two sets of perceptions such that decisions taken on the basis of one having a greater probability of being optimal than those based on the other. Extra information acquired by search activity can make these 'perceptions' approximate more and more closely to reality in exactly the way that increasing the size of a sample increases the probability of estimating correctly the parameters of a given population. Lesourne's example of the way sales of detergents decrease after advertising campaigns as housewives assess their effectiveness in use would seem to be a good example of the dynamics of this kind of perception.

There is, however, another sense in which 'perceptions' can be interpreted, and that is in terms of the meaning attributed to particular objects, or their connotation. Meanings, however, are always interrelated, and unlike a state of incomplete information, for meanings there is no limiting case of complete information, even in a theoretical sense. Attempts to construct a 'verification theory of meaning' under which this would have been possible have, to my knowledge, all failed. To continue the advertising example, campaigns also influence perceptions through the image they create, and which people can borrow to express themselves to other people, or just to themselves. In this respect it is not the objective properties of the product, which are probably not very different from those of the competitor's product, but the meaning of the product to the individual who buys it, and also what he thinks it will mean to other people, which is important. In this case what is important are the meanings attributed by an individual and those he is communicating with, or the way it enables him to situate himself on a social space that is itself charged with meaning. In a different field, it can be argued that the same kind of perceptions show up in the problems older workers have in adapting to new jobs after being made redundant. Ex-coalminers who have difficulty in adapting to less 'virile' jobs are a good example. In Lesourne's paper, perceptions have been introduced into an economic theory of the individual but at the expense of reducing their semantic aspect to one of incomplete information.

The treatment of 'role', it can be argued, poses a similar set of problems. On the positive side it is worth pointing out that traditional concepts of work, which often had strong moral overtones, have not proved well suited to the analysis of the jobs done by people in large organizations. Yet perhaps here there is a danger of 'reification' of roles. This may be because the 'informational' model of role selection plays down the importance of subjective meaning, and plays up that of an objectively existing set of functions that are to be attributed to any given role, and demanded of those who hold it. Lesourne's allowance for innovation in the content of roles owing to the imagination of individuals introduces some flexibility, although, as I should like to argue later, in a more developed semantic model rather more is required.

On a slightly different problem I have tried to apply such a model to the cross-national comparison of industrial relations institutions.[2] The problem involved in making such comparisons is that issues subject to joint decision-making or bargaining are defined differently and divided between institutions differently, and so there is a problem of knowing where to start in making comparisons. I tried to argue that one feature present in all these countries was that the various issues subject to bilateral control were carved up, or defined and distributed between groups of institutions in such a way as to prevent one side (mainly the labour force and unions) from using advantages gained on one set of issues to prise off advantages on another. This, of course, did not prevent the workers or their representatives from trying, and gradually succeeding, to break down these divisions. From the point of view of the present discussion it is a pity that my study related to roles distributed between different institutions rather than those held by individuals. Nevertheless two factors seemed to emerge: the first related to the importance of the way in which issues subject to joint control were defined, and in which the 'rules of the game' surrounding each set were articulated, and the second related to the importance of power relationships in defending a particular definition of the issues in question.

A third feature of Lesourne's model which appears very promising is the analysis of some ways in which the relationship between consumption patterns and utility can change through time, without postulating empirically inaccessible changes in the utility function. In this case changes in the utility function are derived from the accumulated experience of past consumption, and the expected experience of future consumption.

It would have been interesting to see this part of the model related back to the earlier ideas on role selection and passage through roles. In the context of informational models such a need may appear less urgent, but one of the factors which semantic ones bring to the fore are the way roles are not just sets of allocations but mean something to other social actors holding their roles, creating sets of expectations in their eyes which become obligations for the role-holder. Some of these are of course restricted to technical functions, but a large proportion also relate to expected standards of behaviour, self-presentation, and consumption. Also roles change as children become bachelors or spinsters, who then may marry, become parents and then grandparents, and as young executives win promotion and rise through the levels of the organizational hierarchy.

Finally, the idea of a semantic model does raise the question hidden by the expression 'the theory of the individual' as to 'which' individual we are dealing with, 'when' and 'where'. This is not just a rhetorical question, because one of the main implications of meaning-based, as opposed to information-based, models is that the concept of 'the individual' is relativized because he has to define himself on a meaning-charged social space. Even if he wanted to adopt a totally neutral position, he could not prevent others from reading his actions in a certain way, and orienting their dealings with him as a function of this.

Semantic models differ from 'informational' ones in a number of respects. While the informational models, like those of job search, introduce only such information as increased income, and whose acquisition bears a cost, building on a given model of rationality, semantic models are of a rather broader scope, and seek to establish the *subjective meaning* of the situation in which a given actor finds himself.[3] In the case of Weber's study of the protestant ethic, for example, the analysis starts with an attempt to reconstitute the world in the way protestants of the period would have interpreted and understood it, and to reconstitute the identity they would have given to themselves in this, and then to see how individual behaviour produced the social phenomenon of capitalism.[4] Another difference is that while the usual informational model leaves the concept of the individual intact, semantic models relativize it. This is so because if the individual's environment influences his action, it does so through its subjective meaning, and the subjective meaning of his relation to it. Thus, the definition of the individual is not independent of his meaning-charged environment, and in social interaction there is no state in which 'the individual' exists independently of one type of definition or another.

I think this implication of models based on the actor's interpretation of the meaning of the situation he is in, is incompatible with the fairly radical form of methodological individualism underlying the model of individual action in economic theory. One may or may not accept the full generality of Wittgenstein's argument on the impossibility of 'private languages', but it does seem to be inconsistent to treat meaning as a form of rule following – one must have rules for the correct application of words if they are to be meaningful – and at the same time to put forward a concept of 'the individual' who is in the last resort able to confront reality independently of the social relations in which he is set. In this sense empiricism, which allows the individual person to observe reality in the same way as any other individual, and which allows facts to be built on these observations independently of conceptual terms (except in so far as these provide short-cuts), is a methodologically individualistic theory of knowledge. Semantic models are based on a rather different theory of knowledge, and thus the difference between these two approaches would appear to be something of an epistemological obstacle to a fuller synthesis, and to the development of a theory of individual action that might serve as a bridge between the different approaches and methods of economics and sociology.

However, the practical importance of this should not be overstated since most empirical research is based on fairly limited problems and to some extent the specification of the parameters of the models used, and the delimitation of the research problems, mean that the simpler and more readily quantifiable informational models offer a reasonable approximation to the more complex semantic ones. However, there are areas, such as that of the comparative analysis of the working and effects of labour market institutions in bargaining and in job regulation, where this may be less true.

Notes

1. Some of these problems have been the subject of an interesting article by G. G. Granger which appeared in Dianoia in 1973. Professor Granger kindly gave me a copy of the French version 'Sur le traitement comme objets des faits humains'.

2. 'Industrial Democracy and Industrial Control in West Germany, France and Great Britain'. Forthcoming.

3. The rules in 'semantic' models are typified by linguistic rules. In another context I have tried to argue that these have the same social properties as Durkheim's social norms of 'generality', 'independence of the individual' and capacity to exercise a 'constraint' over him. Vide D. Marsden, 'Critique de l'Analyse économique des Faits Sociaux: le cas de la recherche sur le marché du travail', CNRS, LEST, Aix-en-Provence, 1976, 400 pages, roneo.

4. I chose Weber for simplicity only. I could have taken any of a number of more recent studies of working-class 'images' of society and their influence upon behaviour.

• Comment

Feliciano Hernandez Iglesias

University of Sevilla, Spain

As we start reading the paper by Jacques Lesourne, we learn that his objective is not the extension of economic analysis to the social phenomena, as proposed by Becker, and traditionally avoided by economists. The recent developments of economic theory to explain new aspects of human behaviour like demography, crime, health, or institution, assume very few simple hypotheses that impose concrete restrictions on human behaviour which may be tested by existing statistical methods. The purpose of the paper under discussion is completely different. Taking an approach to economics which he associates with the French 'Economie Politique', he intends to substitute a new 'model' for the present treatment of the individual in economic theory. This implies a knowledge of the limitations of the theory that has to be reformed. What are these limitations?

Using the terminology of the paper, I shall concentrate on those which can be placed under the title of 'the individual', the second of five concepts constituting the pillars of the proposed new theory.

The first alleged deficiency of the orthodox theory is that it deals with 'slices' of individuals. One should, instead, consider complete human beings, drinking, eating, voting, etc. at the same time. In other words, the usual method of partial equilibrium analysis should be abandoned and replaced by some sort of 'wholistic' method. This is a very old theme on which it would be inappropriate to spend much time here. Let me say only that partial equilibrium analysis is nothing but applied general equilibrium. Why? A simple dialectic argument may serve for the present purpose. It is true that, in general, a disturbance in a part of a socio-economic system brings about a general response. Therefore, after a while any feedback from the rest of the system will be reflected in our partial sub-system (say 'the drinking slice' of the individual). Thus, it will not escape our examination even if we do not look at the rest of the system. Because these feedback effects are frequently important, we can observe and measure them. It is this interdependence between the various economic sub-systems which underlies both the possibility and legitimacy of the partial equilibrium analysis. However, we know that care is needed in specifying the relevant changes of parameters. For example, the controversy over the Marshallian demand curve originated in the search of a proper description of the behaviour which takes into account the reaction of the rest of the economic system following a price change. The practical solution to this problem was rendered possible by Slutsky's compensation proposed in 1915. Schumpeter made this point clear when he said[1] that Marshall can be considered one of the founders of the general equilibrium analysis and recalled that, in the 'Memorials', Marshall explicitly declared his intention to dedicate the rest of his life to present as much as he could of note XXI of the appendix of the 'Principles' in a realistic way. This is how we came to know that the Walrasian system lies behind our partial equilibrium exercises. It is impossible to analyse any of the cases of practical interdependence relevant to the problems we want to solve without using some kind of 'slicing'. Partial equilibrium analysis is nothing but applied general equilibrium.[2] Therefore, Lesourne's critique of the common practice of economists is nothing but a repetition of the old criticisms[3] of partial equilibrium analysis.

Turning our attention to the details of this model, we find a proposal for a new definition of the individual whose general characteristics include four elements. Three of them are already common among the basic concepts of the present economic theory. The 'individual social state' is nothing but another name for the environment which, of course, includes variables of 'the Becker type'. The utility function is a mapping from a satisfaction vector onto the utility line similar to that found in the works of Becker, Lancaster or Fisher-Frisch-Theil. The satisfaction scale itself is undefined as to the particular dimensions which one should consider. For instance, which one of the three approaches referred to above is best? All we know is that from the perceived world, we have to pass through an intermediate step – the satisfaction scale – before writing the utility function. This two-step procedure and its advantages are well known and thus do not require further comment. We are left with the difference between reality and its perception as the only potentially new element in the proposed model.

It is important to grasp the difference between objectively measured variables and perceived ones, since any explanation of human behaviour must include perceptions. To take the effect of perception into account we need data on the perceived variables, or lacking them we have to use inference of the 'errors in the variables' type. The trouble with this kind of inference is that it raises serious problems when we have to use more than one equation at a time. Only in those studies in which the models were kept simple enough to use methods of inference based on a single equation could the difference between measured variables and their true causal counterparts be maintained. Among these are the studies of the consumption function by Friedman, Ando-Modigliani and others. It is not, therefore, out of forgetfulness on the part of economic theorists that this aspect has not received more attention, but because of the econometric difficulties of its implementation. On the other hand, at the purely theoretical level, the perception gap has been frequently used. Money illusion, which has been an element in many theories of macroeconomic equilibrium, is based on the difference between nominal and real changes in magnitudes. Whenever the economic agents do not perceive the changes in real magnitudes and act on changes in their nominal counterparts, there is money illusion. This was used by Keynes and can be found in the recent Nobel Lecture by Friedman.[4]

It is in the discussion of the constraints on individual behaviour that one expects to find the most innovative aspects of the proposed 'model'. In effect, Lesourne claims that one of the deficiencies of the present economic theory is that it ignores most of the constraints he enumerates. The truth is that the claim cannot be accepted. Income and technical constraints are, of course, a common feature of economic studies. Time constraints were introduced in 1965 by Becker and have, since then, been fruitfully used in many studies.

Moreover, these are not the only kinds of constraints introduced in economic analysis. The health constraint has been studied by Grossman (1972), who used the concept of investment in health as a particular form of human capital. Working with a model in which the relationships between the time constraints and health investments were explicit he obtained important empirical results concerning behaviour on the health market. Regulation constraints may not have received as much attention as they deserve but the author of these comments, a former student of Stigler, cannot believe that there is any economist not aware of the extensive literature on the economics of regulation.[5]

Constraints on the structure of roles which it is socially acceptable to play may seem the most alien to the hard core of economic analysis. As has been pointed out by Cheung (1970), J. S. Mill was right to say that, when an activity is a customary practice, political economy has no laws of distribution to investigate. Cheung adds:[6] 'While the persuasiveness of Mill may yield peace of mind, subsequent economists have frequently employed custom as an excuse to avoid analysis'. So, Lesourne is in good company when he asks for the introduction of socially acceptable behaviour as an element in the modelling of the economic individual. The literature on property rights[7] incorporates and analyses the behaviour imposed by 'custom'. The reader should note, however, that the proper attitude of the economic analyst may not be to incorporate custom constraints in his models but to examine their economic significance.

Capability constraints may look new provided we do not recognize the usual term, namely 'ability', which has received much attention in the studies related to the human capital approach (Griliches and Mason, 1972).

Finally, we should recall that Stigler wrote his famous article on the economics of information back in 1961, and that this was followed by a fairly extensive literature on the same theme (Stigler, 1961). We do not need to urge economists to take the constraints on information into account; these are already frequently incorporated in the present economic studies.

It is therefore inaccurate to say that current economic theory omits most of the constraints examined. On the contrary, it incorporates all of them and the way it is done is not simply by formulating them as given limitations, but very frequently by placing them in a theoretical choice context which is the proper language and method of economic analysis. This is particularly true of the economics of politics and regulation. There is more to it than the mere formalization of seemingly obvious individual constraints. The treatment of these subjects by economic analysis goes a long way towards the study of the efforts of individuals and groups to change the existing rules, an aspect to which

Lesourne refers at the end of the subsection 'Changes in utility through time' (see also Stigler, 1975).

In the second part of the paper, when we move from the description of the model to its application in a dynamic context, given the absence of new elements, the treatment is, as one would expect, quite familiar. Imperfect knowledge introduces the possibility of change through learning. Individuals learn to forecast the future environment, the consequences of their actions, and to perceive the external world differently. Habit becomes a source of change in the satisfaction scale (probably very difficult to disentangle from changes in perception) and these changes of course allow the individual to attain a different level of utility. Among these numerous dynamic elements in the modelling of individual behaviour, we shall only examine the last one.

That there is a possibility of inertia effects in consumption is more obvious than it is easy to prove. The presence of lagged variables may be due to a mechanism of investment in some form of human capital and this can provide an interpretation of the observed behaviour as a reaction to changes in environmental variables (Michael, 1972). Changes in preferences are not necessary. Let us be clear about this important question. It is one thing to change the region in the satisfaction scale (using Lesourne's terminology) but quite another to change the utility function. One of the advantages of using a two-step procedure like Becker or Lancaster to define the utility, is that it avoids arbitrary changes in the utility function itself. This is ignored in the paper under discussion, since explicitly announced changes in the utility function are formulated mathematically as movements from one region in the satisfaction space to another.

The reason for maintaining the hypothesis of stable preferences as against ad hoc shifts in the utility functions can be found in Becker's contribution to the present volume. We may add here, as a general concluding comment, that the need for simple hypotheses stems from the very nature of scientific method. Many years ago Poincaré said that the task of the scientist was to describe the world, and since he had no time to describe everything he had to concentrate on those aspects which had some probability of repeating themselves. The scientist has to choose, and simple facts are the only ones likely to repeat themselves; so the criterion of choice must be simplicity. This simplicity requires abstraction from the detailed and complex circumstances of immediate perception. Poincaré's message was echoed by economists some years later. 'A hypothesis is important if it explains much by little, that is, if it abstracts the common and crucial elements from the mass of complex and detailed circumstances surrounding the phenomena to be explained and permits valid predictions on the basis of them alone' (Friedman, 1953).

Before yielding to the temptation of reforming economic theory each time it looks unrealistic, we should remember the words of Poincaré (1909): 'The elements (in sociology) are men and they are too different, changing, capricious and complex. How shall we find the interesting facts? We need a method to choose. Many have been proposed, but none has produced results. Each new thesis contains a new method, which, by the way the brilliant doctor rigorously avoids applying it, leaves sociology as the branch of science with most methods and least results.'

Notes

1. Schumpeter (1954: part IV, ch. 5, section 2).
2. See Becker (1971: 5).
3. For a reassessment of recent critiques by French economists, see Riboud (1975).
4. We can read there that the negatively sloped Phillips curve occurs when employers and workers suffer money illusion: 'Unanticipated changes in aggregate nominal demand and in inflation will cause systematic errors of perception on the part of employers and employees alike that will initially lead unemployment to deviate in the opposite direction from its natural rate' Friedman (1977: 469).
5. See the proceedings of a conference held in honour of George Stigler on the 'Economics of Politics and Regulation', *Journal of Law and Economics* XIX (2) (August 1976).
6. See Cheung (1970: 57).
7. See Cheung (1969).

References

BECKER, G. S. (1971) *Economic Theory* New York: Alfred A. Knopf.
CHEUNG, S. N. S. (1969) *The Theory of Share Tenancy.* Chicago: University of Chicago Press.

––, (1970) 'The Structure of a Contract and the Theory of a Non-exclusive Resource', *Journal of Law and Economics* 13, (April).

FRIEDMAN, M. (1953) 'The Methodology of Positive Economics', in: *Essays in Positive Economics.* Chicago: University of Chicago Press.

––, (1977) 'Nobel Lecture: Inflation and Unemployment', *Journal of Political Economy* 85 (June).

GRILICHES, Z. and W. MASON (1972) 'Education, Income and Ability', *Journal of Political Economy* 80 (May).

GROSSMAN, M. (1972) *The Demand for Health: A Theoretical and Empirical Investigation.* New York: Columbia University Press for the National Bureau of Economic Research.

MICHAEL, R. T. (1972) *The effect of Education on Efficiency in Consumption.* New York: Columbia University Press for the National Bureau of Economic Research.

POINCARÉ, H. (1909) *Science et Méthode.* Paris:

RIBOUD, M. (1975) 'Le Concept de surplus: de l'équilibre partiel à l'équilibre général.' Thèse Complémentaire, University of Paris I.

SCHUMPETER, J. A. (1954) *History of Economic Analysis* Oxford: Oxford University Press.

STIGLER, G. J. (1961) 'The Economics of Information', *Journal of Political Economy* 69 (June).

––, (1975) *The Citizen and The State.* Chicago: University of Chicago Press.

3

Anomalies of Rationality:

Some Unresolved Problems in the Theory of Rational Behaviour

Jon Elster

Historisk Institutt, Oslo, Norway

The 'rational-actor' approach to human behaviour is, without little doubt, the best available one, but many problems concerning its scope and resolving power remain to be settled. There is, perhaps, no general theory that can be singled out as *the* main competitor to the rational-choice model; however, there are several, mutually incompatible, alternatives. A very general and abstract theory of action will permit us to distinguish between the main contenders. Any single piece of human behaviour may be seen as the end product of two successive filtering devices. The first is defined by the set of structural constraints which cuts down upon the set of abstractly possible courses of action and reduce it to the (much smaller) subset of feasible actions. The second filter is the mechanism that singles out which member of the feasible set shall be realized. Rational-choice theories assert that this mechanism is the deliberate and intentional choice for the purpose of maximizing some objective function, be it a real one (like profits) or a purely notional one (like the utility function representing preferences).

Most of the material presented here is covered in much greater detail in my *Logic and Society*, London: Wiley, 1978, and especially in my *Ulysses and the Sirens. Studies in Rationality and Irrationality*, Cambridge: Cambridge University Press, forthcoming.

This two-step model immediately suggests two alternatives to the rational-choice approach. The first is the line of argument that denies the *importance* of rational choice, and indeed of the second step in general, and asserts the all-importance of the structural constraints. In an extreme version this could mean that the constraints jointly have the effect of narrowing down the feasible set to a single point: in a weaker and more plausible version that the constraints define a set which is so small that formal freedom of choice within the set really does not amount to much. The second alternative denies the *reality* of rational choice, and asserts that the mechanism that singles out one member of the feasible set is a causal rather than an intentional one. To these two alternatives we may add a third, which denies the *stability* of rational choice. I believe that rationality often is unimportant, inefficient and unstable, but also that there is a hard core of important cases where the rational-choice model is indispensable. I also believe that this model is logically prior to the alternatives, in the sense that the social scientist should always be guided by the postulate of rationality, even if he may end up by finding it to be violated in many particular cases. This is a 'principle of charity', similar to the one often used in interpretation. One should never take textual contradictions at their face value, but always consider whether the context gives a clue to consistency. Similarly, one should always look very closely at apparently irrational behaviour in order to see whether there could not be some pattern there after all. Needless to say, charity should not be stretched too far; there may arrive a point where the observer simply has to admit that to the best of his understanding the behaviour has no rational motive.

Structuralism

The methodological school that denies the *importance* of rationality is structuralism. This term may either be taken as a general term, or as designating the French school of linguists and anthropologists, notably Claude Lévi-Strauss. I shall here understand it in the former sense, and I am not really certain whether the French structuralists are structuralists in this sense.

A typical statement is the following: 'the structuralist would emphasize the bounding of political activity by social structure (including class) and values (including ideology). The behaviorist would emphasize political decision making within these bounds. The structuralist would study the fence around the cattle; the behaviorist would study the activity of the cattle within the bounds of the fence'.[1] There are some ambiguities in this formulation. I believe one should be very hesitant in accepting the notion that *values* are constraints; they belong to the second filter, not to the first. (Two exceptions may be mentioned: the values that determine visibility of alternatives and the values that are lexicographically superior to other values.) Also, I propose a somewhat different definition of the structuralist: not someone who studies the fence around the cattle, but someone who asserts that the cattle have very little freedom of movement within the fence.

It is not surprising that Marxists tend to be structuralists in this sense. In the history of the working class the structural constraints of budget and calories have jointly sufficed to narrow the feasible consumption bundles down to a very small set. Economic constraints on resources also have important consequences for political behaviour, mobility and education. However, let us look at some problems that arise here. Of the many interpretations of the labour theory of value,[2] consider the 'Hegelian' interpretation stating that values can be determined independently of prices and the 'Ricardian' interpretation stating that prices are independent of the composition of final demand. The first interpretation is valid only on the assumption of fixed coefficients of production, which is indeed a structuralist assumption denying the reality of the producer's choice. The assumption, however, is completely unjustified. The second interpretation, on the other hand, becomes vacuously true if we deny the reality of the consumer's choice. I do not think this is what Marx had in mind. Rather, I believe he wanted to argue that the long-term equilibrium prices were independent of changes in demand, a statement that is true in the open Leontief system, but false in the closed. In other words, for the labour theory of value Marx needed the unjustifiable assumption of fixed coefficients of production, but not the assumption – justified on Marx's time – of fixed coefficients of consumption. Even the latter assumption has, of course, become wildly unjustified in the 100 years that have passed. It is very rarely the case that economic and legal constraints are so tight that workers have no freedom of choice between widely different alternatives. The degenerate Marxist structuralism – a *frère ennemi* to the equally degenerate Marxist functionalism[3] – usually solves this difficulty by invoking values or ideologies as constraints, i.e. the very move I warned against above.

As a general theory structuralism, as defined here, cannot be defended. There is no general reason why the constraints should be exactly so strong as to bring about a uniquely determined action, or even a very small set of possible actions. On the other hand there are many cases in past history where the approach is strongly appealing. No historian today would show anything approaching to the insensitivity of Marie-Antoinette when told that the crowd rioted for lack of bread: why don't they eat cake? Nevertheless there may be a danger of seeking complicated explanations based on motivation and mentality, when a simple analysis of the feasible set would show that no other course of action than the observed one really was possible.

Games without solutions

I now proceed to the first of several of arguments that deny the very *existence* of a uniquely defined rational behaviour. To state the argument, an excursion into the history of the notion of rationality will prove useful.

The two main theorists of rationality in the social sciences are, I believe, Max Weber and John von Neumann. Among Weber's main legacies to the sociological tradition is the notion of instrumental rationality, or ends-means rationality. Rationality is to choose the best means for a chosen end, *given the initial conditions*. The assumption of given conditions I refer to as the assumption of a parametric environment, and the corresponding notion of rationality as parametric rationality. There is something strange or even contradictory in the notion of parametric rationality. A parametrically rational agent believes himself to be free optimally to adjust to a constant environment, and at the same time he can hardly fail to be aware of the fact that this environment is made up in part of other agents similar to himself. He could then, of course, assume that the others are trying optimally to adjust to what looks to *them* as a constant environment, and then adjust optimally to their optimal adjustment, but this would only mean the re-emergence of the paradox at a higher level.

Von Neumann's great contribution was to cut short this infinite regress, through the notion of strategic rationality. The strategically rational actor sees himself as a player in a game which, in the ideal case, is defined by perfect information, in the sense that all players have full knowledge about each other's preferences and information. No one can rationally assume himself to be one step ahead of the others; everyone has to take account of the fact that all are equally rational. The notion of an equilibrium point is the crucial technical concept which circumvents the infinite regress; it is defined as a set of individual strategies each of which is optimal against the others. If all players but one choose their equilibrium point strategies, then the remaining player can do no better than to choose *his* equilibrium strategy; and this holds regardless of who this 'one player' is assumed to be.

The notion of parametric rationality, whatever its shortcomings, has at least one advantage: it is usually well-defined. There are, of course, maximization problems without solutions, as when the objective function is not continuous or the feasible set not compact. An important case is the non-existence of optimal plans in certain planning contexts.[4] In most applications, however, the assumption of given initial conditions produces a unique action which is *the* rational thing to do, or at least a set of actions which are equally and maximally good. These actions may be self-defeating, when based upon assumptions about other agents that are incompatible with these agents' assumptions about themselves, but at any rate they are well-defined. Strategic rationality in this respect is much more problematic, given the pervasive importance of *games without a solution.*

I shall discuss three varieties of such games: variable-sum games without equilibrium points; variable-sum games with several equilibrium points; and constant-sum games without a von Neumann-Morgenstern solution. Of these the second variety, to which most space will be devoted, is certainly the most important one.

A simple game without any equilibrium point is the following. 'Each player writes down a number. The player who has written the largest number receives from each of the other players a sum of money equal to the difference between the largest number and the number written down by that player.' It is intuitively clear, and it can be rigorously proved,[5] that in this *fuite en avant* there can be no equilibrium point. The economics of hyperinflation may in part be understood as a game of this general form. In this case there is no equilibrium point because the strategy set is not compact, as in the cases where parametric rationality also fails to define a uniquely characterized behaviour.

Much more important are the no-solution games where there are *several* equilibrium points, none of which can be singled out as *the* solution. John Harsanyi[6] has recently proposed a new approach to n-person non-cooperative games, where many games that would previously have been described as unsolvable, now receive a well-defined solution. This solution concept have many surprising features, some of them acceptable, others less so.[7] Nevertheless, even Harsanyi does not claim to have fully solved *all* games. He recognizes that there are 'bargaining deadlocks' where the players must resort to their maximin strategies, even if these are not optimal against each other. Harsanyi speaks of the pair of maximin strategies as being *the solution*, but adds that one might want to use a weaker term such as 'quasi-solution'. Finally, he remarks that 'One may even argue that it is just another way of saying that such games have *no* true solution.'[8]

This indeed is what I am arguing. The maximin strategy should not be called a rational strategy, for that would mean that if the other players are rational, then it is not rational for you to be rational. (One might say, perhaps, that there is no strategy which is *more* rational than the maximin strategy, but this is not sufficient for the maximin strategy being rational.) Use of the maximin strategy amounts to throwing up your hands and seeking a way out of the infinite regress of 'I think that you think that I think . . .'. When we use the maximin strategy we should always anticipate that the other players may be able to anticipate our doing so, and to exploit our weakness, just as we presumably have reflected upon the possibility that they might use their maximin strategy and leave themselves open to manipulation. Each of the players knows that all are rational, and nevertheless he must treat the others as if they were not, which is in itself irrational. Each of the players finally *acts*, but this is a result of causal pressures building up or of mental fatigue, not of rational choice.

An example may prove useful at this point. In economic theory there is a well-known problem concerning the link between labour-scarcity and labour-saving bias in technical progress. From Marx to Hicks[9] it was taken for granted that entrepreneurs had an incentive to economize on the scarce factors, not only through substitution, but also through biasing their innovations. In a classic contribution Salter[10] then showed that when substitution had taken place, all factors were equally scarce at the margin, so that entrepeneurs had no special incentive to bias their search one way rather than another. Two lines of argument were brought forward to answer this contention. One is linked to the names of Kennedy, von Weiszäcker and Samuelson,[11] stating in essence that there are constraints on the set of possible innovations that make the bias a rational one. The other was proposed by William Fellner,[12] arguing that it was rational for entrepreneurs to bias their innovations if they expected the wage rise to continue into the future. The latter argument has recently been criticized by Paul David[13] on the grounds that it neglects the importance of free riders in technical change. I will show that David's argument, when further elaborated, shows that the game played by the entrepreneurs is a game without solution.

The reasoning behind the Marx-Hicks theory must have been roughly the following. It is beneficial for all capitalists if all capitalists introduce labour-saving innovations, for then the demand for labour will fall, and wages accordingly. Therefore, an increase in wages may be expected to bring about labour-saving innovations so as to reduce wages to their former level. This reasoning would have been valid if the capitalists acted as one actor, but it breaks down when applied to decentralized decisions. If all other capitalists are going to bias their innovations, the individual capitalist can act as a free rider; if they are not, his action can only have an infinitesimal impact on the wage level, assuming perfect competition. Now if the wage level is expected to rise in the future, then it may be rational for the individual entrepeneur to bias his search, as argued by Fellner. The problem, however, is why the entrepreneur should have these expectations. The only rational basis for such expectations must be that the other entrepeneurs are *not* going to bias their search, for if they did wages would not go on rising. Now if each entrepeneur biases his search on the assumption that he is the only one to do so, then of course wages will go down, not up. Next time around, each entrepeneur – having learned from this experience – will perhaps not bias his search, assuming that the others are giving a bias to theirs. Then, of course, wages will go up, not down as anticipated. We have, in other words, a game with the features of 'Chicken':[14] if everyone else introduces labour-saving innovations, then it is rational for the individual not to do so; if no one else does so, then it is in his interest to do so. In this situation there is no behaviour that is *the* rational one, at least not if we are talking about strategic rather than parametric rationality. Other examples could also have been given, but the labour-saving problem brings out the essentials quite well. As long as the entrepreneurs believe that they are, each and individually, acting in an environment of other entrepreneurs who just go on acting as they did last year, then the notion of individually rational behaviour, given this belief, makes sense; the belief itself, however, is not very sensible. And as soon as the belief is supplanted by the more rational insight into the strategic and symmetric nature of the situation, then the notion of rational choice simply evaporates, and guessing has to take over.

Von Neumann and Morgenstern proved the existence of a solution for constant-sum two-person games on the assumption that the preferences could be represented by a von Neumann-Morgenstern utility function. A standard counter-example of preferences that cannot be represented in this sense is given by the *lexicographic preferences*, where a vector $(a_1, a_2, \ldots, a_n)$ is preferred to $(b_1, b_2, \ldots, b_n)$ if and only if for some i, $a_i > b_i$, while for all $j < i$, $a_j = b_j$. Peter Fishburn[15] has shown that in constant-sum games with lexicographic preferences there are (i) cases where player I has a maximin strategy and player II a minimax strategy, but these are not optimal against each other, and (ii) cases where neither player has a maximin or minimax strategy. The last case illustrated by the following game, where payoffs to player I are represented by three-dimensional lexicographic preferences:

		Player II		
		s_1	s_2	s_3
Player I	t_1	1, 0, 0	0, 0, 0	0, 1, 1
	t_2	0, 0, 0	0, 1, 1	0, 1, 0

Assuming that I chooses t_1 and t_2 with probabilities a and $(1\text{-}a)$, and that II chooses s_1, s_2, s_3 with probabilities p, q, r, then the expected three-dimensional payoff to I is

$(ap, r{+}(1\text{-}a)q, ar + (1\text{-}a)q)$.

If a=0, then the worst that can happen to I is (0, 0, 0), namely if II sets $p = 1$, $r = q = 0$. If $a > 0$, then the worst that can happen to I is (0, 1-a, 1-a), for $p = r = 0$, $q = 1$. But this means that I cannot choose a so as to maximize this minimum outcome. For any positive a there is a smaller a guaranteeing him a better minimum, but going to the limit and equating a to 0 does not give the best minimum.

Maximizing, satisficing and natural selection

The existence of rational behaviour may also be questioned on grounds related to the cost of information. In order to present this argument in the proper setting, I shall first sketch some of the developments in the theory of rational behaviour that led up to it. In logical, and partly in chronological, succession I believe that five distinct positions within this development may be distinguished. The *first position* is the classical maximization approach, assuming total certainty, no information and transaction costs, instant and faultless calculation, and so on. The importance of this paradigm as an idealized standard should always be kept in mind. The capacity for global maximization, using if required indirect strategies ('one step backward, two steps forward'), is a feature distinguishing Man from the other animals and from the process of natural selection that has fashioned them both.

The *second position* is the theory of satisficing or limited rationality, associated with the name of Herbert Simon. The arguments for this view are partly empirical, partly logical. Empirically it is rarely the case that businessmen deliberately search for the global maximum in their feasible set; rather, they tend to set themselves some goal such as a minimum rate of profit, and then adopt the first course of action that happens to come into their mind (perhaps as a result of some search process) and that satisfies this minimum requirement. Logically it can be argued that the abstractions implied by the classical maximization model are too heroic, and that the model could never be realized even in principle. The inevitable elements of friction, noise and entropy make the global maximum unattainable and the search for it a waste of time that could have been spent more profitably.

The last remark brings us immediately to the *third position*, a modified maximization approach that takes some account of the objections of the satisficers.[16] This position is that satisficing, properly understood, is simply a species of maximization with such elements as the cost of information and transaction included. The abstractly optimal position, e.g. the solution to a technical problem that might be optimal from an engineering viewpoint, may be economically irrational because it is too costly and time-consuming. It has been said, for example, that this technical perfectionism is the reason why French firms regularly lose contracts to American competitors.

The *fourth position* is the third turned on its head; not satisficing-as-maximizing, but maximizing-as-satisficing. The Chicago school of economists have argued that maximizing really is the result of satisficing, in the sense that profit-maximizing firms are just the satisficing firms that are selected by the market because they happen to use the optimal rules of thumb. Armen Alchian, Milton Friedman and Gary Becker have presented several versions of this argument, one which denies that firms have maximizing intentions and one which says that we might as well assume that firms have such intentions, because they behave as if they did.

The *fifth position* is represented by a fundamental and somewhat nihilistic paper by Sidney Winter.[17] The main effect of his paper is to destroy the third position and implicitly to restore the second, but he also has important comments on the fourth. Winter's point is that the attempt to re-define satisficing as a form of maximizing leads to an infinite regress, because the 'choice of a profit maximizing information structure itself requires information, and it is not apparent how the aspiring profit maximizer acquires this information, or what guarantees that he does not pay an excessive price for it'.[18] At some point this infinite regress must be cut short by some guess or intuition, unsupported by formal reasoning, and why not then make this cut-off point as close to the action itself as possible? The last question is crucial, for if the infinite regress could be shown to converge, in the sense that the deviation from the 'real optimum' grows rapidly smaller for each new level in the information hierarchy, then we would not have a deep problem. I do not see, however, how one can argue for such a convergence, and then the problem remains entire. The use of formal methods in such cases is likely to produce precision in the last decimal when we are uncertain about the first.

Winter also has cogent objections to the natural-selection theories of rational behaviour. These theories, it will be observed, operate at the level of the second filter defined above. They are not strictly speaking *alternatives* to the rational-choice mechanism, as the traditional or random behaviour to be discussed below. Rather, they show how natural selection can *simulate* rationality. Winter's central idea is this: from the fact that in an initial situation a rule of thumb employed by a given firm is the most profitable, we can never conclude that it will remain the most profitable when that firm expands relatively to other firms and thus changes the initial situation. He also shows that under plausible conditions maximizers and non-maximizers may coexist in market equilibrium, and that maximizers may become extinct. Both of these possibilities are, of course, contrary to the assertion that all firms will exhibit profit-maximizing behaviour because non-maximizers are eliminated by competition.

The result of these various considerations seems to be that for the analysis of business decisions, and probably for many everyday problems as well, Simon's theory of satisficing is the most adequate. This theory can neither be derived from the assumption of profit-maximizing intentions, nor be used to support an assertion that behaviour will tend to be profit-maximizing. It goes without saying that many subproblems will be optimally resolved by standard maximizing methods, because we 'see' at once that the calculation will be worth while, but I do not believe that the large problems facing the firm or the individual can be solved in this way.

Traditional behaviour and random behaviour

In some cases we know that rational behaviour in a given situation would be, but nevertheless something different is observed. Here the problem is not, as in the preceding cases, that the notion of rational behaviour is ill-defined, but rather that it is not observed to take place. In a well-known article Gary Becker[19] distinguished between two such (second-filter) alternatives to rational choice: behaviour governed by the tradition and behaviour governed by some stochastic mechanism. I shall examine, quite independently of Becker's original purpose in making the distinction, the status and importance of these two categories.

This volume is about the economic versus the sociological approach to human behaviour. The difference between the two shows up very clearly in the study of crime and the study of education. In both cases the sociologist, or some caricature thereof, argues that the choice of a criminal career or of higher education really is no 'choice' at all, but that the individuals are *propelled* into certain channels by subculture-specific norms and values. The economist, by contrast, tends to assume that individuals are *attracted* by differential rewards associated with the possible courses of action. The sociologist, that is, looks at the action as a product of its causal antecedents, the economist as motivated by future rewards: causality versus intentionality. A testable implication of these views is that on the sociological view changes in the reward system would have little efficacy for inducing changes in behaviour, whereas the economist takes it for granted that one can make people behave (through self-interest) in virtually any manner, by making suitable modifications in the reward system.

More specifically, William Cobb[20] and Gordon Tullock[21] among others, have distinguished between two hypotheses that purport to explain why some people become criminals: the 'economic hypothesis' that assumes maximization of expected utility, and the 'sociological' hypothesis (Cobb calls it 'the sickness hypothesis') that links criminal activities to internalized norms. According to Tullock there is no doubt which fits the data best; he also states that many of the sociologists who started out to prove that punishment does not deter crime, ended up by finding the contrary. Raymond Boudon[22] has argued in a similar way concerning the choice of educational career. Whereas writers like Pierre Bourdieu and Jean-Claude Passeron[23] have seen differential choice of educational career as a cultural mechanism for reproduction of class inequalities, Boudon argues convincingly that to a large extent working-class youths avoid higher education simply because it is too costly.

The sociological hypothesis, in the crude form sketched above, can certainly be invalidated by empirical evidence. In addition we can adduce a simple conceptual argument and a more important theoretical one. The conceptual argument originates with Becker:[24] you cannot abide with tradition if the environment changes so as to make the traditional behaviour lie outside the feasible set. The theoretical argument amounts to a distinction between two ways in which values can influence behaviour. The simplistic sociological theory, which no one perhaps has ever held explicitly, says that values *directly* determine behaviour, by singling out one member of the feasible set. A more plausible theory would be, of course, that values determine preferences and that preferences and the feasible set jointly determine behaviour. This, I believe, could be used for a more useful formulation of the difference between the economic and the sociological approach. The sociologist typically assumes that there are very large socially determined differences in preferences between individuals; that, for example, workers and women use higher rates of discount when evaluating the present utility of future rewards. The economist, on the other hand, would tend to think that preferences are basically similar, and that most of the observed differences in behaviour can be explained by differences in the opportunity set. Another, not quite equivalent, way of stating the distinction is to say that for the sociologist the most efficient method (dollar for dollar) of bringing about, say, educational equality would be to work on the value system, whereas for the economist manipulation of the reward structure is likely to be the more efficient method. A third formulation, equivalent to none of the others, could be to say that for the sociologist social change typically begins with changes in the value system, whereas for the economist changes in the feasible set are prior to and induce (endogenous) change of preferences.[25]

This reinterpretation tends to close the gap between sociologists and economists, in the sense that the modified – and much more sensible – sociological position admits that for any given individual, action is determined by preferences, even if preferences vary over individuals. The gap could – and should – also be closed from the other end, by getting economists to admit the reality of traditional, stereotyped and rigid behaviour. I return to this problem below: here I only make the polemic point that people sometimes act stupidly out of stupidity and rigidly out of rigidity.

On the (simplistic) theory of traditional behaviour, actions will remain the same following a change in the feasible set, assuming that the traditional behaviour remains feasible. On the rational-choice theory, changes in the feasible set will typically induce a change in behaviour. On the third approach, to be discussed now, behaviour could change even with a constant feasible set (and without any assumption of a change in preferences). This is the theory that behaviour is sometimes *random*, in the sense of being realized according to some probability distribution over the feasible set. Random behaviour in this sense is assumed in many models of social mobility, in the Asch-Cohen model for conformity and in Rapoport's model for sequential Prisoners' Dilemmas, to name but a few.[26] In all such models the individual is seen as the bearer of *states* rather than of *intentions*, and his behaviour as governed by causal antecedents rather than by future rewards. Both traditional and random behaviour belong to the causal rather than the intentional image of Man.

The interpretation of such models is often ambiguous. Are the stochastic models just useful approximations to some underlying deterministic mechanism (as in coin-tossing), or is it exactly the other way around, so that when we assume deterministic causality we do so in spite of our knowledge of random disturbances? Actually both answers may be true simultaneously. At the deepest level coin-tossing presumably is governed by the objectively random quantum processes; at a more aggregate (but still microscopic) level these processes can be given some very complex deterministic representation; and at the molar level this approximation is represented by a stochastic process again, but not by one that would bear any general relation to the deeper random process. (The situation is somewhat similar to the cases where a real process in discrete time is mathematically represented in continuous time, which for computational purposes is then represented in a discrete time that bears no significant relation to the original discrete process.)[27] This implies that such stochastic models in the social sciences have a rather unsatisfactory status; they describe rather than explain.

There is one exception to this statement: the case where the agent deliberately acts randomly. In this case the transition probabilities (or whatever) would be more than a compact description of some unknown underlying determinism; they would stem directly from the assumption of rationality. A typical example would be the use of mixed strategies in game theory. Now John Harsanyi has recently argued[28] that only equiprobabilistic mixed strategies will be chosen by rational actors, and that these are generated by some objectively random mechanism inside their heads rather than by deliberate choice. The notion of rationality underlying this argument is, however, hard to accept.[29] I, for one, certainly think the efforts of Raymond Boudon[30] to explain choice of education or relative frustration through models involving mixed strategies very worth while.

By way of a conclusion, we may assert that both the cases discussed by Becker may be, but are not necessarily, genuine exceptions to rational-choice theory. There may be cases where values, norms and traditions have a direct impact upon behaviour, but in most cases the influence is mediated by the preference structure. Also, there may be cases where random behaviour stems from a deliberate choice to act randomly.

Rationality and time

The simplest definition of rationality says that a rational individual is one who, when placed before the choice between a number of options to be realized at time *t*, makes his choice according to complete and transitive preferences at *t*. This definition is doubly static; time enters neither in the object of the preferences nor in the preferences themselves. I believe this definition inadequate to cover our intuitive notions of rationality; some temporal consistency requirements should be added to the instantaneous or static ones. To be precise, we should require rationality both in our *choices of successions* and in our *successions of choices.*

A choice of successions is a plan for the future, e.g. an allocation of income or consumption over several years in the future. Philosophers and economists impose rather different consistency requirements on such plans. Philosophers typically require that a rational individual should consume equally in each year, i.e. that there should be no discounting of the future.[31] Economists tend to take it for granted that individuals have time preferences, and require only that these be consistent, in the sense that the plans should not be inherently unrealizable.[32] For an example of time preferences leading to inherently unrealizable plans, take the individual who always wants to allocate half his fortune to consumption in the present year, and then divide the rest evenly over his life. When the second year arrives he will not carry out his first-year plan, but rather use half of the remaining half for consumption in the second year, leaving the rest for equal division over the future, and so on. It is easy to show that a necessary and sufficient condition for avoiding such reconsideration of past decisions is that time preferences are exponential. For the philosopher, then, rationality means no time preferences; for the economist it means exponential time preferences.

Actually I think inconsistent time preferences a basic fact of life, for several sets of reasons. First, *mortality* makes it rational to attach greater weight to the present than to a future in which I may no longer be around: this is the case for having time preferences. Also, the fact that our life expectations change when we move on in life without dying, necessitates a constant change in our plans: this is the case for being inconsistent. Secondly, *weakness of will* is an inescapable feature of the human condition, making not only for time preferences, but also for inconsistency, e.g. through the mechanism described by Phelps and Pollak.[33] That is, to the extent that we are rational, recognition of our limited but unknown span of life implies inconsistent time preferences; and to the extent that we are subject to akrasia, we cannot help acting in this doubly irrational manner. There is, however, an escape clause to the last statement. If we are able to anticipate our later inconsistencies, we may take precautions against them now, e.g. by precommitting ourselves so as to make later reconsideration impossible. This, perhaps, should also be included in the notion of a rational man: to the extent that he is irrational, he should be able to act so as to minimize the harm done to his later self by that irrationality.

Some of these considerations carry over to the case of a rational succession of choices. In some sense we feel that an individual with constantly changing preferences is not really a rational individual, even if at any given point of time his preferences are transitive (and his time preferences consistent). On the other hand we certainly do not want to impose a requirement of constant preferences. We do not want to label as irrational people who change their mind for good reasons, only people who do so for bad reasons or for no reason at all.

Among the good reasons we should include experience and training. *Experience* can be formalized as a difference between ex ante and ex post preferences.[34] A given consumption bundle may look more (or less) attractive after the actual consumption experience than it did before. The larger the part of the commodity space already explored, the smaller, presumably, the induced change in preferences after each choice. *Training* has been formalized as a distinction between utility and consumption capital.[35] Training does not change the enjoyment that I derive from a given amount of time spent on, say, listening to music, everything else being the same. It does, however, make a difference in the 'everything else' by increasing the consumption capital that enables me to get more enjoyment out of a given time spent listening to music.

Among the bad reasons we should include the sheer desire for novelty and its converse, pure inertia; also the sheer desire to be different and its converse, pure conformism. If a person always wants to be in New York when in San Francisco and vice versa, this is clearly irrational. If someone has a consuming desire for novelty and change, he can be led to 'improve himself to death'[36] by a series of small changes, each of which is an improvement in terms of the current preferences. A pure conformist and a pure non-conformist may unsuccessfully chase each other in their preferences.[37] In such cases the individual is in the grip of causal forces operating 'behind his back', and governing his change of preferences in a way he does not understand. We should require of a rational individual either that he be not subject to such causal forces, or that he be able to anticipate their effects and to exploit them for his own purposes. The latter case once again may require precommitment, taking purposive action now in order to bring about or to avoid certain changes of preferences later on. If 'choice depends on taste and taste on past choices',[38] then a rational man should take account of the fact that his present choice will have an impact upon his future taste.

For both the problems under discussion, choices of successions and successions of choices, we have arrived at somewhat similar conclusions. Ideally, choices of successions should be rational, in the sense of exhibiting no time preferences (over and above what is justified by mortality) and at least in the sense of not exhibiting inconsistent time preferences. Ideally, a succession of choices should be rational, in the sense of not being subject to causal forces changing the preferences of the individual (over and above what is rational through experience and learning). Now weakness of will and fixed character traits may be so strong as to be impossible to undo. In this case the rational individual should opt for a second-best solution: given my character as it is, how can I best exploit the causal laws defining it, for the purpose of realizing my rational ends?

Charity

As strongly argued by Donald Davidson, there is a general *presumption of rationality* in the study of human affairs: 'if we are intelligibly to attribute attitudes and beliefs . . . we are committed to finding, in the pattern of behaviour, belief and desire, a large degree of rationality and consistency'.[39] In order to gather the very evidence on which rationality could be denied in the case of a given individual, we must assume him to be rational if the outwardly observable behaviour is to be translatable into evidence. Irrational behaviour only makes sense against a background of rationality; and the pattern may often be reinterpreted so as to make the irrationality appear in a different part of the behavioural system.

This general argument corresponds to what has for a long time been the standard practice among economists. They have worked according to what has been called a *principle of charity*, saying that one should always assume, as a working hypothesis, that any given piece of behaviour, however ill-adapted and strange at the surface, may have a rational explanation. The social scientist should be prepared to spend time and imagination on thinking up rational explanations for the action he observes, and only after repeated failure should he tentatively label the action as irrational.

The successes of the principle of charity are numerous. An example is the resistance to technical change in underdeveloped countries. Instead of arguing that such resistance must stem from the irrational traditionalism of landlord or peasant, it may be explained as the rational response to techniques which combine higher average yields with larger dispersions around the average,[40] or as the rational choice of a landlord who fears that the productivity increase will enable the sharecroppers to repay their debts and to liberate themselves from the state of semi-serfdom.[41] The lack of responsiveness of peasants to price changes appears as rational once we take account of the price fluctuations in the past that make it rational for the peasant to form cautious expectations about prices. The mercantilist policy of protectionism was irrational if we assume that absolute wealth was the goal, but not if we replace that goal by power (and relative wealth). 'If power is the aim, mutually beneficial trade which enriches also the enemies is undesirable.'[42] Among the gambits utilized by the principle of charity some may be briefly mentioned. People may have different goals from what we initially assumed. What would be irrational for a profit-maximizer, could be rational for a power-maximizer or a utility-maximizer. People may act in terms of probability distributions, not in terms of average values. What would be irrational in a uniform climate, may be rational in a changing one. People may act in terms of net profits, not in terms of gross profits. What looks irrational at a first glance, may appear as rational when we take account of the cost of information and of transaction. People may have changing preferences rather than inconsistent preferences. Consumption choices inconsistent with the axioms of revealed preference may be explained on the assumption of changing tastes. People may deliberately refuse to adapt themselves, because of the 'psychic costs' involved. 'The greatest of all monopoly profits is a quiet life.'[43] Finally, people may deliberately randomize, as seen above.

Some of these gambits stretch charity to the limit. Take, for example, Douglass North's analysis of *ideologies*, which he sees as 'a way of economizing on the costs of information and therefore . . . in general a rational response to the costs of information about the broad range of issues' that face the agents.[44] This, I submit, is carrying the presumption of rationality too far. It may be the case that some businessmen discriminate systematically against minorities because they have decided that in the long run this will save them more money than if they take the trouble of evaluating each case on its merits, but I find it hard to believe that anyone could seriously contend that this is the pattern for *all* cases of ideological prejudice. Douglass North again, in another context, explains peasant conservatism as a 'cost-benefit decision: the psychological and transaction costs of instituting the three-field system counterbalanced the significant benefits it promised'.[45] I simply refuse to believe that peasants living at subsistence would deliberately sacrifice an improvement in their standard of living for the sake of 'a quiet life'. As stated above, people sometimes act stupidly out of stupidity, and not every apparently ırrational behaviour can be fitted into the mould of rationality.

Notes

1. A. S. McFarland, *Power and Leadership in Pluralist Systems*, Stanford: Stanford University Press, 1969, p. 135.

2. Cp. my 'The Labour Theory of Value', *Marxist Perspective*, forthcoming, for a further consideration of these issues.

3. For this notion, see my *Ulysses and the Sirens*, op. cit., ch. I.

4. See, for example, G. M. Heal, *The Theory of Economic Planning*, Amsterdam: North-Holland, 1973, ch. 13.

5. G. Owen, *Game Theory*, Philadelphia: Saunders, 1968, p. 73.

6. J. Harsanyi, *Rational Behavior and Bargaining Equilibrium in Games and Social Situations*, Cambridge: Cambridge University Press, 1977.

7. Harsanyi sets up for discussion the following games, among many others:

	B_1	B_2	B_3
A_1	6,4	0,0	0,0
A_2	0,0	4,6	0,0
A_3	0,0	0,0	2,3

	B_1	B_2
A_1	3,3	1,3
A_2	3,1	1,1

In the left-hand game the strategy pair (A_3, B_3) emerges as the solution, a surprising but – on reflection – acceptable fact. In the right-hand game Harsanyi's solution is that each player uses each strategy with probability 50 percent. Personally I tend to think that the strategy (A_1, B_1) in this game should be a constraint on all possible solution concepts to such games; i.e. if a given concept comes with a different solution, it cannot be accepted.

8. Harsanyi, op. cit., p. 138.

9. Cp. especially J. Hicks, *A Theory of Wages*, London: Macmillan, 1932, p. 129.

10. *Productivity and Technical Change*, Cambridge: Cambridge University Press, 1960, pp. 43-44.

11. See notably C. Kennedy, 'Induced Bias in Innovation and the Theory of Distribution', *Economic Journal*, 1964.

12. 'Two Propositions in the Theory of Induced Innovations', *Economic Journal*, 1961.

13. *Technical Choice, Innovation and Economic Growth*, Cambridge: Cambridge University Press, 1975, p. 36, n. 2 and p. 54.

14. See, for example, A. Rapoport, *Two-Person Game Theory*, Ann Arbor: Michigan University Press, 1966, p. 37 ff.

15. 'On the Foundations of Game Theory: The Case of Non-Archimedean Utilities', *International Journal of Game Theory*, 1973.

16. See, for example, W. H. Riker and P. C. Ordeshook, *An Introduction to Positive Political Theory*, Englewood Cliffs: Prentice Hall, 1973, p. 21 ff.

17. 'Economic "Natural Selection" and the Theory of the Firm', *Yale Economic Essays*, 1964-65; also S. Winter, 'Optimization and Evolution in the Theory of the Firm', in: R. H. Day and T. Groves (eds.), *Adaptive Economic Models*, New York: Academic Press, 1975.

18. Winter, 'Economic "Natural Selection" ', op. cit., p. 262; also Winter, 'Optimization and Evolution', op. cit., p. 83.

19. *The Economic Approach to Human Behavior*, Chicago: Chicago University Press, 1976, ch. 8.

20. W. E. Cobb, 'Theft and the two Hypotheses', in: S. Rottenberg (ed.), *The Economics of Crime and Punishment*, Washington: American Enterprise Institute for Public Policy Research, 1973.

21. G. Tullock, 'Does Punishment Deter Crime?', *The Public Interest*, 1974.

22. *L'Inégalité des Chances*, Paris: Armand Colin, 1974. (The English edition of this work, *Education, Opportunity and Social Inequality*, New York: Wiley, 1974, has a less extensive discussion of this particular issue.)

23. See, in particular, their *La Reproduction*, Paris: Editions de Minuit, 1970.

24. Becker, op. cit., p. 160, 164.

25. Cp. my 'Note on Hysteresis in the Social Sciences', *Synthese*, 1976.

26. See R. Boudon, *Mathematical Structures of Social Mobility*, Amsterdam: Elsevier, 1973; J. L. Snell, 'Stochastic Processes', in: Luce, Bush and Galanter (eds.), *Handbook of Mathematical Psychology*, vol. III, New York: Wiley, 1965; A. Rapoport et al., *The 2 x 2 Game*, Ann Arbor: University of Michigan Press 1976, for a survey of such models.

27. R. Bellman, *Adaptive Control Processes*, Princeton: Princeton University Press, 1961, pp. 67-68; for brief and perceptive remarks on the relation between stochastic and deterministic models, see ibid., p. 130 ff.

28. Harsanyi, op. cit., p. 114, 117.

29. Cp. note 8 above.

30. R. Boudon, *Effets Pervers et Ordre Social*, Paris: Presses Universitaires de France, 1977, ch. IV and ch. V.

31. See, for example, T. Nagel, *The Possibility of Altruism*, Oxford: Oxford University Press, 1970.

32. See, for example, R. H. Strotz, 'Myopia and Inconsistency in Dynamic Utility Maximization', *Review of Economic Studies*, 1955-56.

33. E. S. Phelps and R. Pollak, 'On Second-Best National Saving and Game-Equilibrium Economic Growth', *Review of Economic Studies*, 1968.

34. See, for example, R. M. Cyert and M. H. DeGroot, 'Adaptive Utility', in: Day and Groves (eds.), op. cit.

35. G. Stigler and G. Becker, 'De Gustibus non est Disputandum', *American Economic Review*, 1977.

36. C. C. von Weiszäcker, 'Notes on Endogenous Change of Tastes', *Journal of Economic Theory*, 1971: 356.

37. See A. Gibbard, 'A Pareto-Consistent Libertarian Claim', *Journal of Economic Theory*, 1974: 388 ff, for this example.

38. M. Gorman, 'Tastes, Habits and Choices', *International Economic Review*, 1967: 218.

39. D. Davidson, 'Psychology as Philosophy', in: J. Glover (ed.), *The Philosophy of Mind*, Oxford: Oxford University Press, 1976, p. 108.

40. C. R. Wharton, 'Risk, Unvertainty and the Subsistence Farmer', in: G. Dalton (ed.), *Economic Development and Social Change*, New York: Natural History Press, 1971.

41. A. Bhaduri, 'A Study in Agricultural Backwardness under Semi-Feudalism', *Economic Journal*, 1973.

42. A. Gerschenkron, *Europe in the Russian Mirror*, Cambridge: Cambridge University Press, 1970, p. 65.

43. This dictum by John Hicks is quoted after A. O. Hirschman, *Exit, Voice and Loyalty*, Cambridge, Mass.: Harvard University Press, 1971, p. 55.

44. D. North, 'Institutional Change and Economic Growth', *Journal of Economic History*, 1971: p. 122.

45. D. North and R. Thomas, *The Rise of the Western World*, Cambridge: Cambridge University Press, 1973, p. 42.

• Comment

Yannick Lemel

Institut National de la Statistique et des Études Economiques, Paris, France

First, I should stress that it is difficult for someone who has no philosophical training – and this is my situation – to contribute valuable comments on the impressive paper by Jon Elster. So I shall not examine every problem discussed in it but I shall confine my remarks to the illustration of the gap between the model of 'rational-action' and the kind of behaviour this model is intended to describe.

I shall start with the abstract theory of action stated by Elster at the beginning of his paper. Human behaviour may be seen as the product of two filtering devices. The first is a set of constraints which define the subset of feasible actions within the set of possible actions. The second is 'a mechanism that singles out which member of the feasible set will be realized'.

Assume C is the set of all possible actions and $\mu \in A$ a parameter defining the particular set of constraints for a particular person. The family

$$\mathcal{C} = \{C\mu / C\mu \subset C \text{ and } \mu \in A\}$$

will be the family of all subsets of feasible actions. If we consider 'homo-economicus' then C will be $\mathbf{R}^n$, μ will be the n-tuple of prices and income and the family of feasible sets will be defined by:

$$C\mu = \{x/x \in \mathbf{R}^n \text{ and } \Sigma p_i x_i \leqslant I\} .$$

A rational homo-economicus is no more than the utility function representing preferences. Rational behaviour is then defined by a mapping:

(1) $U : C \rightarrow \mathbf{R}$ and the second filtering process will be the maximization of the function:

(2) the rational man chooses x_μ in C_μ so that

$$U(x_\mu) = \max \ \{U(x)/x \in C_\mu\}.$$

This well-known model is a mathematical expression for Elster's sentence: 'rational choice theories assert that this mechanism for the second filter is the deliberate and intentional choice for the purpose of maximizing some objective function'.

Now my point is this. It seems to me that most of Elster's anomalies of rationality are in fact examples of situations in which 'the purpose of maximizing some objective function' is clearly not a 'deliberate and intentional choice'. In other words, these anomalies of rationality are perhaps no more than the inability of equations (1) and (2) to represent the totality of our mental processes when we are engaged in deliberate and intentional choice. In fact, it means that the mathematical model of rational choice is not a sufficiently elaborate one: all the assumptions about rationality need to be spelt out in a mathematical form to complete equations (1) and (2).

Let us consider first the difference between the causal and the rational mechanisms for singling out one member of the feasible set.

The causal mechanism corresponds to the situation in which the resulting action is well defined every time some particular piece of information about the actor is known.[1] (Note that 'traditional behaviour' is one type of causal behaviour.) Then, if $\lambda \in B$ is the parameter which completely defines the actor, the second filter will be represented in case of a causal actor, by a mapping of $A \times B$ in C:

(3) $g : A \times B \rightarrow C$

$(\mu,\lambda) \rightarrow g(\mu,\lambda)$

subject to the particular condition:

(4) $g(\mu, \lambda) \in C_\mu$. How are (1)-(2) and (3)-(4) related?

In fact, the most general representation of the second filtering process will be a mapping of the family A into C:

(5) $f = A \rightarrow C$

$\mu \rightarrow f(\mu)$ subject, of course, to the particular condition that:

(6) $f(\mu) \in C_\mu$. The function f represents a revealed preference. The works of Ritcher[2] and others have shown that there is no great difference between (1)-(2) and (5)-(6). When the function f is 'congruent', i.e. satisfies the condition:

(7) if $f(\mu_1) \in C_{\mu_2}$ and $C_{\mu_2} \subset C_{\mu_1}$, then $f(\mu_1) = f(\mu_2)$, there exists a utility-function U such that (1)-(2) are identical to (5)-(6). This function U satisfies:

(8) $\max \{U(x)/x \in C_\mu\} = f(\mu), \forall_\mu$.

Function g is a special case of the second filtering process representated by f. So, every time g is congruent, we can find a function U and construct a rational model so that the two formal models of behaviour will be indistinguishable.

Rational behaviour and causal behaviour are not very different from a mathematical point of view. The condition of 'congruence' is not a very stringent one. Nevertheless, it is clear that a rational actor is not a causal one. Elster, speaking about 'parametric rationality' writes: a 'rational agent believes himself to be free to adjust optimally to a constant environment' (omitting that this environment is made up of other agents similar to himself and doing the same thing). So the rational actor must be free but the causality and rationality models as defined earlier do not take account of this problem.

The rational actor defined by Elster (and I think this definition is right) is by essence free. When this actor has to choose between two feasible actions, his freedom is not the same as when he has to choose between 1,000,000 among which the first two are included. In the case of a congruent f, to choose $f(\mu_1) \in C_{\mu_2} \subset C_{\mu_1}$ and to choose $f(\mu_1) \in C_{\mu_1}$ is not equivalent from the point of view of freedom. The second opportunity is preferable because C_{μ_1} is larger than C_{μ_2}; it does not matter whether the actor chooses the same action in both cases.

For the free rational actor, the value of a choice is clearly linked with the set of feasible points within which the choice must be made, and it is not restricted to the particular action chosen. This kind of preference is not built into the framework of utility functions. So the rational model is unsatisfactory. It is necessary to build a new, more elaborate model in which the value of a chosen action and the value of the set of feasible actions are distinguishable. This can easily be done with two separate utility functions linked to each level of the problem.

Consider now rationality, time and random behaviour. As Elster writes the usual definition of rationality is inadequate to cover our 'intuitive notion of rationality' because it is a static one.

Imagine an actor who selects different objects from the same set of feasible actions from time to time at random. In such a case it is impossible to distinguish random from rational behaviour even if the actor each time selects the object with the deliberate purpose of maximizing some objective function. In such a case, model (1)-(2) is still valid but it is unable to represent a process taking place through time because there is no mention of time in equations (1)-(2). This is another example of what I mean. Until now, economists and sociologists have not given a complete enough expression of their intuitive notions of rationality. Elster claims implicitly that they have not built the intuitive concept of an 'intention', which is something which necessarily persists through time, into their mathematical model of rational action.

Elster's paper provides a good survey of all the intuitive ideas our models of rationality must incorporate. Let me finish with one intuitive notion which is not in the paper. A rational actor is able to examine the costs and returns of each course of action, to compare these and choose the most advantageous one. Such an intuitive concept cannot easily be expressed in terms of the model of rational actor: the utility function classifies the *net benefit* of actions. This is a mistake. If we were able to construct models adequately representing the actor weighing costs and returns, we should have a tool with which to integrate economics and work of sociologists like Blood and Wolfe or Homans for example.[3]

Notes

1. Of course, I assume that the particular situation associated with this information is temporally anterior to the action. See notably D. A. Pierre and L. D. Haugh, 'Causality in Temporal Systems', *Journal of Econometrics* 5, 1977.

2. See, for instance, M. K. Ritcher, 'Revealed Preference Theory', *Econometrica* 34, July 1966.

3. G. S. Homans, *Social Behaviour. Its Elementary Forms*, London: Routledge and Kegan Paul, 1968. R. O. Blood and D. M. Wolfe, *Husbands and Wives*, Glencoe, Illinois: The Free Press, 1960.

• Comment

Duncan MacRae, Jr.

University of North Carolina, USA

An analysis of rational models by a philosopher of science can be especially valuable because this viewpoint should permit a comparison of the limited perspectives of the various social sciences from 'outside'. Thus, Elster's initial point, that we may consider human action as involving choice within a set of structural constraints, gives promise of synthesizing approaches that have been characteristic of economics and sociology. Lesourne makes a similar point.

If we consider human action in this way we must then try to estimate the limits that these structural constraints place on choice. A methodology based on the observation of constraints alone as independent variables, such as a sociological survey using statuses and roles as predictors of behaviour, can encourage the conclusion that only constraints matter – even if much of the variance is left unexplained. Conversely, a methodology centering about the observation of changes in system equilibria (such as changes in price and in quantity produced) can lead us to see nothing but choice – even if historical and cross-national comparisons might reveal changes in the parameters of the model.

Even if we combine these approaches, as we should, we cannot expect a synthesis immediately, unless the two together explain essentially all the variance. As long as they do not, each discipline will tend to claim all the unexplained variance as lying within its own domain, and claim priority for its own approach in efforts to explain that residual variance. One resolution of these disputes might be in the realm of practice or experimentation: whichever discipline can propose the most useful and successful interventions, presumably in the service of social values, will 'win the game'.

Elster's second point is that rational action may sometimes not be precisely definable. In strategic games where players must play simultaneously, or in sequences of moves that may be reduced to simultaneous plays, a player may know the *conditions of play* completely yet not know the material results of his choices, even as statistical expectations for mixed strategies. In these cases we can do little with rational models.

When such 'impossibility' conditions arise, a useful strategy of analysis is to ask how frequent they really are – to look for related models that are solvable and that correspond to reality. Thus, if we can treat sequences of plays as sequences, under some conditions we may be able to assume that players respond primarily to the *present* situation rather than to anticipated *future* situations. Models of this kind include the Richardson-type model of arms races, economic models of the 'cobweb theorem' type, or models of alternation of political party control involving political, social, and economic variables.

Elster's observation that decisions are based on *subjective* probabilities seems to introduce the same risks of indeterminacy into economic models as does the consideration of *perceived* situations. Whether indeterminate or not, however, these phenomena are real; the actors we observe may fail to see the world as a scientific observer sees it, or to estimate the consequences of their acts as he would.

As scientific observers, however, we may feel that people would be better off (at least in self-interested behaviour) if they *did* view the world in an 'objective' fashion. Thus, Elster suggests that politicians may be selected for the low degree of distortion of their judgements. I should like to believe this was true, especially if undistorted estimates led them to seek the *general* welfare rationally; but the conjecture requires empirical test.

Another mechanism for increasing the 'objectivity' of decision-makers' estimates is of course education. Practice in estimation of probabilities, and in use of the principles of estimation, might conceivably reduce the disparities between subjective and objective probabilities when the latter were knowable. This sort of instruction is analogous to the instruction that d'Iribarne proposes for the consumer and citizen.

A third significant point of Elster's is that satisficing cannot easily be defined as a form of maximizing. He cites Sidney Winter in this connection. We may construct models of rational search for information, and under some conditions they may predict convergent behaviour regardless of the starting point. But Elster correctly stresses that they may not; in this respect his argument parallels that of Lévy-Garboua in noting that convergence or equilibrium may be reached at a choice that is far from the best. With a wide and multidimensional dispersion of the qualities of objects, relative to the consumer's motivation to search, some subspaces of the distribution of objects will presumably never be searched.

This distinction brings out a difference between rational choice models and Skinnerian models of reinforcement, which may deserve investigation – or may possibly be illuminated by the psychological literature. The rational-choice model implies that the organism learns by *comparison* of alternatives; the reinforcement model permits the strengthening of a response in terms of the *absolute* degree or reinforcement afforded by a single stimulus. Between the two (though not in the Skinnerian model) there may be a 'cognitive map' that guides the organism to the initial choice of a stimulus, and perhaps allows it to reject a reinforcing stimulus in favour of a possibly better one. But we are led in this way back to the difficult problem of accounting for perception and cognition.

A final significant problem raised by Elster concerns charity. He noted that it is difficult to explain charity as the result of narrowly defined (material) self-interest. Economists in our seminar immediately responded that this involved no problem, since more general maximands could be postulated to account for altruistic behaviour.

Why, then, is it narrow, material maximands that we see used most often? Many economists seem to believe that altruism is a very scarce resource, and that material gain or at least self-interest dominates human action (note that I am referring here to self-interest as commonly defined, and not to the tautological 'self-interest' that would include any and all maximands of rational action). I suggest that there is a valuative question at stake as well as a scientific one – a question that arises also in d'Iribarne's paper. Welfare economics, which is closely associated with positive economics, *defines* a chooser's welfare in terms of the satisfaction of his preferences. If he were able to sacrifice his own welfare (in the ordinary, not the economic sense of the term) for others through altruistic action, economists would no longer so easily be able to define welfare as identical with preference satisfaction. Some economists do try to find self-seeking motives (in the ordinary sense) for charity, heroism, sainthood, and the like; but these efforts are not easily accepted by non-economists. They involve alteration of the commonsense notion of 'welfare' – which, unlike scientific concepts, cannot be given a completely arbitrary name or deprived of a name that links it with widely shared values. I treat these questions more fully in *The Social Function of Social Science*, Yale University Press, 1976, ch. 5.

Part II

PREFERENCES AND CHOICES

4

Perception and the Formation of Choice

Louis Lévy-Garboua

University of Paris XIII, France

In the standard works of economists, objects of choice and preferences are assumed to be perfectly known. Those who wish to find out how they are determined are told that this task is the basic responsibility of psychologists and sociologists. In fact, this attitude is no more than a way of evading the issue because economic theory is developed without reference to the writings of such specialists as if formation of choice was a meaningless or unimportant question, as though ostensibly at least there were no such things as beliefs, habits, impulses, addictions, social norms, influences or errors, and as if misperceptions did not exist. Instead of asking whether all actions conform to the rational behaviour assumption, I shall attempt to explain how such actions are decided by applying the economic approach to perception defined as the selection of objects of choice.

After reviewing the present standpoint of economics vis-à-vis the formation of choice (section 1), the economic approach is used to deal with this problem (section 2). Several applications of the proposed model are subsequently explored and classified under two headings, i.e. stability of choice (section 3) and misperception (section 4).

1. Economics and the formation of choice

Economists traditionally locate the boundary of their discipline downstream of the formation of choice and take the preferences of individuals as given. Although this point of view has become a firmly rooted habit within the profession, I contend that recent advances of the economic approach have made it obsolete. The arguments for rejecting choice formation outside the realm of economics would seem to be of three kinds: (i) formation of choice is a non-economic question; (ii) it is a meaningless question; and (iii) it is an unimportant question for an economist. I shall comment on each of these arguments in turn explaining why today they are no longer valid.

1.1. Is formation of choice a non-economic question?

It is by no means certain that economists have ever been profoundly convinced of the validity and general applicability of the rational behaviour assumption. However, they regarded this as adequate for any study of market behaviour and it meant that they could avoid dealing with such difficult questions as human emotions, irrationality and the deterministic forces of society. These were therefore confined to the category of non-economic questions and no further reference was made to them. The weakness of this position was that the boundaries of economics were not clear-cut. When some economists began to analyse non-market or illegitimate behaviour, many of their peers no doubt felt that they were going beyond the limits of reasonable subject matter. A number of psychologists and sociologists, whose prolonged study of individual and collective behaviour patterns had instilled in them a greater measure of caution, must also have felt that these economists had become victims of an overuse of their intellectual faculties and had finally lost sight of their limitations. In fact, it is a narrow understanding of the rational behaviour hypothesis which has on every occasion given rise to sterile controversy on the boundaries of economics.

The rationality to which I am referring now is not a behavioural assumption of limited applicability, better suited for explaining market decisions than non-market decisions, for instance. Rather, it is seen as an axiom of unparalleled generality, supporting the application of the economic approach to all kinds of human behaviour.[1] The power of the economic approach vis-à-vis other approaches in social sciences stems from the fact that *economicness* is a universal characteristic of all physical and living systems which does not depend upon the nature of the environments and goals.

Even now, however, most economists do not perceive the full generality of their approach since they are reluctant to admit that economicness is embedded in human beings. Therefore, they fail to apply the rational behaviour assumption to the decision process as a whole, i.e. the implementation of choice (action) *and* the formation of choice. This shortcoming of traditional economics has resulted in the failure to explain many kinds of human behaviour. This in turn has given rise to a growing movement of criticism and departure from economic analysis, and from the hypothesis of rational behaviour, whether we call it Weberian, Galbraithian, Radical or Determinist, and to a growing interest for sociological thinking. I believe that the economic approach performs a better understanding of all kinds of behaviour than any alternative theory provided we use it to explain how choices are formed effectively rather than deciding, once they have been made, whether they are 'rational' or 'determined'. This has the merit of replacing the usual interminable controversy by verifiable propositions.

1.2. Is formation of choice a meaningless question?

Economists probably believed that they could afford to overlook the formation of choice if the objects of choice seem to be *obvious*. On the other hand, those actions whose motives did not seem sufficiently clear (e.g. religious behaviour) were rejected as being outside the scope of economics.

The selfish pursuit of gain was first seen as an obvious object of choice for producers and workers in a competitive economy. There is no denying the validity of this hypothesis. However, economists are often accused of having reduced human motivation to this one goal or, in other words, of having reduced Man to nothing more than a homo economicus. Before going any further, it should be remembered that every human science has rightly attempted to restrict the nature of the goals which condition action. Sociology has placed prime emphasis on social status, psycho-analysis on sexual pleasure, anthropology on the conservation of species, and sociobiology on altruism. It goes without saying that these various motivations are not independent of one another. They stem perhaps from the single principle of action capable of producing within the same individual patterns of behaviour of increasingly comprehensive nature as he internalizes more complex interactions with his environment (see Becker, 1976; Boudon, 1977). It is no less clear that the general goal(s) of human activity break down into a large number of practical aims, depending on the problems to be solved. However, as soon as the objects of choice increase in number and variety, their obviousness disappears and the question of choice formation arises.

Consumer choices are typically multidimensional. However, the traditional theory of consumer behaviour has preserved the obviousness of objects of choice by treating these as homogeneous and stable goods. Every consumer is thus confronted with the (finite) set of existing goods as the practical objects for his decisions. This is no longer true with the new theory of consumer behaviour. The commodities, instead of being goods, are now considered as being values.[2] Since the latter are non-material and non-directly communicable elements, they are likely to be perceived by individuals in a manner which is both more costly and more diverse.[3] The goods themselves are considered as complex, differentiated and unstable items and the services which they are expected to provide are linked with the characteristics which describe them.[4] The basic services or characteristics to which they correspond therefore replace the goods as practical objects for purchase decisions. But there is no reason to believe a priori that these are perceived and evaluated in an identical manner by every consumer nor even that they are finite in number. However, it is essential that these objects be 'objective', i.e. obvious and known to all, if one wishes to avoid dealing with the formation of choice. The assumption made by Lancaster (1966, 1971), that the characteristics of goods are technical and objective, can thus be considered as a way of postponing the problem of choice formation.

Hence, the dilemma of being torn between the desire to simplify economic theory and that of ridding it of oversimplified and ad hoc hypotheses. This second aspect deserves at least some attention. Additional encouragement can be derived from the fact that utility is an extremely flexible concept which does not insist that objects of choice be decided once and for all, nor that they belong to a limited category. On the other hand, the ranking of any two objects of choice on a scale of preference is regarded as stable since it would be difficult to understand how an individual could understand and adapt to a constantly changing environment if this were not the case. Utility is seen in this context as a general and vague means for orienting human activity. It can be applied to a great variety of objectives, whether monetary or psychic, individual or collective, manifest or latent. In addition, it is a neutral term which goes with various scientific and philosophic views and is not just utilitarianism.

The theory of the formation of choice put forward in this article is based simply on the idea that individuals are confronted with a collection of alternatives, e.g. goods, and that they attempt to make the best choice by basing their evaluation of these alternatives solely on *perceived* objects of choice (or characteristics or information). This selection procedure is obviously sequential. It is stopped once the marginal cost of the search equals or exceeds the expected marginal return.

1.3 Is formation of choice an unimportant question?

If formation of choice used up few resources, economists could have overlooked it without regret. At first sight such a viewpoint does not appear absurd. The process of choice formation in fact utilizes flows of information and matter-energy which are not primarily designed to modify the individual's environment at the time when they are brought into play but rather to prepare the ground for a future change. It is thus inconceivable that one should exhaust resources just to obtain knowledge of a situation, and before the corresponding process of action has been initiated.

This knowledge can be acquired through the action itself (experience) or before (inspection). In the latter case the individual draws little on external resources and utilizes mainly on his own human resources. Economists have thus been able to regard the formation of choice as an inexpensive activity to the extent that experience was merged with action and the role of human resources ignored. Since the emergence of the theories of human capital, of learning by doing and of the allocation of time, such reasoning is no longer possible. What is more, the possibility of storing and retrieving information throughout the life-cycle, particularly via the experience one acquires, would suggest that formation of choice might well be a pervasive activity.[5]

2. An economic approach to the formation of choice

A study of choice formation must bear on some specification of the factor which ultimately gives an orientation to human activities. In the economic approach this is provided by the preferences of individuals, which can be expressed by saying that 'any person confronted with several alternatives chooses the one which he prefers'. One can then build up a well-ordered utility function which attains a maximum for the alternative preferred. If one adds that the preferences are given, one obtains the rational behaviour hypothesis. The economic models of search have extended this hypothesis in the direction indicated by Stigler (1961). They examine what happens when each individual is confronted at each moment of time with a sample of options rather than with the whole collection. This assumption is based on the fact that time is needed to visit each market and evaluate each good.[6] The statistical decision rule then applies, provided the sampling is random, and it explains why a sample is better than a census and why, when the cost of search rises, less search is made before coming to a decision.

Unfortunately, all of these models assume that individuals *know* what they 'prefer', whereas one needs only to simulate a few concrete decisions, as psychologists do,[7] to realize that the main difficulty is in forming or knowing preferences. Economists, who have hitherto overlooked the imperfection (i.e. the selectivity) of any kind of perception, doubtless miss the essential point with regard to choice formation, *i.e. the uncertainty which the decision-maker feels with regard to his intrinsic preference*. To know this, one's information needs to be complete and faultless.

In the rest of this article I shall explore this new direction, which introduces *perception* into the economic analysis of decision-making.

Psychologists, when their simulations produce paradoxes, tend to conclude that choice is 'irrational'. In fact, a detailed discussion of the examples which they provide suggests that in every instance certain systematic factors of choice orientation have been omitted. What has in fact been attributed to chance circumstances or to 'irrationality' should be ascribed to these factors.[8] It would seem that the rational behaviour hypothesis can and should be retained to explain choice formation when preferences are not stated in advance. The economic approach can be applied in this context when perception of the objects of choice is imperfect and their evaluation costly, since it basically amounts to considering that observed behaviour patterns are not entirely due to chance or to uncontrollable factors arising from the individual's environment. These individuals have a certain latitude for orientating their actions in the way they desire and for modifying their environment.

2.1. A sequential model of choice formation

Let us assume that an individual, at the time of making one decision, is confronted with a collection of options. These are complex objects, for instance goods, activities or persons. However, each alternative is analysed by the decision-maker as a mix of more simple objects of choice (characteristics) which are the services expected from this decision (the information out of which the former can be evaluated). Moreover, perception being selective, these characteristics do not become apparent all at once but *gradually*. A new quantum of characteristics is perceived at each successive step of the search. The individual therefore revises his evaluation of the collection of options[9] as a result of what he has just perceived. Since his preferences are assumed to be stable throughout the whole process, the revelation of new objects of choice (information) is the sole factor capable of modifying a previous evaluation.

At the end of each step all the options are ranked in decreasing order of preference. However, instead of being definitive as economic theory would normally assume, this ranking can be revised just as long as there is imperfect perception of the alternatives and the individual retains some uncertainty as to his intrinsic preference. Note ($Z_1(j)$, $Z_2(j), \ldots Z_i(j) \ldots Z_n(j)$) the services (in utility terms) expected from the alternatives that have been ranked respectively in 1st, 2nd, . . ., ith . . ., nth position[10] at the end of the jth step. The subject's intrinsic preference denotes the alternative which he would choose if his perception were perfect. The one which is ranked 1st at the end of the jth step has a probability prob $(1, \infty/1, j)$ of retaining this position at the end of an infinite time of search. If this conditional probability were equal to 1, the subject would be certain of making 'the right choice' and would delay his decision no longer.[11] The maximum expected utility would then be equal to $Z_1(j)$. Since the individual is generally uncertain about his choice, the expected maximum utility depends not only on the evaluation $Z_1(j)$ but also on the conditional probability of not being mistaken prob $(1, \infty/1, j)$. This last value is a measure of the subject's *confidence* in his choice at the end of the jth step.

To lack confidence in one's choice means that one feels that one may be making a mistake in taking the decision which seems the best at that particular moment. The cost of error can be evaluated accurately once the consequences of the decision taken have been fully experienced. If a consumer chooses a defective car, he will bear the cost of replacing it with a better car. If a student embarks upon a course of study which is too difficult for him, he will drop out unexpectedly and fail to capture at least part of the benefits that he had expected. If a person chooses an unsuitable spouse, he will have to bear the cost of marital discord and possibly divorce.

An individual who takes a decision without being fully confident of his choice revises downwards his evaluation of the expected present value by an amount which is equal to the present value of the expected cost of error, given the subjective probability of an error. From $Z_1(j)$, the utility of choice drops to the lower value:

$$U(j) = Z_1(j) - \lambda[1 - \text{prob}\,(1, \infty/1, j)], \quad \lambda > 0. \tag{1}$$

[12]

λ is the compensation in utility terms which the individual requires in order that he choose the alternative which seems to him the best at the end of the jth step, despite the fact that he is certain that this is a wrong choice. There is no apparent reason for λ to be dependent on j. By using conf(j) to denote the confidence of an individual in his choice at the end of the jth step, a loss function L can be defined as follows:

$$L(j) = \lambda[1 - \text{conf}(j)] + C(j), \tag{2}$$

where

$$\text{conf}(j) = \text{prob}\,(1, \infty/1, j), \quad 0 \leqslant \text{conf}(j) \leqslant 1, \tag{3}$$

and where $C(j)$ represents the total cost of search up to the jth step.

Since the search for new objects of choice (characteristics) is costly, once the observer has reached the jth step he will only continue his search if he anticipates that the marginal return will outweigh the marginal cost. The expected marginal return is the value of the increase in confidence expected from the revelation of new parameters. Expressing the marginal cost of search as c, the observer makes his decision when:

$$\lambda[E\ \mathrm{conf}(j+1) - \mathrm{conf}(j)] \leqslant c, \tag{4}$$

where E denotes the expected value of the variable which it precedes.[13]

The optimal stopping rule (4) is also obtained by minimizing the loss function associated with the choice:

$$L(j) \leqslant EL(j+1).^{14} \tag{5}$$

The value of the confidence or of the loss associated with the choice is a highly subjective quantity. One individual, in possession of the same data as his fellow, could nonetheless have far greater confidence in his choice. However, the influence of psychological traits is doubtless more superficial than it would appear since beliefs are in the main based on past experience. This will become apparent when we express confidence in relation to the decision parameters.

2.2. Perception of alternatives and confidence is one's choice

The perception of a new quantum of characteristics changes the decision taken at the end of the preceding search step if, and only if, the re-evaluation of at least one alternative not ranked number one places it above the alternative which was given first preference. For example, at the end of the $(j + 1)$th step, the option ranked in ith position at the end of j steps overtakes the one which was in first position, i.e.

$$Z_i\ (j+1) > Z_1\ (j+1), \quad \text{where } i > 1, \tag{6}$$

whereas

$$Z_i\ (j) \leqslant Z_1 (j).$$

During choice formation this comparison takes place before perception has occurred. Condition (6) therefore applies to the values anticipated for the new evaluations of expected services. Ex ante and ignoring the nature of the new characteristics to be perceived, an additive expression of the utilities would appear to be justified:

$$EZ_1\ (j+1) = Z_1\ (j) + z_1 \quad \text{and} \quad EZ_i\ (j+1) = Z_i\ (j) + z_i, \tag{7}$$

where z_1 and z_i denote the expected outcomes, in terms of utility, of a supplementary search phase on the corresponding evaluations of alternatives 1 and i.

By using (7), the condition required for pursuit of the search to bring about a change of decision can be expressed simply as:

$$z_i - z_1 > Z_1(j) - Z_i(j) \geqslant 0, \quad \text{where } i > 1. \tag{8}$$

Thus, the perception of new characteristics modifies the choice if, and only if, at least one of the options not selected previously contains more of these (in terms of utility) than the option selected and if the differential endowment of the former in new characteristics is greater than that of the latter in characteristics already perceived. In order to be decisive, the characteristics not yet perceived must either be very unequally distributed between the options or, if this distribution is not very unequal, embody a high degree of utility (within the range of variation actually found in the collection of objects).[15]

The decision to continue to search depends on the subjective probability of observing one or more inequalities such as (8). Moreover, before any new perception, the events described by the inequalities (8), when i varies between 2 and n, are mutually independent. This is equally true of contrary events. By utilizing (3) and (8), the subject's confidence in his choice at the end of the jth step can be expressed as follows:

$$\text{conf}(j) = \prod_{i=2}^{n} \text{prob}\,(z_i - z_1 \leqslant Z_1(j) - Z_i(j))$$

$$= \prod_{i=2}^{n} h_{ji}. \tag{9}$$

Note that:

$$h_{ji} = \int_{-\infty}^{+\infty} \int_{-\infty}^{z_1 + Z_1(j) - Z_i(j)} \overset{1}{f_j}(z_1)\, \overset{i}{f_j}(z_i)\, \mathrm{d}z_1\, \mathrm{d}z_i, \quad \text{where } i > 1, \tag{10}$$

by using $\overset{i}{f_j}(z_i)$ to express the density function of the services from the ith object which the search should reveal at the end of the jth step.

Prior to any perception, no information on the objects can influence the probabilization. Thus

$$f_j^1 = f_j^i = f_j, \quad \text{for every } i. \tag{11}$$

By applying (11) to (10) and by calculating the double integral, one obtains:

$$\begin{aligned} h_{ji} &= \int_{-\infty}^{+\infty} \left(\int_{-\infty}^{z_1 + Z_1(j) - Z_i(j)} f_j(z_i)\, dz_i \right) f_j(z_1) dz_1 \\ &= \int_{-\infty}^{+\infty} F_j(z_1 + Z_1(j) - Z_i(j)) f_j(z_1) dz_1 \\ &= h_j(Z_1(j) - Z_i(j)), \quad \text{with } h_j' \geqslant 0. \end{aligned} \tag{12}$$

$F_j(z)$ is the cumulative density function associated with the distribution of services revealed by the search and h_j an increasing function of a single variable.

In short, confidence in one's choice at the end of the jth step can be expressed as follows:

$$\text{conf}(j) = \prod_{i=2}^{n} h_j(Z_1(j) - Z_i(j)), \tag{13}$$

in which each of the terms is given in equation (12).

Equation (13) shows that confidence in one's choice is greatest when the evaluation gaps between the various options are highest. However, these gaps do not all have the same weight, since $(Z_1(j) - Z_i(j))$ increases with i. Thus, h_{ji} increases with i. Evaluation gaps concerning the objects ranked at the top affect confidence to a far greater extent than those concerning objects ranked at the bottom of the list. Moreover, if distribution of services revealed by the search are fairly much concentrated around zero, the values for h_{ji} tend rapidly towards 1 when $(Z_1(j) - Z_i(j))$ increases.[16] As i increases, the h_{ji} functions flatten out in the neighbourhood of 1 in the probable variation interval of their argument. They therefore contribute very little to establishing or modifying confidence, with the result that bottom-ranked alternatives tend to be 'omitted' in subsequent evaluations.

As the optimal stopping rule shows, what counts in choice formation is the *increase* in confidence and not its absolute value. The process will converge on a decision if this increase diminishes with search after some point.

Equations (12) and (13) show that confidence depends on the result of previous search (via evaluation gaps $(Z_1(j) - Z_i(j))$) and on the observer's belief in the probable revelations from his future search (via the functions f_j and F_j). Expectation of future events is itself linked to past experience. The subject draws upon his prior knowledge and his first search phases in order to get some idea of the shape of these distributions. He revises his belief at the end of each phase as a result of the new observations he has made. If the jth step confirms the previous ranking, at least as far as the leading alternatives are concerned,[17] the individual concludes that this is probably because he has already perceived the decisive characteristics. He therefore concludes that his chances of finding others during the course of subsequent phases are even slimmer than he had thought during the preceding phase. The f_j distribution is then more concentrated around zero than f_{j-1}. When f_j approaches the distribution totally concentrated around zero, the growth of the h_{ji} slows down as they get closer asymtotically to 1.[18] The confidence gain a person expects from continuing his search will therefore diminish progressively once he begins to notice a degree of stability among the top-ranking alternatives. This conclusion will be further strengthened if evaluation gaps between top-ranking alternatives do not diminish. Equation (12) shows that these h_{ji} are increasing and concave functions of their respective arguments, which are in fact these gaps. Thus, when previous choices are confirmed by observation, this tends to put an end to the search.

3. Stability of choice

A person's belief in the correctness of his opinion and his choice stems from the fundamental asymmetry which exists between what is perceived and what is not perceived. Once the individual has stopped his search, it is as if what he does not perceive did not exist and could not have existed in the sense that his behaviour henceforth no longer depends upon this and becomes stable. Having attained this position of equilibrium, the individual *believes* in his choice and tends not to change it. Thereafter the only factors which can reduce his confidence to the point of triggering off a new process of search and causing a change of decision stem from experience and changes in the environment.[19]

3.1. Confidence and decision changes

It is to be expected therefore that opinions which are not or cannot be followed by any action are more stable than those which are put to the test. An individual's belief in his religious choices is generally much more deeply rooted than his belief in his market choices, because it is impossible for him, during his lifetime, to have any experience of death and the origins of the world, whereas he can always try out new products. Once a person has acquired confidence in a system of religious beliefs via his education, he has no longer any inherent reason to change this.

Thus, if preferences are stable, the only factors likely to cause decision changes are experience and environmental changes. The occurrence of a disaster, the introduction of new products on the market, a migration or a change of job, family events or any change in social environment may give rise to a revision of earlier choices. The economic approach analyses the manner in which such factors influence observable behaviour in terms of their price and income effects, as for example Stigler and Becker (1977). However, our analysis puts the accent on informational resources and costs of perception. The phenomena mentioned above are in particular responsible for bringing about a change in the objects of choice, revealing decisive characteristics and uncovering new markets or new alternatives.

Economic growth, in particular, causes frequent changes in a person's environment. When the growth rate increases, the rhythm of change speeds up and confidence begins to waver in the choice of actions undertaken; whilst certain events support, and others contradict, this. This kind of situation therefore encourages more decision changes. However, the expected marginal return from the search for the best option is low because new unforeseen and destabilizing changes are anticipated. Under such conditions, randomness can become an optimal decision rule. An individual will not hestitate to experiment despite his lack of confidence in his choice. This analysis therefore reveals a negative effect of economic growth on consumer welfare of which mention is seldom made.

3.2. Habit and resistance to change

Experience can also cause habit formation and resistance to change. Suppose for example that a person, having used a brand, feels that the services it provides fulfill, and even exceed, his expectations. If the information acquired about this brand is *specific*, experience will only increase the satisfaction expected from it without having any effect on the evaluation of the services provided by substitute products. If Z_1 and Z_2 are used to denote the ex ante evaluations of the two leading choices and E the experience acquired with regard to the first brand, the evaluation gap can be said to have passed from $a(0) = Z_1 - Z_2$ prior to use to $a(E) = Z_1(E) - Z_2 \geqslant a(0)$ after use. Experience has thus confirmed the choice made and increased confidence in it. A change of decision at this point in time would involve a higher cost of experimentation than before trial of the product. This cost in fact corresponds to the loss of utility incurred by forgoing the services of brand number 1 in order to try those of brand number 2, and this can be expressed in the following terms:

$$c(E) = [Z_1(E) - \lambda(1\text{-prob}(1, \infty/1, E))] - [Z_2 - \lambda(1 - \text{prob}(2, \infty/1, E))]$$
$$= a(E) + \lambda[\text{prob}(1, \infty/1, E) - \text{prob}(2, \infty/1, E)], \qquad (14)$$

where prob $(i, \infty/1, E)$ $(i = 1, 2)$ denotes the probability, posterior to experience of brand number 1, that product i be intrinsically preferred to the others. It will be easily seen that:[20]

$$\lambda[\text{prob}(1, \infty/1, E) - \text{prob}(2, \infty/1, E)] = \lambda[h(a)\, h(a + Z_2 - Z_3) \ldots h(a + Z_2 - Z_n)$$
$$- (1 - h(a))\, h(Z_2 - Z_3) \ldots h(Z_2 - Z_n)]$$
$$= A\ [a(E)], \qquad (15)$$

where the perception index (E, in this case) has been omitted after the h function for the sake of simplicity. A is a positive and non-decreasing function of $a(E)$. The marginal cost of experimenting with brand 2 is therefore increased as a result of trial of brand number 1 in so far as this has *maintained* or *increased* the evaluation gap between the known product and the unknown products:

$$c(E) = a(E) + A\ [a(E)], \quad \text{with } c' > 0. \qquad (16)$$

The incentive to experiment further lessens once the first test has given 'satisfactory' results. The satisficing behaviour assumption is therefore compatible with the economic approach. It is not necessary to apply the full test procedure to reinforce belief in one's choice, since brand 2 will always remain unknown despite the fact that it might have proved more satisfactory than brand 1 had both been compared under identical conditions. *All other things being equal*, provided the experimental product lives up to the consumer's expectations, it tends to become his regular brand.

3.3. Perceptive abilities and addictions

By strengthening the consumer's confidence in his choice, experience will stimulate demand for a product considered satisfactory. Generally speaking, this demand stabilizes rapidly since confidence has an upper bound. It may, however, happen that demand for a particular good will continue to increase with use, reflecting a continual increment in its expected marginal utility. In such cases, consumption of the good becomes an addiction. Stigler and Becker (1977: 77-81) have suggested an explanation for this intriguing phenomenon by drawing a distinction between 'beneficial addictions', such as music addiction and 'harmful addictions', such as drug addiction. In their view, listening to music results in the accumulation of a form of specific human capital, i.e. the ability to appreciate music, which reduces the cost of producing 'music appreciation'. In a similar manner, addiction to heroin produces a disinvestment in another kind of specific human capital, i.e. the capacity for euphoria, which increases the cost of producing 'euphoria'. Although the consumption of music appreciation increases with experience, whereas consumption of euphoria diminishes, the input amounts required by these consumptions are liable to increase over time. The trouble with this explanation lies in the overly vague specificiation of the good produced, i.e. music appreciation and euphoria, which can be given misleading interpretations.

Our analysis would suggest that addictive goods have special perceptive properties, as a result of which their expected marginal utility relative to that of other goods continues to increase. Music and heroin have this much in common – they both widen the horizons of perception and produce perceptive commodities which we may call 'life dimensions'. Cultural goods, drugs and gambling which stir the imagination all fall within this category, although music, as opposed to heroin, is a beneficial addiction because supposedly it does not diminish one's ability to enjoy other dimensions of life.[21] Unlike heroin, the consumption of music enables musical ability to develop with no adverse effect on other perceptive abilities. The beneficial effect of music is specific, whereas the harmful effect of heroin is general. Since musical experience is specific, the expected marginal utility of music time (and that of the 'musical dimension') is likely to increase continuously relative to the marginal utility of other goods (and life dimensions). On the other hand, since the experience of heroin is general, the decrease in the expected marginal utility from a dose of heroin has an immediate and identical effect on that of other goods. Thus, the harmful effect of heroin does not result in a drop in the demand for heroin. This theory suggests that demand for heroin *appears* to be inelastic because the result of this product's general harmfulness is to rise prices of the other dimensions of life as well as the price of the 'euphoric dimension'.

4. Misperception

By overlooking the formation of choice, economic analysis has restricted human behaviour to a naive psychological pattern and has been incapable of explaining with any relevance a great number of behaviour patterns linked to misperception. The introduction of this forgotten factor throws light on a number of questions ranging from the market mechanism to the role of influence on choices.

4.1. Perception of characteristics and the market mechanism

The new theory of consumer behaviour explains the choice of market goods by regarding these as complex objects which can be broken down into simpler elements. Despite the central role played in this by the idea of a 'relevant characteristic', as developed by Lancaster (1966, 1971) and by the 'hedonists' (see, for example, Maynes, 1976), it is hard to find a clear and convincing definition of it. The foregoing analysis of choice formation supplies an answer to this question.

Let us suppose that all the physical characteristics embodied in a collection of goods are directly observable. Those which should be perceived first of all are either those which are relatively very abundant in certain brands or those which embody a high degree of utility. The economicness of the perception process has the effect of 'maximizing' the evaluation gaps between goods from the collection right from the first steps of observation. As a result, confidence in one's choice increases rapidly whereas the a priori probability of perceiving decisive characteristics[22] by continuing the search diminishes. Since the cost of observation for all these characteristics is by definition nil, all the decisive characteristics will be perceived finally and non-decisive characteristics will be 'overlooked'. On the other hand, if directly unobservable characteristics exist, they would never be perceived, although some of them might have proved decisive. In more general terms, *the cost of perceiving certain decisive characteristics may be too high for them ever to be revealed by the consumer's personal search*. Several procedures tend to be created to offset this lack of perception.

Producers' actions are an effective means for offsetting consumers' misperceptions. As Akerlof (1970) has pointed out, producers are much better informed than consumers about the qualities of their brand. Knowing the tastes of their clientele and the properties of the goods which they manufacture, they are able to perceive decisive characteristics which purchasers will not themselves notice. In view of this, it is in their interest to point out the existence of such characteristics on the market-place in so far as their perception does not diminish the expected marginal utility of consumers and swings the choice of some of them in favour of their brand. Labelling, product presentation, advertising, brand and price strategy are all means for reducing the cost of perceiving decisive characteristics which are both beneficial and difficult to observe directly. One or other of these procedures will therefore be used to *signal* a property of this type on the market-place, provided it is perceived by the procedure and the marginal cost of signalling does not exceed the marginal return.

As has just been mentioned, *advertising* will sometimes reveal to consumers decisive characteristics which had escaped their perception. It thus modifies the evaluation of the services expected from the advertised brand.[23] This is the role of informative advertising. It is particularly important in the case of the launch of a new product or for one which has a unique feature. In other cases the content of the advertising message is of little informative value. It may possibly suggest pleasant associations, e.g. an atmosphere of exotism or femininity, but it will reveal no decisive characteristic inherent in the brand. This type of advertising is designed to strengthen consumer confidence in the choice of the brand when this is subject to severe competition. When several brands are perfect substitutes, the evaluation gaps between them are very slight. As a result, the confidence of potential purchasers is also very slight, so that any increase in expected confidence provided by some external and costless signal becomes important. Rather than choose a brand at random, potential consumers will therefore rely on advertising.[24] The rationale for this behaviour is that, in a competitive environment, advertising is taken to be a quality signal.[25] Persuasive advertising of this kind is therefore suitable for brands with perfect substitutes as well as for those seeking to remind consumers of their reputation.

However, producers will not remedy all kinds of consumers' misperceptions. In particular, they will not spontaneously reveal the existence of unpleasant or harmful characteristics in their products whenever these are decisive but difficult to observe. However, although thorough inspection of the whole collection of brands in competition would be too expensive for a single consumer to undertake, this becomes worthwhile for a group of consumers if the number of beneficiaries is much greater than the number of brands to be tested.[26] *Consumer associations* have been set up with the object of revealing decisive characteristics which producers would otherwise conceal.

This analysis shows that all those decisive characteristics which are *perceptible*, given the present state of technology and belief, tend to be revealed either by producers or by consumers. Conversely, non-decisive characteristics with an avoidable production cost tend to be eliminated from the market since, because consumers overlook them, producers can thereby cut out a cost without adversely affecting demand for their products. In other words, all perceived characteristics which could have been eliminated from the production process are therefore relevant, i.e. decisive for at least one consumer. This is a partial confirmation of Lancaster's hypothesis whereby all consumers perceive the same relevant characteristics in market goods. However, this results not only from the technology, but also from the market mechanism. Yet the market itself can only make perceptible what individuals are capable of perceiving at any given moment.

Certain characteristics tend to be naturally or socially imperceptible. If a commodity has characteristics the effects of which are *remote*, these tend to be underestimated and possibly overlooked. Remote events in fact appear more unlikely than those which are closer in time. Without knowing the details, the consumer is virtually certain that random or unexpected changes will occur and modify his environment between the time when he attempts to evaluate a 'future characteristic' and the time when he will actually reap the benefit from it. The extent of unexpectable change, and therefore the uncertainty affecting any evaluation of future benefit (cf. equation (1)) increases in relation to its remoteness. Consequently, analysis of this kind of misperception suggests that the use of a discount rate does not imply that individuals prefer the present to the future, all other things being equal,[27] but that future characteristics are less highly evaluated than present characteristics and that, beyond a certain threshold of remoteness, they are no longer even perceived.[28] Similarly, an essential effect of *social norms* is to increase the extent to which individual behaviour patterns are foreseeable by considerably reducing the extent of admissible responses to various stimuli. When education and the system of rewards and penalties are effective, members of the community perceive illegitimate or non-conformist objects of choice as much more improbable than others, and even impossible. Therefore, this means that their bundle of choices is restricted to legitimate and conformist objects.[29] Social norms thus act basically as a perception mechanism.

4.2. Choices subjected to influence

Individuals are not equally endowed with an ability to perceive. This is likely to be increased by education, the experience acquired with age and through the specialization of activities, perspicacity, prior knowledge or acquired information. If every individual had the same intrinsic preferences, some of them would always make the right decisions. They could in fact take their personal search farther than others since their perception costs are lower. Those less good at decision-making would therefore stand to gain from picking out those who were best at this and imitating them. The best decision-makers would, for their part, also stand to gain from this since they would thereby acquire influence power and social prestige instead of a sum of money. By applying the principle of economicness to the organization of society, it is possible to predict the probability of such non-market exchanges and analyse the mechanism of choices subjected to influence. This analysis still holds as an approximation when intrinsic preferences differ among persons. In fact, each individual ignores both his own intrinsic preferences as well as those of others, so that he does not know exactly who has the same intrinsic preferences as himself. What is more, if he gets selective information from someone else, the services which this is assumed to indicate tend to play a more decisive role in his instantaneous preferences than the one they would have played in his intrinsic preferences. It follows that instantaneous preferences, as a result of this information-push, are much more *uniform* than intrinsic preferences.

The following discussion excludes purchase of particular or general information which forms part of the personal search methods analysed previously. Thus, it focuses on the information-push which normally occurs through inter-person relationships and conspicuous consumption. Unlike a purchase of information, the cost of an information-push is borne by the best informed individual. In order to understand the rationale of his action, one needs to analyse the benefit he gets from it. The essential features of this type of behaviour can perhaps be best expressed in terms of a *communication* between two persons.

When A transfers a message to B he makes an investment, in the sense that, for the moment, he is forgoing resources (his own time and non-disseminated information) in the hope of increasing his utility at a later date.[30] By revealing his own choice to B, A is wagering on the fact that this information will have a decisive *influence* on B's behaviour. The wager will be won if B, when the time comes for him to take a similar decision himself, finds his confidence increased in the alternative chosen by A to the point where he stops his search and *imitates* this choice. After which A will be able to measure his success by observing that B's effective choice is modelled on his own and is posterior to it. An objective observation of this kind, which is not always accompanied by an explicit acknowledgement on the part of B, is the best indication of A's influence on B.

The influence of one person on another has a value for the person exerting the influence which is the sum of two terms. The first represents the value to A of the information fed back by B, i.e. the fact that his choice was identical to A's, since the latter's confidence in his initial choice and thus the utility he derives from this (as expressed in equation (1)) are increased by confirmation of this kind. The second term represents the value to A of a change in his social environment, i.e. the influence which he has had over B's decision. To use the terminology of Becker (1974), this corresponds to an increase in A's social income in terms of utility. A's influence on B therefore has an informational value and a real value for A. Added together they constitute the marginal returns on A's investment in communication. If A accepts to transfer the information he possesses by indicating his choice to B and to other persons, this means that the marginal cost of this information-push is lower than the expected marginal return.

Divulging one's own decisions is a risky investment since it is difficult to communicate to another person the confidence one has in one's own choices. In most cases a prerequisite is to disclose one's true preferences by following one's own precepts, in order that the information which one supplies to others appear authentic. But this alone is not sufficient since one must also reveal one's ability to perceive and prove that it is higher than the average ability of the group. Individuals who have acquired the power to influence others are therefore those who have trained themselves in perception (at least with regard to certain decision areas) and who have invested in a reputation of being 'good decision-makers'. In some respects such people resemble 'researchers'.

A researcher is in fact a person who comes up with new knowledge, ideas, patterns or techniques and thereby influences future decisions made by members of the community. He has sharpened his perception in a given area, i.e. with regard to a certain collection of objects, which consequently enables him to reveal gradually the hidden characteristics overlooked in current observation. Moreover, he agrees to bear the cost of building up a reputation. For example, the scientific researcher agrees to use rigorous and generally accepted methods, submits his work to criticism, publishes articles, etc. Once his reputation is made, his discoveries are regarded by his peers with increased confidence. In fact, information communicated by the researcher has a social utility only in so far as it is perceived by members of the community, which supposes that they are able to expect from this an increased confidence in their future decisions which will outweigh the effort required to understand the message. Since this latter cost may prove very high in view of the difference in training and ability between the researcher and the average person in the group, this information is generally transmitted via 'intermediaries'.[31] The researcher communicates his discovery to a restricted group likely to understand it; the members of this group will subsequently adapt the exposition so that this becomes comprehensible to a wider group, and so on. The power to influence other individuals is thus vested in this entire group of researchers and intermediaries.

The foregoing analysis applies in fact to a number of areas of social life and in particular to the consumption of goods. Social psychology has often emphasized the influence exercised by certain 'leaders' on the behaviour of other consumers. These leaders obviously correspond to the researchers and intermediaries mentioned above. Such persons have succeeded in creating for themselves a reputation of good taste, intuition, modernity, etc. They spread the use of new products by taking the risk of being the first to buy them, of shocking others, of being criticized or envied because in return they receive a non-monetary benefit, i.e. social prestige and influence.[32]

Ever since Veblen (1934) it has been recognized that objects of consumption have become a prime vehicle for social prestige. What is meant by this is that they are more effective in producing influence than human capital, regarded as the objects of the relationship between individuals. The cost of another person's perception of objects is in fact much lower for conspicuous consumption than for objects embodied in human beings. The sight of goods consumed by others speeds up choice formation more effectively than does current inter-person communication. This analysis adds to the now more traditional explanations involving the movement of the relative price of time and goods, the need to authenticate the information communicated and its more or less 'public' character. Its advantage is that it enables one to predict that the prime vehicles for social prestige and influence will be artistic and cultural objects, i.e. all those objects which, by their nature, appeal to perceptive abilities and enter into the production of 'life dimensions'. The 'stylish', 'attractive' or 'modern' provide an inexhaustible variety of characteristics, messages and sensations and, by communicating these, the leaders' power to influence is able to renew itself. The acquisition of 'beneficial addictions' could therefore prove to be a way of becoming a social leader.[33]

If certain consumers influence others, the degree of variation in preferences will diminish. This tendency toward uniformity may be very great if one considers the amplification of original influences by intermediaries and the fact that the researchers themselves form a restricted group. Since our analysis of decisive characteristics shows that these are not given objectively, i.e. independently of consumer preferences, it follows that the taste of the most influential among them will have far greater weight than that of the remainder in determining the supply of characteristics. This power of influence therefore also has an indirect effect on the definition of an object's relevant characteristics.

Notes

1. This viewpoint is illustrated by the works of Becker (see his paper in this volume, p. 7 'the economic approach is a comprehensive one that is applicable to all human behavior') and McKenzie and Tullock (1975).

2. For an exposition of the new theory of consumer behaviour see Michael and Becker (1973), or Lévy-Garboua (1976a).

3. This point is not clearly dealt with in the theory of household production. An essay by Schultz (1975) does, however, go some way towards this.

4. Lancaster (1966) confuses the services expected (objects of choice) and the characteristics (useful or descriptive information). The usefulness of such a distinction will be seen later.

5. Much more so than the first models of search would indicate.

6. Search for the lowest price is analysed by Telser (1973) and others. Nelson (1970) also examines the search for the best quality good.

7. See for example Lindsay and Norman (1972: 534-39).

8. A discussion of this kind will be found in Lévy-Garboua (1976b: 21-25).

9. It is represented by an evaluation vector expressed in utility terms.

10. If several options score equally, the ranking is done at random.

11. If two alternatives were intrinsically indifferent, prob$(1, \infty/1, j)$ would only be equal to 1/2 although the subject were certain of his choice. However, the corresponding probability would be zero for the $(n-2)$ alternatives not preferred.

12. If two alternatives score equally the rank figure '1' which appears in the probability term of equation (1) will simply be replaced by '1 + 2'. In which case, the formula is unchanged since $Z_1(j) = Z_2(j)$.

13. It is easy to show that:

$$E\,\text{conf}(j+1) = \sum_{i=1}^{n} \text{prob}(i, \infty/i, j+1)\ \text{prob}\,(i, j+1/1, j).$$

14. $EL\ (j+1) = \lambda[1 - E\,\text{conf}\,(j+1)] + C(j+1) = \lambda[1 - E\,\text{conf}\,(j+1)] + c + C(j)$.

15. By developing all the implications of inequality (8), one could justify the proposals put foward by Lancaster (1971: 140-56) with regard to the method for determining what (perceived) characteristics are relevant in a collection of close substitutes.

16. Let us assume that the distribution of services revealed by the search tends towards the distribution δ_0 which is totally concentrated in $z = 0$. In this case, one sees by applying (12) that: $h_{ji} \to H_0\ (Z_1(j) - Z_i(j))$, where H_0 is the Heavyside function which assumes value zero when its argument is negative and 1 when it is positive or nil. As $Z_1(j) - Z_i(j) \geqslant 0$ for every $i > 1$, $h_{ji} \to 1$, and all the more rapidly as $(Z_1(j) - Z_i(j))$ assumes higher values.

17. We have just seen that the alternatives ranked lowest as a result of previous search tend to be rejected and contribute little to any increase in confidence.

18. Cf. note 16.

19. Experience and changes in the environment may also confirm the previous choice.

20. The calculation for prob(2, ∞/1, *E*) is similar to that for prob(1, ∞/1, *E*) as set out in subsection 2.2. It should, however, be noticed that:

$$\text{prob}(2, \infty/1, E) = \text{prob}(z_2 - z_1 > Z_1(E) - Z_2).\ \text{prob}(z_3 - z_2 \leqslant Z_2 - Z_3) \ldots \text{prob}(z_n - z_2 \leqslant Z_2 - Z_n).$$

21. The 'researcher' who derives personal satisfaction from identifying new dimensions could also be considered an 'addict' (see subsection 4.2).

22. A decisive characteristic is defined as one whose perception changes the consumer's choice. Cf. subsection 2.2.

23. This argument will be found in Lévy-Garboua (1976a: 97-98) and Stigler and Becker (1977: 84-85).

24. Advertising for detergents provides a perfect illustration of this.

25. This argument will be found in Nelson (1974).

26. Let m be the number of consumers and n the number of brands. Thorough inspection of the products involves an average cost $\bar{c}$ and it provides the average consumer with a benefit which, for the sake of simplicity, can be measured as the evaluation gap between the best choice (U_1) and a brand selection at random ($\bar{U}$). Taking into account the average transaction costs C involved in collective consumer action, the condition for this to be profitable can be expressed as follows:

$$m\ (U_1 - \bar{U} - C) \geqslant n\bar{c}.$$

27. Stigler and Becker (1977: 89) also appear to support the hypothesis that a zero discount rate is consistent with stability of preferences.

28. This is why the use of decreasing exponentials to estimate the present value of a stream of future services provides satisfactory results.

29. Gintis (1972: 277) sees the 'structure of ,availabilities' of economic bundles as having a decisive influence.

30. In order to simplify the argument and confine it to what is strictly necessary to our present context, I assume that there are only two periods (thus ignoring the frequently cumulative nature of communication) and A's utility gain derives from B's reply, treated in binary fashion, i.e. imitation of A or non-imitation of A.

31. If the cost of perceiving the message is too high, individuals who try to understand it will learn nothing from the first phases of their search. This will confirm their impression that it is of no value and strengthen their initial beliefs.

32. These non-monetary benefits may be followed by other monetary benefits, deriving from their association with an upper social group and access to a variety of information.

33. This conclusion throws a new light on subsection 3.2. In particular it demonstrates that 'life dimension' is no ordinary commodity.

References

AKERLOF, G. A. (1970) 'The Market for "Lemons": Quality Uncertainty and the Market Mechanism', *Quarterly Journal of Economics* 84 (August).

BECKER, G. S. (1974) 'A Theory of Social Interactions', *Journal of Political Economy* 82 (November-December).

––, (1976) 'Altruism, Egoism, and Genetic Fitness: Economics and Sociobiology', *Journal of Economic Literature* 14 (September).

BOUDON, R. (1977) 'Déterminismes Sociaux et Liberté Individuelle', in: *Effets Pervers et Ordre Social.* Paris: PUF.

GINTIS, H. (1972) 'Consumer Behavior and the Concept of Sovereignty: Explanations of Social Decay', *American Economic Review* 62 (May).

LANCASTER, K. J. (1966) 'A New Approach to Consumer Theory', *Journal of Political Economy* 74 (January-February).

––, (1971) *Consumer Demand: A New Approach* New York: Columbia University Press.

LÉVY-GARBOUA, L. (1976a) 'La Nouvelle Théorie du Consommateur et la Formation des Choix', *Consommation* (July-September).

––, (1976b) 'Une Introduction à l'Economie Sociologique', Mimeo. Paris: CREDOC.

LINDSAY, P. M. and D. A. NORMAN (1972) *Human Information Processing. An Introduction to Psychology*. New York: Academic Press.

McKENZIE, R. B. and G. TULLOCK (1975) *The New World of Economics* Homewood, Illinois: Richard D. Irwin, Inc.

MAYNES, E.S. (1976) 'The Concept and Measurement of Product Quality', in: N.E. Terleckyj (ed.), *Household Production and Consumption* New York: NBER, Columbia University Press.

MICHAEL, R. T. and G. S. BECKER (1973) 'On the New Theory of Consumer Behavior', *Swedish Journal of Economics* 75.

NELSON, P. (1970) 'Information and Consumer Behavior', *Journal of Political Economy* 78 (March-April).

––, (1974) 'Advertising as Information', *Journal of Political Economy* 82 (July-August).

SCHULTZ, T. W. (1975) 'The Value of the Ability to Deal with Disequilibria', *Journal of Economic Literature* 13 (September).

STIGLER, G. J. (1961) 'The Economics of Information', *Journal of Political Economy* 69 (June).

––, and G. S. BECKER (1977) 'De Gustibus Non Est Disputandum', *American Economic Review* 67 (March).

TELSER, L. G. (1973) 'Searching for the Lowest Price', *American Economic Review* 63.

VEBLEN, T. (1934) *The Theory of the Leisure Class.* New York: Modern Library, First edition, 1899.

• Comment

Bayesian-Consumer-Econometricians

Frank Stafford
University of Michigan, USA

The paper by Louis Lévy-Garboua is a very thought-provoking piece and adds to the growing interest in alternative approaches to consumer behaviour. These alternative approaches embrace statistical learning-by-consuming, reinforcement or other dynamic elements. As in any area of economics it is usually the case that a greater level of model complexity leads to reduced prospects for predictive results. Perhaps with this in mind George Stigler and Gary Becker have argued in so many words that economists should resist the temptation to give up on the assumption in conventional theory that tastes are exogenous.[1] Economists should be more steadfast on the issue of stable preferences because, they argue, a wide range of predictive results can be derived with exogenous, temporally constant preferences and, perhaps, even identical preferences across individuals provided the analyst does not suffer from a weak imagination in identifying income and substitution effects. This I can certainly agree with, and in many cases the conventional model is adequate if good data, a reasonably specified model,

Research for this paper was supported in part by grants from the NSF Special Projects Division and from the NSF Office of National R & D Assessment. The research reflects the author's views and not necessarily those of any Federal agency.

and econometric luck are all present. However, the Stigler-Becker paper also includes examples which require substantial modifications of conventional theory in, for example, the form of stocks of music capital or euphoric capital.

These modifications add greatly to the complexity of consumer choice theory and can be viewed as models which further weaken the predictions of conventional demand theory (which were weak to begin with). These conventional theory predictions are about what will happen in response to changed opportunities as reflected by changes in income and price. Adding state variables to the problem and calling them music appreciation capital, better knowledge, or calling them altered preferences should be judged in terms of predictive power relative to some alternative, simpler model. In this case there are some predictions because the capital approach has, for example, predictions which depend on the horizon of the decision-maker. To be specific, an older person who suddenly 'discovered music' would be less likely to become 'addicted' because the expected gains from a stock of music capital would be realized over a shorter remaining life.

In the Lévy-Garboua model and in a variant which I propose for further work, the state variable approach is used to represent *purposive* learning;[2] consumers act to develop stocks of information about preferences. The approach could easily be modified to assume that preferences are few and well-known, but the methods or technology for satisfying them is known only imperfectly, particularly when there is rapid technological change in the form of new products. Either of these approaches appears consistent with the class of behaviours discussed by Becker and Stigler; habits, addiction, advertising as well as such phenomena as 'fads', and consumption experiments and others. A major goal of conventional theory, to predict responses to price and income change, is attained in the more complex model but may be more difficult to identify since information levels of consumers condition their responses. That is, in the model which I sketch out, a lower price of a good lowers the cost of learning about that good, and hence the learning effect could result in a larger short run response to a price fall than the long run response, even for non-durables. This may be particularly true if the lower price is expected to persist because the capital stock of better-known technology or preferences for the good will be expected to apply to a larger share of the budget through time. Note that here the capital stock of consumer skills model has a similar prediction, but in the learning-by-consuming model the stock can be thought of as the consumer's level of information about own preferences.

Suppose that the coefficients of the utility function are not completely known. In particular one's utility is a function of the quantities consumed of various (K) goods ($X_1, \ldots, X_K$) and of the coefficients in the utility function ($V_1, \ldots, V_N$) which are random variables with a multivariate prior density function. This density function is updated by sample evidence which is acquired by purchasing and consuming the goods. Purchasing a good embodies some fixed cost of search, transactions and the like; a variable cost per unit of the price per unit, plus the possible opportunity losses from underconsuming and overconsuming the good relative to other goods. If we imagine marginal utility from the good to diminish over some range at a rate determined by utility function parameters (which are known only imprecisely) then there is an expected opportunity cost in utility terms from overconsuming any particular good by virtue of uncertainty in the prior (beginning of period) utility function coefficients ('Try it, at the margin you'll hate it' – or at least not like it as well as you thought you would). In this way the expected cost of experimentation involves the density function of the coefficients of the utility function as well as the price of the good.

To keep things possibly tractable consider a quadratic utility function in which the arguments are separable. Here the consumer has an a priori specification of

$$U_{kn} = V_{0kn} + V_{1kn}x_{1n} + V_{2kn}x_{1n}^2 + \epsilon_{kn},$$

for good k in period n. There is a joint density function on V_{0kn}, V_{1kn}, V_{2kn} which is truncated or otherwise assigns a zero density to $V_{2kn} \geqslant 0$ (non-diminishing marginal utility). Otherwise, only the budget constraint would prevent an infinite expected value to sample information derived from consuming X_1 in the given period.

Given current knowledge of preferences as embodied in utility function coefficients, there would be normal incentives to avoid overconsuming a single good because expected marginal utility in a single period for a given good would diminish over some range. However, our Bayesian-consumer-econometrician would like to gain better information about his utility function parameters, and the confidence ellipse on the utility regressions can be shrunk by adding another observation to experience which has built up to this period's prior density function. Of course old consumers who have lived and consumed a lot may behave as if the period's prior density functions were tightly drawn, and if a world of changing prices is added they would have relatively more incentive to learn about new price developments than simply learning more about their druthers.

If the consumer is confident of the specified functional form extreme values of the arguments would provide greater expected incremental precision to the coefficients, but extreme values, particularly on the high side, are expensive in the usual sense besides increasing the risks of overconsuming (or underconsuming certain necessary goods like vitamins) and given a stochastic term in the utility 'regression' the information gain would never be complete. Young consumers have a higher shadow price to information since they have a longer horizon to capture the benefits and since their prior density functions are more diffuse. Hence, it would be logical that they would experiment more, and if there are fixed costs to sampling any of some goods and if borrowing on future income is difficult, they could logically engage in different experiments in different periods – an entire year's 'savings' might go for a single back-packing trip one year and *even if successful* next year's 'savings' might go entirely for theater tickets. As in the Lévy-Garboua model incremental sample evidence provides (at *some* point though not necessarily throughout the range of possible sample sizes) diminishing marginal information value and this would provide further disincentives to departures from a stable consumption pattern as consumption experience increases so long as prices remain stable.

Our Bayesian consumer econometricians probably realize early in life that getting good data is expensive, and if someone else has invested in an 'experiment' it may be useful to ask his advice (only his advice because to use his data is pure and simple stealing). A person's advice could be particularly valuable if you believe his utility function might be similar to yours, based, perhaps, on previous advice which turned out to be good (predictive). If experiments run by what Lévy-Garboua would likely call certain highly regarded consumer-researchers are viewed as applicable by many other consumers, the possibilities for public good like aspects of information abound and can explain consumption fads. Consumer researchers are particularly useful in conveying information about large, discrete decisions like housing and children.

How does one explain bad habits? Apart from the tendency to define some habits as 'good' and others as 'bad' it would seem that habits would be thought of as consumer dogmatism concerning utility function coefficients combined with high prices of the goods not consumed at all. If the coefficients are treated as virtually known parameters, at least for some consumption goods, then change or variety is expected to provide only trivial incremental information relative to the cost of experiments. The consumer subjectively 'believes' in the superiority of a certain consumption pattern and repeats this pattern year after year.[3] In Lévy-Garboua's terms habits reflect behaviour when utility function coefficients are treated as essentially known parameters,[4] as long as prices are stable. With a new set of prices old habits could be broken because a lower product price lowers the cost of experimentation. The consumer could, after experimentation, eventually settle down to a new set of habits.

What also concerns observers of other people's behaviour is the tendency for what appears to be unstable shifts in consumption patterns. A person who tries drugs may learn to like it and become addicted to a new consumption pattern whereas he has previously been 'addicted' to admirable pursuits – hard work, a nutritionally balanced diet, and so on. Abrupt shifts and nearly discontinuous behaviour as a response to changes in exogenous variables is common in the context of dynamic models and our illustrative model implies an abundance of state variables – the utility function coefficients – and given the usual non-linearity of the relations which update prior density functions via sample evidence to reach posterior density functions, such a model is likely to be very difficult to solve analytically. Furthermore, solutions are likely to be characterized by watershed effects wherein small displacements in the state variables can send a person down a qualitatively very different path. An example of such behaviour in a non-stochastic model, is given in a recent human capital accumulation model[5] wherein a small upward displacement in initial human capital, particularly for those with little financial wealth, can induce an abrupt change in the optimal life cycle from one of little work and training to one of an extended training period followed by a period of rapidly rising labour supply which exhibits a high lifetime average. These results obtain despite the use of what most economists regard as well-behaved mathematical functions. The point is that a model of dynamic learning of preferences or of home technology, like any dynamic model, is likely to give rise to such watershed effects or to multiple optimal consumption paths.

Other aspects of the approach outlined above may include predictions of ordinary consumer theory. These predictions are applicable to consumers who know about the utility or home technology parameters of all the goods available to them and simply alter consumption in response to prices and income. On the other hand, a purposive learning model seems better suited for analysis of new goods. If new goods are introduced at a rapid rate the shadow value of knowledge or better precision on utility function coefficients of currently available goods is expected to depreciate more rapidly, and there would likely be less incentive to learn fully the utility function or technology given at a point in time if change is expected. Rapid introduction of new products makes old consumers look young as they attempt to learn about the new products. As L-G notes, randomness can become optimal. I would not want to go this far in my speculation without a clearly defined and analysed model, but it seems likely that the expected rate of introduction of new goods would have important behavioural consequences in such a model. Furthermore, consumption experimentation will result in apparent intransitivities if interpreted by the conventional economic model of the consumer.

Because trying out new products to learn about them is costly we would expect rich consumers to try out a wider variety of consumption goods and to have succeeded in finding a larger number that they like. In this case the effect of income should not be simply to encourage greater consumption of the same number of goods but also to encourage consumption of a larger number of goods and a wider variety of goods over time. Situations wherein none of a particular good is consumed have a quite different interpretation in the learning-by-consuming model from that given in the usual consumer model.

In summary, one should be reluctant to complicate the consumer behaviour model since greater complication has a major cost: greater ambiguity and less clear-cut predictive power (not to speak of more intellectual baggage for the analyst). However, once we take that step and add non-trivial[6] state variables we are led along the lines of the Stigler-Becker paper, and if the state variables represent levels of information one is led along the lines of the model in the Lévy-Garboua paper or along the lines of the Bayesian-consumer-econometrician model which I have sketched out here. I believe this approach is more likely to be illuminating than approaches which do not include imperfect knowledge. In the approach which I propose, preferences, though stable for a given individual can differ across individuals, and knowledge of the preferences and incentives to learn about them is affected by prices of goods. As prices of goods change over time and as consumers respond by re-assessing their preferences through consumption experiments there will be a rich variety of behavioural responses. This learning process broadens the consumer model to represent paths of consumer response to price and income changes rather than simply giving initial and eventual equilibrium.[7] I believe that such a model could be very fruitful in analysing the consumer's response to inflation (pure or mixed) and would have implications for differential responses by consumers who differ by age, education, and in other ways. Before attempting a specific model, it seems reasonable to review some empirical evidence that seems to have a bearing on the general approach.

There is empirical evidence which does appear consistent with an approach which emphasizes learning behaviour. One experimental study of transitivity of preference indicated a substantially greater proportion of transitive responses by older and more educated persons.[8] The author concludes from the evidence that 'an older person is a more efficient utility maximizer than a younger person',[9] and implies that this would justify restrictions on the market activity of teenagers. In terms of a learning model greater apparent intransivities should not be viewed as per se irrational; rather we would expect greater apparent intransitivities to be the consequence of rational investment in information, particularly for young people.

A more interesting study which bears on consumer learning is some work by James Morgan.[10] Morgan utilizes a national survey of 2214 household heads in the United States in 1965. From probability measures he constructs an index of receptivity to change, which basically measures (1) use of a specific list of new (1965-vintage) products (steam iron, electric frying pan, gasoline credit card, coin-operated dry cleaning machines, auto seat belts, new car purchases rather than used car purchases); (2) self-perception of receptivity to new products (respondent says he tries out new products when they first come out, perception of new products as likely to represent improvements, etc.); and (3) attraction of new scientific developments (polio vaccine use by some family members, attitude toward landing a man on the moon, and attitudes toward water flouridation). Variables identified via multiple regression as the most important predictors of receptivity to change were total family income, education of head of family, index of social participation,[11] and age of head of family.[12]

Each of the variables which Morgan found important as predictors of receptivity to change (an index of consumption experiments by the household head) seem consistent with a general learning model of consumer behaviour of the type presented by L-G and the approach sketched out above. Family income allows a wider range of experiments. Education may be thought of as a variable which proxies better ability to process sample information, and hence those with more education may expect a larger incremental benefit per unit of resources used to try out new goods.[13] Younger persons would have a longer horizon to capture benefits from improved knowledge and would therefore experiment more. One reason for observing a lower score on the receptivity to change index for young people is because they would also be busy trying out products which are known to old consumers (e.g. effects of drinking too much gin), and this would divert resources away from trying out new products (such as credit cards or electric frying pans).

Those who interact more with other persons are likely to have more information about how others found new products. If, on average, the others were pleased with new products, then those who interact more would have incentives to adopt them. If the consumption experiments of others were typically failures then these products would be avoided. Those with higher social interaction would know enough not to try a lot of bad, new products. However, they may still adopt those few products which turned out to be successful and would therefore have a greater apparent receptivity to change. It is hard to know what kind of process is operating without better data on what people learn about new products through social participation as measured in the Productive Americans Study.[14]

Notes

1. 'De Gustibus Non Est Disputandum', *American Economic Review*, March 1977: 76-90.

2. In the paper by John Cross, 'A Stochastic Learning Model of Economic Behavior', *Quarterly Journal of Economics*, May 1973: 238-66, is an example of what can be called a passive learning model.

3. The gambler in Michael Rothschild's paper, 'A Two-Armed Bandit Theory

of Pricing', *Journal of Econimic Theory*, October 1974: 185-202, can settle down to habitually playing the 'wrong', but known, slot machine. Also it is easy to show that the optimal scale of evaluation of alternatives can imply a sample size of zero. See Frank P. Stafford, 'A Decision Theoretic Approach to the Evaluation of Training Programs', Technical Analysis Paper, ASPER, US Department of Labor, May 1975. Here the analogous consumer behaviour is not even trying particular good. (Some 'bad' programs may be dispensed without evaluation.) At the same time the consumer may not even question the consumption of some goods. (Some 'good' programs do not warrant the cost of any evaluation.) In the consumer case, however, the 'good' goods are consumed, and learning may take place about their relative desirability but not about desirability of those not consumed (evaluated).

4. In Bayesian terms, what L-G refers to as confidence is precision, which is the inverse of the post-sample variance. Unchanged or fixed beliefs or preferences are likely to be prevalent for religious preferences since these are less subject to experiential revision – the cost of sampling is high, particularly on the existence of afterlife.

5. H. E. Ryder, F. P. Stafford and P. E. Stephan, 'Labor, Leisure and Training Over the Life Cycle', *International Economic Review*, October 1976: 651-74.

6. An example of a 'trivial' state variable is the intertemporal budget constraint common in many consumer models.

7. Whether or not there are differences in predictions from passive learning models (e.g. John Cross, op. cit.), versus purposive ('rational') learning of the type implied here is an interesting research issue.

8. See Arnold A. Weinstein, 'Transivity of Preference: A Comparison Among Age Groups', *Journal of Political Economy*, March/April 1968: 307-11 and a summary of the results in Jack Hirschleifer, *Price Theory and Applications*, Prentice Hall, 1976, pp. 55-56.

9. Weinstein, op. cit., p. 311.

10. James N. Morgan, 'Receptivity to Change', in: *Productive Americans*, University of Michigan, Ann Arbor, Michigan: Survey Research Center, 1966, ch. 13.

11. Social participation as defined by Morgan would likely reflect level of interaction with others in a variety of contexts – religious services, vacations, volunteer work, meals away from home, and participation in sports or hobbies.

12. Morgan, op. cit., p. 220.

13. This could go the other way if there were a simple environment. Better learners would then know all there is to know and the payoff to additional experimentation would be zero.

14. Analysis of use of new products is currently underway by John P. Robinson. He is using data from the Time Use Study of the Survey Research Center of The University of Michigan (1975-76). That survey included information on use of pocket calculators, microwave ovens and other new home technology.

5

Social Sciences and the Reconstruction of Welfare Economics

Philippe d'Iribarne

Centre National de la Recherche Scientifique, Paris, France

The economic approach of welfare problems is characterized, for most of the works relevant to it, by the fact that it constitutes a science totally autonomous with respect to other social sciences. This autonomy is based on two facts.

(1) On the one hand, that a person's welfare is directly connected with the physical characteristics of consumption, with no specification of the physiological, psychological or social properties of consumer goods. Apart from some rare exceptions, no variable corresponding to the approach of these other sciences is introduced in the representations which welfare economics elaborates: in their most classical form the utility functions use quantities of goods as arguments, and when one tries to extend the field covered by the theory one uses physical variables such as time.

(2) On the other hand, that the empirical data which are used concern merely the person's choices, all the information corresponding to the motivations of these choices being excluded (and being studied by the other social sciences). It is a matter of principle. It is asserted that the economist, while he knows well that a person's choices are conditioned by different mechanisms the study of which is relevant to physiology, psychology or sociology, is not supposed to give attention to these mechanisms *because these choices which result from them contain all the information he needs.*[1]

Now, some researches on questions such as the influence of economic growth on welfare and the volume of waste in Western societies,[2] starting with the classical framework of welfare economics, have proved that it is not possible to keep this framework just as it is if one wants to take into consideration the empirical data. It was necessary to abandon the idea of building a welfare theory totally autonomous with respect to the other social sciences. It was also necessary to abandon the ideas of using only the observed choices as empirical data, and of neglecting the analysis of the factors conditioning them, developments that led us to re-examine utility theory fundamentally.

Difficulties related to the existence of learning

When Pareto introduced an operative definition of welfare based on observed choices, he did it by using the idea of learning; he thought that, with sufficient learning, a man is able to make the best choices from his point of view: when one deals with 'actions repeated in a large number', men act according to their 'tastes' (Pareto, 1909). Thus, Pareto wrote, 'a man who buys for any food the first time may buy more than what he requires to meet his needs, taking the prices into consideration; but the second time he buys, he will correct his error, at least partly; and so, little by little he will at the end buy exactly what he needs. We consider him at the moment when he has reached this state'.

As a general rule, a man makes his choices in accordance with the information, conscious or unconscious, he can have on the different accessible states. The limits of this information (a) restrict the feasible domain within which choices take place, and (b) lead to uncertainties and errors when he compares different states.

Experience allows a man to extend the information he can have. It thus allows him on one side to enlarge his practically feasible domain (for example Archimedes found the idea of using mirrors to set the enemy fleet on fire) and on the other side to take into better account for his choices the respective effects of different states (the child will henceforth rather not go near the fire). It is only after a certain number of trials, of which each gives a more or less satisfactory result (owing to the information following these trials), that a man is apt to adopt a behaviour leading to the most satisfactory state that exists, considering the constraints other than information he has to meet, including the state of his environment and his own faculties of adaptation. The learning process has by then reached its final stage (it can be said that it has completely converged).

It is only among choices which are the result of a completely converged learning that behaviour observation will enable us to classify, in terms of welfare, the state which has been chosen relative to those which have been refused. The problem then remains of distinguishing between converged choices and other choices.

A choice can result from completely converged learning only when of course, as Pareto observed, a sequence of situations of similar choices has led to a stable choice. Choices which do not recur often (durable goods: car, domestic equipment, housing) give but a limited reliability. Moreover, the repetition and stabilization of choices are not sufficient conditions. As a matter of fact, they can simply correspond to an interruption in the learning process at a level where a maximum welfare has not been reached.

First of all, the domain within which learning took place may be more limited than the theoretical feasible domain. It is often so in terms of consumption. The individual learning and trials are restricted to a domain related to usual social practices. These practices are determined by cultural models, the efficiency of which is strengthened by rationalizations. These rationalizations, by suggesting that trials too much different from cultural models would have bad consequences, discourage such trials. For instance, cultural models relative to food carry beliefs with no connection to reality such as 'meat is necessary for health' which dissuades people from trying food without meat. Naturally enough, the way cultural models develop is not independent from human experiences. But the simple fact that these models change over time shows that it is difficult to speak of a learning which has converged with regard to them. Thus, the observed choices allow us to identify the consumption producing the highest welfare only in domains which are more restricted than those determined by financial constraints alone.

Moreover, an interruption of the learning process may occur in a behaviour which does not provide the highest welfare possible, even within the domain of behaviours effectively experienced. Such a situation is met when the outcome of the experience is long delayed and (or) when the causal links between the behaviour and its results are not very apparent (as in the effects of food or tobacco on health, and especially the effects of over-calorific food on the shortening of life). Particularly, learning can hardly be successful when some experiences improve the aptitudes of the person who lives them and thus have a long-term effect in addition to their short-term effects. Let us take the example of learning a difficult sport or the practise of a musical instrument. From the first trials one acquires aptitudes which will facilitate satisfactory performance later on. But one does not feel this positive effect immediately, whereas one does feel completely the unpleasant aspect of these trials. In these conditions someone who takes into account only the immediate outcome of experience is very badly informed of the respective advantages of various possible options (behaviour leading progressively to satisfactory aptitudes and results, as well as behaviour not leading to them). An action whose appreciation requires the acquisition of aptitudes may be rejected after the first trials, and this will prevent the learner from reaching a state where it can be appreciated. A state may be stable although it is situated at a level of welfare which is much lower than the one which could have been obtained through a behaviour leading to the acquisition of the necessary aptitudes. One can meet such cases within all types of consumption which may have 'poetical effects' ('cultural' consumption, television). One will meet analogous cases each time that the first experiences have tolerance effects which makes it difficult to go backward (cf. drugs, alcoholism).

One must therefore avoid considering that every behaviour is the result of a learning process that has absolutely converged, and corresponds to a choice providing the person who chooses with the highest welfare that he can reach. In matters of consumption, it is very likely that one will not find learnings which have absolutely converged for the essential categories of the budget (food, housing, transport, spare-time activities, health-action). It is therefore not possible effectively to define the relations between consumption and welfare by using merely people's choices and without distinguishing reliable choices from unreliable.

Such a situation has important consequences for the very definition of utility as well as for the methods of welfare economics.

Giving up the notion of 'satisfaction' as a reality different from observed choices, is generally considered an important advance made by utility theory. This sacrifice can be accepted in so far as learning phenomena do not exist. But as they do exist, it is necessary to use a notion which stands in the background of these choices and helps us understand them, but is not identical to them. So it is in any case, as soon as one has welfare concerns, meaning by that something which is not without connection with the meaning of this term in ordinary language. A 'choice' made in the most complete ignorance of its consequences (for instance, a child putting its fingers in an electricity socket) and which, in fact, is more an attempt than a proper choice, can hardly be considered as revealing that what has been chosen provides a higher welfare than what has been rejected. Otherwise, one would have to give to 'welfare' a meaning which can often be completely contradictory to its usual meaning. One is indeed allowed to build a scientific theory by defining the objects one wants, and by giving them the names one wants (provided that one is self-consistent and that one avoids ambiguities). Thus, to study economic equilibrium one can legitimately use a theory of choices which does not rest on the notion of welfare.

But the situation is different when one wants, as did Pareto and most of the economists who consider that utility is indeed an indicator of satisfaction in the usual sense,[3] to build a theory of welfare while having in mind the ordinary concepts of welfare and satisfaction. It then becomes necessary to build a theory which distinguishes between choices resulting from sufficient learning and those which do not, and to use a notion of welfare different from a mere synonym of choice.

The notion of welfare refers then to a reality (what a person feels)[4] which cannot be directly observed. The use of this notion helps to understand what one observes. Moreover, as a feed-back occurs from the feeling to behaviour, it is thus possible to study some features of feeling through an analysis of behaviours:

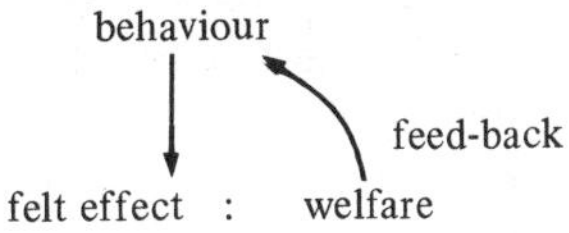

In fact, it is usual, when interpreting the behaviour of numerous systems and especially living systems, to search for an implicit hierarchy which, on the one hand generates their choices when they are perfectly informed and, on the other, directs the progressive correction of errors during learning (and through which errors are defined) when choices are not perfectly informed. Concerning human beings, it will be said that when it is possible to interpret observed behaviours as a gain, when the information is perfect, and as a groping quest for the highest possible states when the information is imperfect, according to a hierarchy revealed by the search process itself, this hierarchy defines a hierarchy between states in terms of welfare. One thus gives an operative definition of welfare.[5]

Besides, to distinguish choices which result from an absolutely converged learning process, it is necessary to analyse the processes which guide the choices. One is therefore led to reject the principle according to which those processes are to be neglected and to abandon the idea of building a welfare economics totally autonomous from the other social sciences.

The interdependencies between the situations of different persons and the elaboration of a comparison in welfare terms based on observed choices

Welfare economics is concerned with the way different people's welfare is affected by the general transformations of the economy, be they associated with the modifications of the consumption of the person we consider or with the modifications of the other people's consumption. To establish comparisons between states, *it is necessary to have an instrument of measure (or at least a scaling) which does not change within the domain defined by the bundle of the states of the economy between which comparisons are made.*

Let us suppose that a man's welfare is affected on the one hand by a set (Y) of factors on which he has no influence (his environment, and especially the behaviour of the other people) and on the other hand by a set (C) of factors on which he can act (his behaviour, and especially his own consumption). Let us consider two states $T_1(C_1, Y_1)$ and $T_2(C_2, Y_2)$ characterized by the set of parameters on which this man on the one hand can act and on the other cannot. If $Y_1 \neq Y_2$ there exists, by definition of Y, no choice possible between T_1 and T_2 which can compare them directly. Direct observation can provide for each Y (state of the environment), a partial hierarchy $E_Y(C)$ between the states generated by a variable behaviour. But it cannot give a total hierarchy $E(Y, C)$ between the obtained states by varying this man's behaviour

(C) as well as the state (Y) of his environment. Especially, if a person's welfare is affected by other people's consumption, the observation of choices does not allow us to define, for measuring welfare, a stable instrument of measure within the domain defined by the different states of the economy.

To order T_1 and T_2, one must find some reliable choices of the person we consider, environment being unchanged, which have consequences identical to the modifications of the environment. The observation of choices made in such conditions enables us to order T_1 and T_2 indirectly.

To say that one finds choices which have identical consequences to choices between T_1 and T_2 means that it is possible to define a set of variables X (X being a vector) completely expressing the significant consequences of the choices (two states for which X takes the same value being always simultaneously preferred or refused when the person has to choose between one of them and a third one), and that to order T_1 and T_2 one tries to order $E(X_1)$ and $E(X_2)$ through a reliable choice between T_1' (C_1', Y_1') and T_2' (C_2', Y_2') such as $X(T_1') = X(T_1)$, $X(T_2') = X(T_2)$ and $Y_1' = Y_2'$. Starting from the person's choices, one brings to light a criterion $E(X)$ concerning the consequences of these choices, and one uses this criterion to compare situations between which no choice can be observed. In other terms one determines a hierarchy in the X-universe and one characterizes the situations in X.

Such a method leads us to elaborate a theory explaining observed choices (a) when they occur at the end of a learning process having completely converged, and (b) explaining them by their consequences. Such a theory has the following elements:

(i) the definition of a set of 'result' variables X;

(ii) the determination of $X(C, Y)$ connecting the results obtained on X with the person's behaviour and with the state of his environment; and

(iii) the determination of a hierarchy $E(X)$ such that, for every environment Y_0, all the behaviour C^* carried to effect at the end of learning process which has completely converged in a domain $\mathcal{C}$, verifies:

$$E\,|\,X(C^*, Y_0)\,| \geqslant E\,|\,X(C, Y_0')\,|\ \ \forall\, C \in \mathcal{C},$$

where $E(X)$ corresponds to a pre-ordering set of equivalent hierarchized classes.

Such a theory being built for a bundle of behaviours and environment states, it will be said that within such a bundle welfare will be higher in a state A (C_A, Y_A) than in a state B (C_B, Y_B) if $E(X_A) > E(X_B)$, with $X_A = X(C_A, Y_A)$ and $X_B = X(C_B, Y_B)$.

If it is built, such a theory not only enables us to compare states corresponding to different environments, in terms of welfare, it also permits comparisons between states corresponding to the same environment, and thus between which a choice is possible, but between which no choice deriving from convergent learning process has been observed.[6]

The limitations of the theoretical framework given by utility theory and its classical extensions

In the most classical formulation the utility function U_i (Q_i), where a person's consumption is represented by a vector Q_i (q_i^1, q_i^2 . . . q_i^η) as defined in the space of goods, uses as arguments only certain physical characteristics (quantities) describing the consumptions of person i.

Therefore to define utility functions, using as arguments physical characteristics of goods which are invariant in the domain we consider, the postulate of independence of utilities must be verified (proposition 1).

Indeed, if this postulate is not verified one has $U_i = U_i(q_i, q_j)$ ($j \neq i$) and thus U_i (Q_i) is not invariant in the domain we consider. Moreover, U_i has no more meaning if one is concerned only with the classical definition of utility, since when using this definition one cannot compare different states for which these Q_j change.

Moreover, to be able to determine utility functions (or more generally to establish in welfare terms a hierarchy among the states) based on a person's choices concerning goods defined by their physical characteristics, without considering the mechanisms through which these characteristics affect his welfare, it is necessary that functions U_i (Q_i) should exist, where the dimensions of Q_i are physical characteristics invariant in the domain we consider (proposition 2).

Let us suppose indeed that, whatever may be the description of Q_i by physical characteristics, there exists a bundle of characteristics Y

external to Q_i which influence U_i.

If the choices of i concerning goods defined by their physical characteristics are only allowed to order the states for which Y is constant, this does not allow us to establish utility functions defined on the bundle of states between which one tries to establish comparisons.

To order the states A and B so that $Y_A \neq Y_B$, relying upon choices of i related to i's consumption, it is necessary to use the intermediate variables X so that:

(a) the observation of the choices of i on Q, and the knowledge of the $X_i\,(Q_i)$ enable us construct $U_i\,(X_i)$, and

(b) the relations $X_i\,(Q_i, Y)$ totally express the influence of Y on U_i.

But to discover the relations $X_i\,(Q_i, Y)$ implies studying some of the mechanisms through which the physical characteristics of the goods a person uses influence his welfare, mechanisms which condition what these relations are.

Considering propositions 1 and 2 so as to be able to establish utility functions defined on the states set of the economy, based only on the choices of a person concerning goods defined by physical characteristics, the postulate of independence of utilities must be verified. More precisely, a description of Q_i must exist, according to physical characteristics, such that no modification of other people's consumption affects the way a person is concerned by a Q_i defined by such a description.

Finally, the fundamental postulate of the 'content' of the theory (a given bundle of goods defined with physical appropriate characteristics provides a person with a well-defined 'material welfare', and in particular there is independence of utilities), should be verified so as to justify the use of its underlying postulates (utility functions of the form $U_i\,(Q_i)$ where the dimensions of Q_i are physical characteristics; observation of choices made on physical characteristics, excluding all others).

Taking external effects into consideration has led us to modify somewhat the situation just described as a matter of the 'content' of the theory as well as the underlying postulates (in any case in applied studies I am not sure that the most rigorous utility theory has been re-examined in consequence). This consideration has led us simultaneously to give up the postulate of the independence of satisfactions and to change accordingly the underlying postulates of the theory:

(a) to introduce into the utility function U_i of i the consumption $Q_j\,(j \neq i)$ of the other consumers, and

(b) to use intermediate variables X such that it is possible to determine U_i (X) using a person's choices as a basis, and that X (Q_i, Y) totally expresses the influence of Y on Q_i. (Thus, with regard to congestion one uses time and money as intermediate variables X. One tries to define the equivalence between one and the other, that is to say the 'value of time' for a person, using his own choices as a basis, and one expresses the influence of other people's consumption on i through their influence on the use of his time. One proceeds in a similar way in all the economic calculations which aim at optimizing the value of environmental transformations enabling people to gain time.)

But this approach, which allows us to consider phenomena which escape the most classical theory, has been treated in a very restrictive way, which enabled theorists to avoid modifying the theoretical and methodological framework of the welfare theory: they are satisfied with taking into consideration only material interdependencies (congestion, pollution and so on) such that the material situation of a person, described by merely physical characteristics, is affected by other people's actions which can also be described by merely physical characteristics.

This way of dealing with interdependencies is consistent with maintaining three postulates which allow economics to remain autonomous as a science with regard to the other social sciences. (While requiring it to abandon its total autonomy with regard to the natural sciences, this point apparently is not well understood.) These postulates are used as a basis for the actual practice of applied economics.

(1) There exists a description of a person's situation in terms of physical characteristics (which may depend on the consumption of the person we consider, as well as on other people's) such that the situation so described provides this person with a well-defined 'material welfare', which in any case remains invariant within a domain corresponding to the set of the states of the economy being compared.

(2) One can use utility functions U_i (X_i) using only the physical characteristics of the person's situation as arguments.

(3) The mechanisms through which a person is affected by his material situation, as described by the appropriate physical characteristics, are not to be taken into consideration when determining the utility functions. Determining them implies only the consideration of mechanisms connecting different physical dimensions and determining the relations $X(Q_i, Y_i)$ between the material situation of a person, his consumption, and other people's consumption; the consumption being defined by physical characteristics. It is necessary to take into account

only those laws that concern the connections between physical dimensions, and thus those that are relevant to the natural sciences and not the social sciences.

One can easily see that the first two postulates are equivalent. Moreover, the third is verified only when the first two are themselves verified. Indeed, if one cannot find some utility function $U(X_i)$ using only physical characteristics of a person's situation as arguments, one must define a function using as arguments the X characteristics corresponding to the psychological and social characteristics. To discover the relationships between the X's and the material characteristics of a person's situation implies then that one must study specific mechanisms relevant to the social sciences, mechanisms which condition what these relationships are.

In maintaining these postulates, the economist very wisely preserves the autonomy of his science. Besides, if he is satisfied with the 'obvious' descriptors of the material situation and with the simple connection between the physical dimensions (as between the intensity of the congestion and the time lost), he is not supposed, just as in the framework of the more restrictive utility theory, to be concerned with the practical motivations guiding the choices. He need not in any case be concerned with the social significance of the material situation on which the choices bear, nor with the psychological processes which led to them.

The psychological interdependencies between the satisfactions of different persons and the impossible autonomy of welfare economics

In most societies and in any case in industrial societies, the life of each person is affected by other people's consumption through social mechanisms (d'Iribarne, 1972, 1973).

A man's consumption influences not only his physical state (e.g. by sheltering him against cold and rain), but also his psychological state. Its influence on social status, well known to economists[7] at least as a peculiarity, is far from being the only such influence and is perhaps not even the main one. Another key influence derives from the fact – since the final consumer is often not identical with the person who buys or prescribes the good consumed – that the latter person's choice is a sign of his attitude to the former. Thus, the food a housewife prepares testifies, according to its degree of delicacy, to her being a more or less good wife and mother (d'Iribarne, 1977). The medicines a doctor prescribes indicate, in relation to their number, sophistication and newness, how much he takes care of his patient (Dupuy and Karsenty, 1974).

Moreover, the objects we use affect our psychological state even apart from our relations with others and from the effects they may have on others. A high-powered car or a highly automatic piece of machinery gives us an added sense of power and makes us feel good even if no one sees us.

The power of these psychological effects of consumption is further enhanced by the fact that even those effects that one might be tempted to describe as purely physical are themselves influenced by 'psychological' factors. For instance, a meal may prove indigestible and we may not like its taste at all if it is not psychologically gratifying. Medicines influence our health not merely by their pharmacodynamic effects, but also by a placebo effect which depends upon psychological factors.

But the 'psychological performances' of goods depend on the significance one gives to them, which is not a 'natural' property but is largely social. Thus, for instance, a person dressed in a dinner jacket will not feel equally comfortable if he wears it at the opera house or at a pop festival. Moreover, allowing for the repercussions of psychological upon physical factors, the physical effects themselves depend to some degree upon cultural factors. For instance, if a person eats a rat, a locust or an earthworm, the reactions of the digestive apparatus will be very different in Western countries from those in societies where such foods are regarded as delicacies.

This fact would be unimportant, when comparing states by using choices, provided the significance of goods remained stable in the domain of states which economic analysis leads us to compare. But unfortunately in many cases, especially in industrial societies, the significance attached at any given moment to a particular bundle of goods is affected by the consumption of other members of society. Thus, it is the relative consumption of a person in comparison with that of other members of society which classifies him in the upper classes, in some particular group of the middle classes, or in the proletariat. It is this relative consumption which helps him become integrated in a higher or lower status group, and influences the reactions of others in anonymous encounters. This phenomenon is only one member of a much larger family. Thus, whether someone is regarded as mean or generous when acting toward someone else (as food prepared by the housewife, medicines prescribed by the doctor) depends on what counts as 'normal'; i.e. what is done on the average in the society and in the social group to which a person belongs.[8] What gives the motorist the feeling of being on top of the world, or otherwise, is the power and speed of his car compared with other cars on the road, the knowledge that he can overtake others or must allow himself to be overtaken.[9]

A detailed analysis of the way people are affected by different types of consumption (food, housing, etc.) enables us to see that in industrial societies these phenomena, far from being a minor curiosity, play a decisive role in the relations between consumption and welfare. Various observations relative to general behaviour, to declarations as well as to psychological equilibrium, confirm this assertion (d'Iribarne, 1976b).

This influence of other people's consumption on the significance of the goods a person uses implies that we cannot find a physical description of reality, relating to variables controlled by the person or to variables affected by other variables which he controls, enabling us to obtain, taking the elements of this description as arguments, a utility function well defined on the set of the economic states which one wants to compare. In such conditions one cannot, even when restricting onself to the comparison of states between which the systems of significances and the psychological characteristics of people stay unchanged, proceed to a hierarchization in terms of welfare without using the variables X and some relations $X(C, Y)$ derived from other social sciences. And this is even more true when one wants to compare states between which changes of significance systems, of psychological characteristics of people, etc. occur; this is what one finds when proceeding to international comparisons of welfare (or even intertemporal comparisons provided they do not concern short periods). Unless one uses the contribution of other social sciences, one can examine market failures only in a very partial way (as one cannot grasp some fundamental interdependencies between the situations of different people). One cannot understand that growth does not bring more satisfaction in the usual meaning of the term (if one corrects the data of the national accounts taking into consideration only material external effects the welfare level of the wealthy countries seems to be high and growing with time) (Nordhaus and Tobin, 1973), and appreciate the volume of waste in industrial societies. To handle these questions correctly one must proceed, together with a change in the propositions of welfare economics as to the properties of reality, to a theoretical and methodological change ending with the closure of economics as a discipline.

In this regard the new consumer economics (researches inspired by the works of Becker and Lancaster) is not distinguishable, in actual practice, from the most classical approach. The variables that it uses as arguments of the utility functions are in fact exclusively physical. Indeed, the use of variables and techniques from other social sciences is no longer rejected in principle (Becker, this volume). In practice, however, this field merely extends the field of 'economic' explanation in the strict sense, without using the other social sciences. Thus, Becker says for instance, 'This approach implies that felonies like robbery and theft are committed mainly by poorer persons not because of anomie and alienation but because their deficiencies in education and other learning reduce the "profit" to them from legal occupations'. From this point of view this approach is profoundly different from the approach we propose, even if the fact of using 'intermediate variables' expressing why goods are used introduces a certain superficial relationship between the two. One will also notice that in its most general form the use of such intermediate variables is by no means a peculiarity, neither of our approach nor of the 'new consumer economics'.[10] In what it effectively works out the new consumer economics corresponds to a specific use of these variables, where the autonomy of economics is preserved. Such an approach, neglecting psychological and social variables, may be sufficient within a field where these variables are fixed. It thus can throw light on some problems. Thus, in a given state of anomie and alienation, one may be satisfied with explanations of crimes and thefts which do not use them as explanatory variables. By locating oneself at a given moment in a given society one may have some chance of thus simplifying these problems. But it means that one will be condemned to furnish only a small part of the explanation of the phenomena.

If the new consumer economics wished to free itself from its present limitations it would encounter the problems we met and one may think that it would be led to resolve them in a similar way. Its defenders would then be obliged to leave the field familiar to the economist, and to acquire an ability in the other social sciences, which requires a great deal of time; and they would be led to proceed cautiously for a long time in fields that are new to them (all this having been experienced to his cost by the author). One may fear that many will prefer, for a long time, to be satisfied with declarations according to which the new consumer economics is not closed in principle to the approach of the other social sciences, while in practice it carefully stays at a distance from them.

Partial hierarchizations and general hierarchization

When one tries to build realistic welfare economics one may wish, at least in principle, to define a complete hierarchy of states which can differ from each other by any characteristic of the social or material environment of the person with regard to whom this hierarchy is being established. It is then necessary to have an instrument of reference which remains invariant while social characteristics vary in any possible way.

Formally such an operation corresponds to the one that obtains when, in the study of a teleological system, one seeks the 'essential variables' of the system, that is to say the ultimate elements of judgement, as well as the criterion, using these elements as arguments, which is associated with it (the criterion which in all circumstances guides the perfectly well informed choices of the system, and in the case of imperfect information directs its groping quest). In the actual state of our knowledge the highlighting of such ultimate elements of judgement seems problematic.[11] The way people are affected by their material and social environment depends on the general answer they give at a given moment through their behaviour and throughout their life by the organization of their personality, to the general problem which the combination of the different elements of their environment sets for them. To define a total hierarchy between states requires that one define, with descriptors available for every culture, modes of personality organization which one would have to order hierarchically. This supposes that, seeking in each society some $E(X)$ appropriate to it, one goes sufficiently further back to find the same $E(X)$ again in different societies. Such a task is for the moment nothing more than a mere direction for reflection and research. It is possible to say that it does not seem to be hopeless. The dominance (except sometimes for the most extreme famine, the hardest winter or great dangers) of what is relevant to the psychological aspects of life (acceptance by others, finding one's identity, etc.) over the physiological aspects (avoiding hunger, seeking comfort or good physical health) seems to be universal.[12] It thus means that it is not absurd to seek a set of such universal properties.

Fortunately, however, not every comparison between states requires the building of a 'general theory of man' including its ultimate elements of judgement as well as a criterion using these elements as arguments.

Let us thus compare a set of states between which common features $\bar{Y}_0$, $\bar{C}_0$ exist and which differ by other features $\bar{\bar{Y}}$, $\bar{\bar{C}}$. Let us suppose that all the influences of the $\bar{\bar{Y}}$'s and the $\bar{\bar{C}}$'s on the ultimate X's work through a set of X' of intermediate variables. One will have $X = X(X', \bar{Y}_0, \bar{C}_0)$ and $X' = X'(\bar{\bar{C}}, \bar{\bar{Y}})$ and it will be possible to define a relation $E_{Y_0C_0}(X')$ enabling us to compare the states belonging to the set. This relation will constitute a partial criterion of hierarchization (Figure 1).

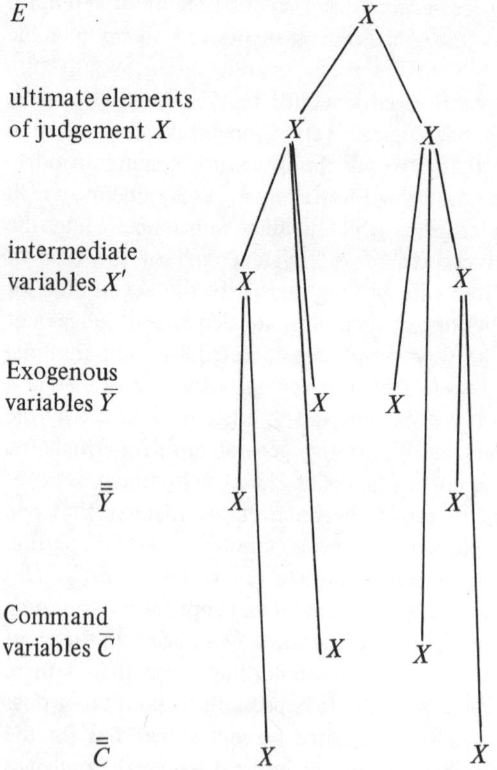

Besides, if in building a theory of man one uses only observations corresponding to states for which $\bar{Y} = \bar{Y}_0$ and $\bar{C} = \bar{C}_0$, one will find that it is sufficient to use the variables X' as ultimate elements of judgement. One will, in fact, have built a partial theory available for only a part of the possible states (the ones for which $\bar{Y} = \bar{Y}_0$ and $\bar{C} = \bar{C}_0$), using the variables (X') apparently forming the ultimate elements of judgement.

In practice, there are many ways to limit the scope of validity of the theory one builds.

(1) One can limit the domain studied by taking into account only parts of the material environment and of personal behaviours (only consumption, or only housing) and by supposing the rest of the environment and behaviour to be given. To separate problems in this way makes the analysis easier, but one must be aware of the fact that it is artificial.

(2) One can limit the diversity of the social environments within which one locates oneself: one will try to compare, in terms of welfare, only states belonging to industrial societies or, more narrowly, to French society of a specific period or to a particular social group.[13] But of course, one can no longer establish comparisons of welfare between people living in different cultures (in particular between people living in 'developed' countries and people living in 'under-developed countries').

(3) One can limit the effects on the X's we consider by comparing states for which some of the effects are invariant. If one considers a parallel evolution of the levels of different people's consumption, an evolution within which modifications of welfare relevant to sign effects are nil, one can bypass these effects. One can thus obtain quantitative indicators much more easily.[14]

Starting with very partial, 'local' theories, unifying very specific families of behaviours, one can try to go progressively further back to more general theories unifying larger families of behaviours.

Let us suppose that one even considers as given the set of social rules of the game and especially the social codes defining the significances connected to behaviours and situations, as well as the way things intervene in the psychological organization of people. One can then build welfare functions by taking the physical descriptors of behaviours and situations as arguments. But then one will have very specific functions of a very particular social state. Let us suppose that one considers, on the other hand, social factors and factors of individual psychology as variables. One will then be obliged to use much more general welfare functions using as arguments 'psychological' variables which characterize the things that behaviours and situations provide. One could pass from these general functions to specific functions by initially fixing the value of parameters corresponding to factors supposed to be constant.

The variables to be used

To reveal the relationships between consumption and welfare, the variables necessary to characterize the sets of consumption exist at three levels:

(a) variables describing consumer goods by physical characteristics independent of the society within which one is;

(b) variables describing what these consumptions 'are' in a given socio-cultural universe, allowing for the social properties with which this universe provides them; and

(c) variables describing the repercussions of these consumptions on the life of the person we consider.

The variables of the first type are included in C as regards the consumption of the person we consider, and Y as regards the consumption of others. The social codes and more generally the social 'rules of the game', ensuring the 'translation' of the variables of the first type in those of the second, belong to X. In practice, according to cases, one has to use a greater or lesser number of stages of the variables X.

The definition of the variables to be used for the *physical description* of consumer goods is not given by immediate experience. These variables must enable us to distinguish two consumer goods when they produce different influences on any aspect of the welfare of the person we consider, while permitting the most simple possible description. *It is only after we have examined through what mechanisms consumer goods influence people's life that we can say how to describe them and how to define homogeneous goods.* Homogeneous goods, as regards the characteristics which determine their utilitarian properties (for example, for clothes: thickness, thermal conductivity), may be extremely heterogeneous as regards the characteristics which determine their social properties (for clothes: the aspect and cut of the cloth, etc.). These characteristics themselves may be far from being evident.

Thus, for instance, the characteristics of built-up space which influence interpersonal relations are not evident, and require a whole research work to be revealed (d'Iribarne, 1976a).

The establishment of a theory corresponds to the highlighting of relevant descriptors, to the definition of operations enabling us to describe any set of consumption goods according to these descriptors, and to the terms of laws enabling us to compare different sets described by using them (the purpose is not, of course, to establish in advance a systematic comparison between all the sets of possible goods). The comparisons relevant to 'economic' concerns, which deal with the social organization of scarce resources, will certainly refer to sets of goods different from those among which one will establish more 'technical' comparisons (relevant to 'efficiency' more than to 'effectiveness'). Thus, one will be concerned with the effects on welfare of transformations of the housing deriving from economic growth, and not with the definition of a satisfying organization of built-up space. One will be concerned with the effects of the growth of food consumption, not with the nutritional advice which must be given to a person. However, the kind of knowledge, with regard to relationships between consumption and welfare, that one has to use in such an economic approach includes the knowledge necessary to these more 'technical' approaches. Thus, to study how the effect of housing on welfare evolves, it is necessary to define categories of housing homogeneous with regard to their contribution to welfare. But it is impossible to do this if one has not seriously studied the housing descriptors relevant from this point of view (and at the present time national accounting, not being able to do it, produces results which are no doubt somewhat absurd).

The social properties of different consumer goods vary from one society to another and from one social group to another. Here the factors which condition the significance given to consumer goods, defining foods for instance as common or subtle, copious or spartan, make an essential contribution. These factors may be more or less conventional social codes (white means joy in some societies, mourning in others). They may also be more objective characteristics of the situation, such as the relations between a person's consumption and the 'normal' consumption of the society we consider, or the visibility of actions undertaken. This latter explains for example that two actions having identical effects on a man's health with be given very different significances and will have, on the whole, very different effects depending on whether it is a matter of rescuing a mountain climber in peril or rectifying a dangerous point on a road (d'Iribarne, 1969). But the passage from physical characteristics to social characteristics can require a much more complex 'translation' than the mere application of a code of significances. Thus, the fact that a built-up space with given physical characteristics is propitious for negative, neutral or positive interpersonal relations, depends on the degree of consistency of the social interactions produced by this framework with the interactions socially prescribed (d'Iribarne, 1976a).

Let us suppose that one tries to compare two situations such that the people whom one considers both have the same relationship with consumer goods (for instance, consumption plays the same part in social status, and the quest for status the same part in the quest for a good relation with fellowmen). Thus, one can use as the variable X the 'social performances' of consumer goods. One has one stable $E(X)$ by taking these performances as elements of X. In fact, the work done by CEREBE up to the present time has always been oriented in such a direction.[15] But it is a specific one. In fact, goods which are similar not only in their physical properties but also in their social properties can play different parts in the life of the people using them. Thus, they can have *very different repercussions on their life.*

This is true for what is obtained in the different dimensions of life (status, interpersonal relations, etc.). Thus, a type of housing unsuitable for neighbourhood relations will be far from always having identical repercussions on interpersonal relations. These repercussions will be very different for those who are very much concerned with neighbourhood relations and for those concerned with other relations. A given consumption level within a given society will not always have the same influence on social status. This influence will be different for those who see in consumption only a means to gain high social status, and for those who can gain it by inheritance or profession.

This is true also with regard to psychological organization. Thus, a material universe providing security will have very different effects on people who feel more or less insecure. A modest status will have very different effects on those who are very much implicated in social competition and on those who have 'retired from the game' in order to seek a more harmonious relation with the world. Having insufficiently studied what part things play in life, we shall not insist on this point. One can nevertheless note that it should lead us to differentiate people not only by the social class to which they belong, but also by the psychological characteristics which seem little connected to this membership. These characteristics are related to the person's history and introduce interdependencies between what is experienced at different moments of their existence (e.g., difficulties occurring at a given moment may sometimes be propitious to a psychological maturation which will have positive effects later on, and sometimes may generate an irreversible trauma). This introduces appreciable difficulties for the hierarchization of states and even for the definition of the adequate variables X. In the future we shall progressively attempt to solve these problems.[16]

Therefore, to compare the effects of different consumption sets on welfare implies that one uses variables and laws defining relations between variables belonging to a vast field of the social sciences. It is necessary to use concepts and laws belonging to sociology, social psychology, and psychology. Besides, the field of social life with which one must be concerned extends far beyond the field of consumption in the restricted sense, for it is so much involved in the entirety of life. When one studies medication, it is necessary in order to understand what is going on, to study the doctor's activity, the norm conflicts that he may encounter, and the medicalization of ill-being (Dupuy and Karsenty, 1974). The study of food consumption leads us to the analysis of a woman's role within society and of conflicts between modern and traditional images of this role (d'Iribarne, 1977). With regard to housing one is led to analyse the organization of sociability (d'Iribarne, 1976a), and as regards television, relations within the family. More generally, the place of consumption in life depends on the way in which relations with others, with oneself and with the world are organised (d'Iribarne, 1978).

Notes

1. Yet some of them ask questions about such a situation (see Houthakker, 1961).

2. Researches conducted since 1967 by the author first alone and then helped by a team: the CEREBE (Centre de Recherche sur le Bien-Etre). One can find the orientations of the research led by the CEREBE concerning relations

between consumption and welfare in d'Iribarne (1972, 1973). These researches try to show, from empirical data, the relations between consumption as a whole, or consumption of specific goods (food, cars, housing, medicine, television) and welfare.

3. For instance, a work of 'pure theory' such as Debreu (1959) or a classic manual such as Scitovsky (1964).

4. In the most general meaning, physical feeling as well as 'moral conscience' feelings.

5. Naturally enough, the attempt to describe a man's behaviour as inspired by a certain hierarchy does not at all mean that one identifies him to a 'rational actor' whose behaviour corresponds to an organized quest of conscious purposes (one does not do it either when one studies a plant or an organ and considers them as teleological systems). It is an implicit hierarchy derived from the observation of behaviour and which may largely be in contradiction with the conscious hierarchies of action that one seeks.

6. On the other hand, it is not supposed to give a general representation of behaviour: it does not explain the behaviours which do not derive from a learning that has converged. The purpose is not at all to establish an ordering in advance over the whole set of choices. It is admitted that these are often very little 'rational' for they are insufficiently informed. The properties of 'rationality' will not be conferred to the behaviour of consumers but to the hierarchy of states in terms of welfare.

7. At least since its analysis elaborated by Veblen (1899).

8. See the analysis of Durkheim (1895).

9. These different phenomena are related to the fact that in all systems of signs, the meaning associated with any given significant depends upon the latter's location in the whole set of significants of the system. When certain features of things signify something, what they signify depends on their relative position compared with the features of other things. More especially, features where higher levels are associated with higher price signal a meaning which has to do with relative and not with absolute performance.

10. See, for example, what Houthakker (1961) says about it, and the remarks of Lancaster (1971) on the duration of this use.

11. Naturally enough these elements must not by any means be confounded with 'ends' consciously pursued by a person in a certain social and cultural context. They are not likely either to be conscious or to occur as 'ends' in the accepted use of this term in our language. One may rather think of the quality of being, which may even be largely incompatible with the rational pursuit of ends.

12. Properties as simple as these can have large implications for the understanding of the relations between consumption and welfare, of economic behaviour variations in connection with cultures, etc. (see d'Iribarne, 1972, 1973).

13. Thus, a study of medicine prescription in privately marketed medicine (Dupuy and Karsenty, 1974) is set in the framework of a very particular social group in the France of 1971. This made it possible to limit the necessary investigations considerably.

14. The author is at present trying to study in such a perspective the relations between expenses and service quality for urban environment.

15. This approach is now changing (see d'Iribarne, 1978).

16. Brief indications on some of them are given in d'Iribarne (1974).

References

DEBREU, G. (1959) *Theory of Value* New York: Wiley.

DUPUY, J. P. and S. KARSENTY (1974) *L'Invasion Pharmaceutique* Paris: Editions du Seuil.

DURKHEIM, E. (1895) *Les Règles de la Méthode Sociologique* Paris: Alcan.

HOUTHAKKER, H. S. (1961) 'The Present State of Consumption Theory', *Econometrica* 29 (October).

D'IRIBARNE, Ph. (1969) 'A la Recherche de Politiques Rationnelles de Santé et de Sécurité', *Analyse et Prévision* 8 (December).

––, (1972) 'La Consommation et le Bien-Etre: Approche Psycho-Socio-Economique', *Revue d'Economie Politique* 82 (January).

––, (1973) *La Politique du Bonheur* Paris: Editions du Seuil.

––, (1974) 'Les Mécanismes du Bien-Etre', *Economie Appliquée* 27 (October-December).

––, (1976a) 'Espace Bâti et Relations Interpersonnelles', Miméo. Paris: CEREBE.

––, (1976b) 'L'Indépendance des Satisfactions; un Postulat Contraire aux Données Empiriques', Miméo. Paris: CEREBE.

––, (1977) 'Consommations Alimentaires et Comportements Socio-Economiques', *Consommation* (April-June).

––, (1978) 'Genèse et Avenir de la Société de Consommation', *Futuribles*, no. 13.

LANCASTER, K. J. (1971) *Consumer Demand.* New York: Columbia University Press.

NORDHAUS, W. and J. TOBIN (1973) 'Is Growth Obsolete? ' in: M. MOSS (ed.), *The Measurement of Economic and Social Performance.* New York: Columbia University Press.

PARETO, W. (1909) *Manuel d'Economie Politique.* Paris: Giard.

SCITOVSKY, T. (1964) *Welfare and Competition.* London: Unwin University Books.

VEBLEN, T. (1899) *Theory of the Leisure Class.* London: The Macmillan Company.

• Comment

Duncan MacRae, Jr.

University of North Carolina, USA

The general theory proposed by d'Iribarne, like Lesourne's, is an ambitious one, and requires a great amount of collaborative work if it is to be formulated precisely and verified. He recognizes the magnitude of the task; and perhaps meetings such as this seminar can further it. He looks beyond the boundaries of economics for the continuation of this task; and, as I shall indicate, I wish to look still further for the collaboration of other social sciences in the task and for the relaxation of certain assumptions characteristic of economics.

d'Iribarne defines his problem in part by the fact that learning (training, *apprentissage*) occurs and thus that preferences are not fixed. To recognize this fact would seem to mean rejecting Becker's axiom of the fixity of preferences. In responding, Becker uses two lines of defense: (1) that it is preferences for underlying 'basic commodities', or Lancaster's 'characteristics' of goods, rather than for goods as such, that are fixed; and (2) that some changes in human choice, that occur even when the objective environment has not changed, can be accounted for by 'human capital' or 'consumption capital' (Stigler and Becker, 1977). These postulated characteristics of the chooser, which may develop slowly and have some stability over time, are presumably distinct from physiological states of satiation such as the absence of hunger. Nevertheless, as in the case of hunger, it is desirable to try to measure such states directly or at least by means more direct than the observation of economic choices.

From the existence of learning, d'Iribarne concludes that a revised definition of utility is needed. Utility or welfare can no longer be associated with preferences in general. Rather, he defines welfare as corresponding to the ultimate (convergent) choice made by the individual under conditions of perfect information. But even if the individual is engaging in a rational search for information, and terminating it when its marginal costs and benefits become equal, he has not in general reached the point defined by d'Iribarne, which corresponds to *perfect* information. The question of comparing the various end-points that correspond to perfect information, to economizing in information search, and to learning, arose also in our discussion of Elster's and Lévy-Garboua's papers.

I wish to go farther than d'Iribarne, however, and argue that in the presence of altruism even the point of convergence he identifies (with perfect information) is *not* in general one of maximum welfare. I set aside the fact that various non-utilitarian (non-hedonistic) definitions of welfare exist – for example, notions of human perfection. But even in a utilitarian (Benthamite) framework, welfare must be defined as a state of feeling or experience which, if not observable directly, can still be inferred by psychological measurement. An altruistic act may then be one that does *not* maximize the chooser's welfare, even though it may well be predictable in terms of some other maximand. We thus return to two points I raised in discussing Elster's paper. First, 'welfare', a valuative term with widespread connotations outside economics, cannot be arbitrarily redefined by economists – even though they have tried to do so in the system of discourse of their own discipline. Secondly, in trying to preserve the artificial correspondence between choice and welfare which they have produced by an impermissible definition, economists are driven to postulate narrow, material maximands and to assert the scarcity of altruism. The question as to what it is that people maximize should be resolved by empirical research; but such research can take place only within a conceptual scheme that *completely* separates 'welfare' from any tautological connection with 'preference satisfaction'.

d'Iribarne further requires that his model include a set of variables intermediate between choice and utility (or welfare). These variables seem to correspond to Becker's 'basic commodities' or to Lesourne's 'satisfactions'. It is important to identify and measure these variables.

Becker noted in the discussion that some of these variables had in fact *been* measured e.g. health in the work of Michael Grossman. But as a non-economist I suggest that the direct techniques of measurement commonly used in other social sciences would be a useful adjunct to economic methods (MacRae, 1978).

The problem of more direct measurement also arises, as I have noted above, in the measurement of welfare or well-being itself. As d'Iribarne points out in the larger work from which his paper is drawn, there is an extensive literature on 'social indicators of subjective well-being', represented by Campbell et al. (1976). Though economists may criticize the validity of indicators based on direct questioning, the general canons of science require that we study systematically the relations among multiple possible indicators of a concept. Such study is all the more necessary when that concept is the core valuative concept on which policy proposals may be based.

One implication of such direct measurement is illustrated by a finding of Easterlin's (1973). He finds that according to the Cantril self-anchoring scale (which may or may not be a valid measure of welfare), respondents in rich countries did not seem much happier than those in poor countries. Such a finding suggests that people define their welfare in terms of national rather than worldwide standards of comparison. A similar disparity in standards of comparison might well exist between generations.

This inference might lead us to reconsider our policies for intergenerational transfers. Tullock has claimed elsewhere that we might not wish to transfer wealth from the present generation to future generations, because future generations are likely to be wealthier in any event. Easterlin's findings lead us to a similar question, but by another path – an argument not of inequity, but of inefficiency in producing welfare. If future generations, like wealthy nations, are likely to derive less happiness from their wealth – to be psychologically impoverished, as it were – then perhaps we should seek other means to maximize welfare over the long run.

Whether this question remains important depends on the replication of Easterlin's findings with various other indicators of subjective well-being. Tullock pointed out in the discussion that recent findings of Gallup (1977) showed substantial differences between rich and poor nations on another indicator of 'welfare'. But whatever the ultimate relation between the various indicators may prove to be, the question of *how* they are related could not even have been raised if we had not defined them, and measured them, as conceptually distinct.

d'Iribarne also deals with a question of practice as well as theory: the possible use of the model he proposes, as a source of information to consumers and citizens as to how to promote their own welfare. This suggestion seems to be the opposite of a proposal often attributed to American policy analysts: to advise only the government and not the individual. I suggest that the most useful theories of well-being should permit both sorts of advice. In our discussion, d'Iribarne replied that the most effective sort of advice by social scientists is that which changes the concepts and causal models entertained by citizens (or elites), and facilitates governmental use of those same new concepts and models.

References

CAMPBELL, A., P. E. CONVERSE and W. L. RODGERS (1976) *The Quality of American Life.* New York: Russell Sage Foundation.

EASTERLIN, R. A. (1973) 'Does Money Buy Happiness? ', *The Public Interest* 30 (Winter).

GALLUP, G. H. (1977) 'Human Needs and Satisfactions: A Global Survey', *Public Opinion Quarterly* 41 (Winter).

MACRAE, D., Jr. (1978) 'Review Essay: The Sociological Economics of Gary S. Becker', *American Journal of Sociology* 83 (March).

STIGLER, G. J. and G. S. BECKER (1977) 'De Gustibus Non Est Disputandum', *American Economic Review* 67 (March).

6

Objectives of Income Redistribution

Gordon Tullock

Public Choice Center, Blacksburg, USA

The purpose of this paper, oddly enough, is not so much to inform its audience as to solicit their assistance for the author. As you may know, I have in recent months been deeply concerned with the demand-revealing process. This has led me to two involvements with income redistribution. First, a great many people criticized the demand-revealing process on the grounds that it allegedly is too favourable to the wealthy and too unfavourable to the poor. I do not believe this is necessarily true. The demand-revealing process can be adjusted in a number of ways, if one does object to its distributional effects.

Indeed, it, like democracy, can be used to generate substantially any 'distribution of power' simply by appropriate weighting of different individuals. In any event, there seems no reason to believe that the demand-revealing process, even if used in the simple and straight-forward form in which it is described in my article with Tideman (1976), would be any less egalitarian than democracy.[1] Democracy in practice is only modestly egalitarian, even if its proponents frequently talk as if it were extremely so (Tullock, 1971). Thus, both democracy and the demand-revealing process involve only rather modest transfers to the poor. There is no reason to believe one is worse than the other on this dimension. People who object to the demand-revealing process on these grounds should also object to democracy.

So much for this particular aspect of the problem. I should like to turn now to the second connection of the demand-revealing process to income redistribution, which is, in my opinion, of much greater intellectual importance. It is also, in my opinion, much more difficult. After all, anyone can design a constitution which will generate any desired degree of income redistribution by simply specifying it in the original document. The problems of income distribution raised by the demand-revealing process, however, are not problems of design but problems of what we want.

Thus, the point of this paper really is to solicit the views of the reader on what our goals should be when we talk about income distribution in society and, in particular, the distribution of burdens and benefits of government activity. I am not able in this case simply to examine my own ideas in this area, because it would appear that my ideas are rather eccentric. I am not particularly in favour of income redistribution. I have vague feelings that some aid should be given to the poor, but clearly my position is not that of the average intellectual.

I am, however, a positive economist and am willing to advise other people on how to achieve their goals. In particular, since a great many people talk about various redistribution objectives, and since the demand-revealing process permits much more precise adjustment of governmental behaviour to desires of the citizenry, it should be possible to achieve whatever goals are desired in the area of income distribution much more precisely with the demand-revealing process than with other methods.

The problem I have encountered, and for which I wish to request your assistance, is that there does not seem to be anything in the literature which indicates what redistribution we should desire, granted this greater precision made possible by the demand-revealing process. In dealing with this problem, I should like to ask the reader simply to take on faith my statements as to what can be done in the demand-revealing process. I am not presently making any particular addition to the existing published literature but merely providing an outline of its conclusions. If you have any doubts that I am correct, you can turn to the above-mentioned article with Tideman, the special issue of *Public Choice* (1977), or the articles in the rather extensive bibliography which is included in the special issue of *Public Choice.*

First, then, the demand-revealing process makes it possible to make use of a close approximation of Lindahl taxes for public goods. Note that I say a 'close approximation'. There is some doubt as to how close an approximation we would be able to achieve, but it seems to me that it is only sensible to assume that the approximation will be very close indeed. If we assume that it is close and then develop a set of criteria we would use on that assumption, and it later turn out to be somewhat more difficult than we expected, we can easily correct our reasoning for this inaccuracy. If, on the other hand, we assume that the approximation is very rough, and therefore only a very crude set of criteria is necessary, if we later discover that the approximation is very good, we will have to go through the whole process again. I would therefore like to ask that you bear with me and assume that the Lindahl taxes will be very closely approximated – indeed, for ease of explanation, we might assume that they will be reached perfectly.

Note that, although we seldom mention this, the Lindahl taxes can be negative. In Figure 1 we show a two-person, A and B, society, in which there is some public good to be purchased which will benefit A and injure B. The demand curve for B, then, is negative, as shown in Figure 1. We sum the two demand curves to get $A + B$ and note the point where it crosses the 0 line. This gives us the optimum shown by 0. We then charge A a tax of A' and B a negative tax of B'.

Note that this procedure, although geometrically different, is a mapping of the usual method of computing the optimal amount of pollution. Furthermore, it gives A and B roughly the same consumer surplus on this social improvement. It is, of course, simply the application of the Lindahl tax scheme, except that one of the taxes is negative.

Distribution of costs and benefits of this sort is not what most people mean when they talk about redistribution of income. In a moment I shall turn to the more normal meaning of redistribution, but I should like to raise questions here as to the appropriate distribution of benefits and costs of government action. In a way, I am going to follow the traditional economic distinction between discussion of an efficient change and of deliberate income redistribution; but, in my case, later I am actually going to talk about deliberate income redistribution. I simply want to clear the decks by talking about certain problems of efficient change first.

Note, then, that although public finance specialists (including myself) have always been deeply enamoured with Lindahl taxes, this has been essentially a theoretical attraction because they are theoretically so nice. Everybody is paying his true marginal evaluation of some particular public good because the different evaluations of the public good by different people lead to their paying different prices for the same quantity. Furthermore, we can, in the demand-revealing process,

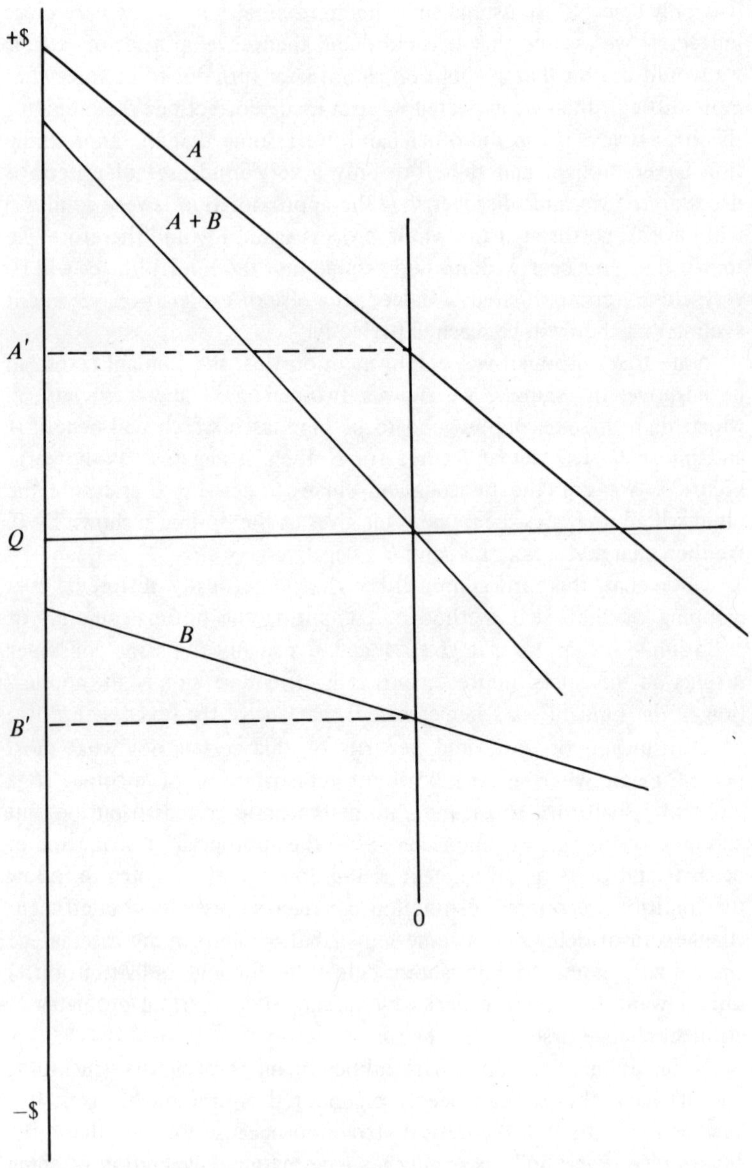

Figure 1

obtain that quantity of public goods which is optimal, so everything seems fine.

When one begins thinking about it, however, it is not so obvious that the Lindahl tax is a sensible tax. Suppose that we have some public good for which *A*'s demand is high and *B*'s demand is low, as in Figure 2. We sum the two demand curves, using the demand-revealing process for the project, find the optimum (which turns out to be 10 units), and charge *B* \$10 (or \$1 a unit) which is the value of the marginal tenth unit to him, and we charge *A* (the high demander) \$100 (or \$10 a unit) which is the value of the marginal unit to him. For \$11 a unit, we can produce the 10 units. *B* is paying \$10 total and *A* is paying \$100, and there is no obvious reason for us to believe that *A* has a higher consumption surplus than *B*. Indeed, the first approximation would be to say that they are probably about the same.

This certainly has little or no resemblance to what happens in the private market. Nor is it obvious to me that distributionally this is a good idea, whatever else may be said about it. Thus, my first problem with respect to income distribution under the demand-revealing process is to ask if it is indeed a good idea to use Lindahl prices, granted we can do so. Before trying to answer this question, remember that just at the moment I am only talking about changes in government process and *not* about the kind of redistribution we think of as assistance to the poor. I will turn to that in a moment. We should assume, then, that the income distribution before we contemplate purchasing this public good from *A* and *B* was one which had been socially accepted, although up to now I have not explained how we will obtain such an income distribution.

We also have the question of what we would do if we decide against the Lindahl price. But there is an even more difficult problem. In many cases of government action, there is a net social benefit of a unitary nature, i.e. we cannot carry the production of the public good out to the point where the marginal price – summing all individual demand, positive *and* negative – is equal to the cost. For example, suppose it were decided to abolish the Common Agricultural Community. Clearly, the benefit from this action would be much greater than the loss, and it is hard to think of any way to regard this as generation of a continuous type of public good.

This raises very real problems for income distribution. As an example, suppose that *A* has an Interstate Commerce Commission-granted monopoly on trucking between two cities in the United States.

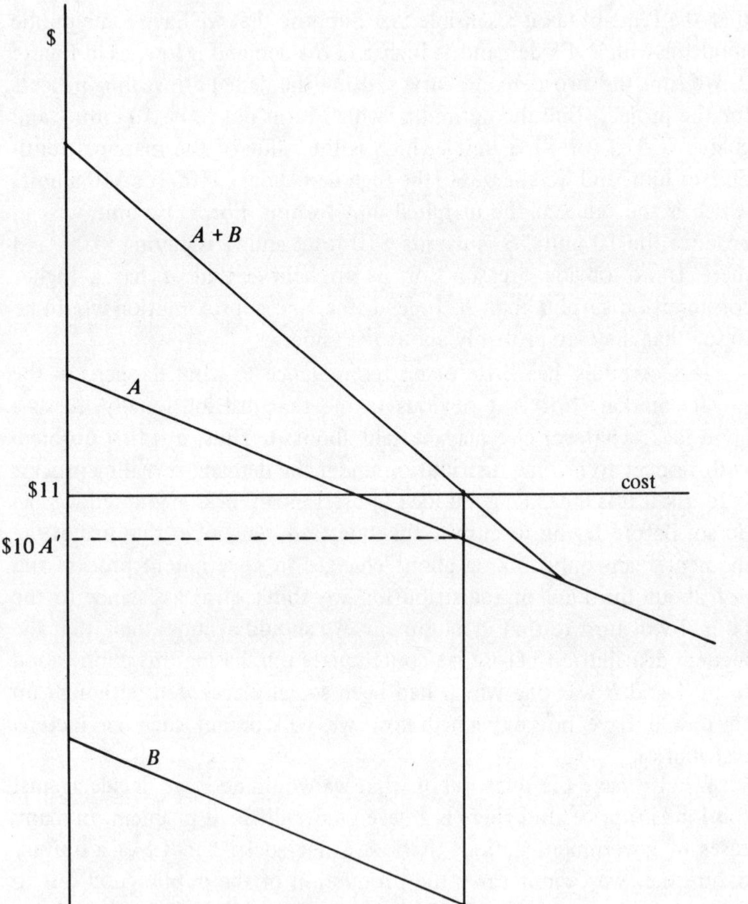

Figure 2

His income from this government-granted monopoly is $10,000 higher than what he would achieve in a competitive trucking market. *B* and *C*, on the other hand, are users of this truck line, and the cost to them of the monopoly is $9,000 and $6,000, respectively. This would, I take it, be roughly the typical situation, although normally there are many more parties involved. If we obtain the actual values the parties would place on the abolition of a monopoly, which is –$10,000 for *A* and a sum of +$15,000 for *B* and *C*, we note that it is clearly a socially desirable act because there is a larger profit than there is cost.

But having decided that it is socially desirable, which is all that traditional economics has done, we now have the problem of determining who should get the $5,000 social profit. Indeed, we could ask who is to get the full $15,000, since it is not inevitable that we will compensate the loser. Nevertheless, most economists have argued in such cases that the loser should be compensated and I am going to adopt this assumption. Note that the problems I raise later would not be changed particularly if we decided not to compensate *A*, but the amount of money to be distributed would be increased.

What, then, do we do with the $5,000? The traditional economic explanation is that we would let it remain in the pockets of *B* and *C*, with *B* getting $4,000 and *C* getting $1,000, and simply compensate *A* for his losses. But surely there is no strong argument for this. Why not divide it into three equal parts and give one-third to each of them? Or, if we think that *A* is a nasty man and should not be compensated, why not arrange that *B* and *C* will each get $2,500? Note that all of this is perfectly possible with the demand-revealing process.

Even these proposals are fairly modest. Why should any one of these three people have control over this fund? Why not contribute it to the well-being of the untouchables in India? Or why not pay it into a fund which is designed, when many further similar contributions are made, to be divided among all citizens of the world on a so-much-per-head basis. Or we could even concentrate it on the poor – that is, this money will be paid (once again, together with similar funds from the elimination of other uneconomic institutions) to, let us say, the 5 million poorest people in the world.

I can find no significant discussion of this problem. What is the objective which would be recommended by a person who believes in a great deal of equality or, for that matter, an economist who does not have any particularly strong feelings about equality but who just wants a 'good' outcome. If you happen to be a property-right devotee, for example, *who* has the property right in this fund?

There is, by the way, another candidate for the money – a candidate whom I would regard as exceptionally deserving, although administratively hard to locate. Presumably the abolition of the United States Interstate Commerce Commission would be the result of entrepreneurial activity by some group or individual. Giving them the bulk of the social profit, or at least enough social profit to motivate this kind of work, would seem to be highly desirable. This would mean that the present situation in which, in general, it is easy to organize a minority to push for some act which is contrary to the public interest, and very difficult to organize one which benefits the public interest, would be reversed. Granted we are going to compensate the losers, there would be no significant interest group organized to avoid this change in the law; and if we used the profit to compensate the political agency that brought about the change, then we would motivate political entrepreneurs to go into this business and we might end up with a massively more efficient government.

The problem here is essentially administrative. Even with the demand-revealing process, very few people are motivated to become well informed. Thus, the reward might well go to the wrong people, and therefore it would not serve its motivating function. Still, I would think some experimentation along these lines would be desirable. Note that if we decide to give half of the social profit to whoever pulls off the political coup that makes the social profit possible, we would still have the other half for other distribution, and the questions I have raised above would still be important ones.

Having whetted your interest (I hope) with these subsidiary, but nevertheless intellectually challenging, problems, I would now like to turn to what I regard as the major problem in redistribution which is conscious, deliberate redistribution of income for the benefit of the recipients.

I should like to begin by pointing out that there is one great advantage of the demand-revealing process: it does not permit transfers which are motivated *only* by the desire of the recipients to receive money. If we look at modern democratic states (and, also, for that matter many dictatorships), we observe an immense amount of transfer from party to party which is motivated entirely by the desire of the recipients, with the people who involuntarily make the contribution not having any interest in the matter at all or being opposed. The Common Market agricultural policy is an example; almost all protective tariffs are further examples; the higher educational system (by which almost all of us are employed) is a procedure for transferring funds to people who will be well above average income anyway from the general population, who have only an average income.

All of these transfers, so far as I know, can be justified only on the grounds that the political process does indeed grind them out because the recipients want them, and under democracy it is hard to organize any opposition to them. It is a case of an intense minority getting transfers from a dispersed and not deeply interested majority. All of these things would vanish if we used the demand-revealing process, because the mild opposition to these various programs of the average man would, when added up, be greater than the intense desire for them by the minority. This seems to me an immense step forward.

Still, so far as I know, there is absolutely no rational explanation for any of these transfers, except that the recipients want them and the political process happens to be such that they can get them. The change in the political process that eliminated them would, I think, be widely supported. Even some professors of economics would be willing to back a program which surely would greatly reduce the demand for professors of economics.

We are thus left with transfers to people who, for one reason or another, attract the favourable attention of the donors. Mainly, these are the poor and the ill. There are other groups, of course, but I trust you will not object if I confine myself to these particular groups. It would be one of the advantages of the demand-revealing process, then, that transfers would be concentrated in a group of people who are at least by some thought to merit the transfer. Farmers, so far as I know, are not thought to merit transfers by anyone except the farmers themselves nor are the beneficiaries of various protective tariffs thought to merit the money by anyone but themselves. However, that is not true with respect to people who are sick and/or poor.

Here again I have frankly to confess that I am not very much of an egalitarian, and therefore I would probably choose a fairly low level of transfers. It is not obvious that I would choose as low a level of transfers to the poor as we actually observe in most democratic states – where the transfer tends to be of the order of 2 to 3 percent of GNP – but, in any event, I would not be in favour of a very high transfer rate. My objective, however, is not to present my own preferences but to use this paper in an effort to solicit the views of people who do believe in considerable transfers, so that, having found out what they have in mind, I can design a political process based on the demand-revealing process, which will tend to generate that outcome.

There is, however, one problem with which I should begin. Suppose that Professor Bleeding Heart tells me that he knows perfectly well what income transfers should be. We should find the world average income and tax everyone who has an income above that amount by 90 percent of the excess, and then use the funds derived to give to all people who have less than the average income 90 percent of the difference between their income and the average income. I have not looked at the numbers recently, but I suppose that the average monthly income in the world is something like $500 per family.

There is nothing easier than designing a governmental structure which does this. We simply put the requirement that this be done into the constitution. To say it is easy to design is not to say that it is easy to implement. I doubt very much if such a constitution will be acceptable in any country which has an average income much above the world average, and I also doubt that we could get world acceptance simply because the wealthier countries – such as the US and France – would object very strongly to this large transfer to poverty-stricken countries such as China and India. Thus, although it is easy to design such a procedure, it is very unlikely that we would get beyond the design stage.

Furthermore, I am sure we would find that although Professor Bleeding Heart regards this as a good system, many other people would have different ideas. What we need, then, is a constitution or a method of making decisions on income transfers which has acceptable elements in itself and which succeeds in aggregating in one way or another the preferences for redistribution of many different people. Selecting one dictator for this subject is an easy course. Furthermore, selecting a single first preference is particularly attractive if we are going to use ours. In other words, we could all stand around and each one of us offer his own personal preference for redistribution.

The fact remains, however, that we are not dictators, not even collective dictators, and there is no obvious reason why our decision as to how much redistribution we think should be carried out is the socially binding one. And, in practice, it would not be. We can only hope to get some particular method of redistribution adopted if there is some procedure of aggregating the preferences or at least a large enough or powerful enough group so that there is some possibility that the procedure will be implemented. Since I take it none of us prefers the dictatorial route, that means that we must aim at a policy which a great many people will adopt.

But note here a particular problem with what we might call Rawlsianism. Since *The Calculus of Consent* (Buchanan and Tullock, 1962) also talks about things 'behind the veil of ignorance', I might be regarded as a premature Rawlsian.[2] There is a difference, however. We talk about establishing a constitution in *The Calculus of Consent* to deal with future problems – these problems, of necessity, not being fully known at the moment. As it happens, we argue that there is a particular set of constitutional arrangements which is more efficient than others, and hence the present discounted value of this constitution from the standpoint of a person who is uncertain of the future would be positive. Furthermore, there is a set of side payments which could be used, granted that we were going to use the optimally efficient constitution, to compensate people who, being able to make calculations about the future, realize that they will not do as well as other people. Thus, in our case we are simply using a sort of variant of Pareto optimality, which we call Pareto optimality in large.

The Rawls proposal, however, does not claim that there is any particularly efficient level of income redistribution; and, indeed, I believe from my personal knowledge of Rawls that he would probably argue that a zero income redistribution would generate the largest total income; hence, in a way – a very special way – it might be regarded as the most efficient. Thus, he is not attempting to solve a problem with a solution which in fact could be to the benefit of almost everyone, but he is suggesting that people act as if they did not know in order to improve their morals. I doubt very much that any practical government is ever going to do this. In a way, Rawls has made a contribution to the way we should think and talk in the event that we decide that we will devote some time to the discussion of what is the optimal income redistribution in some ethical sense. He has not produced a method which we could expect to have any great effect on income distribution in the real world.

In a way, from the standpoint of the egalitarians, this is fortunate, because the Rawls method surely would lead to less income redistribution than we now have. The point of the veil of ignorance is to make it impossible for people to make their decisions in full knowledge of their real-world circumstances. We do not have the veil of ignorance, and decisions are therefore made with this forbidden knowledge. Since the median income is below the average income, this would mean that we would anticipate in a democracy that there would be more money transferred than would be transferred behind the veil of ignorance (Wagner, 1974).

We need then a method of aggregating people's preferences: one method in general use today is the market, another is democracy. For redistribution of income, there is indeed a market solution – voluntary charity – and, in those cases in which there are not large government transfers, it tends to be quite extensive. However, I am going to ignore the market as an income transfer mechanism and concentrate on government or coerced income transfer.

Traditionalists like Anthony Downs sometimes argue that the amount of income transfer generated by simple majority voting is the optimal amount. Downs, of course, then supplements this argument by arguing that a democracy is desirable because it transfers the optimal amount. The circular nature of this line of reasoning is clear. So far as I know there is absolutely no reason to believe that majority voting or any of the variants of democratic government transfer an 'optimal' amount. Indeed, I would argue that they do very badly, since the bulk of the transfers they generate are transferred back and forth within the middle class; and, so far as I know, there are no arguments that would indicate that these transfers are desirable.

However, there is in democracy a very important problem which is normally ignored, i.e. the weighting of the individual votes. Characteristically, in democracies people's votes are weighted either 1 or 0. I can think of no argument for this except tradition, together with the fact that it might be politically extremely difficult to get any kind of agreement on a particular modification. In a way, this particular voting scheme is a Schelling point.

So far as I know, however, no justification has ever been offered for it other than that. There are occasional justifications for weighting all votes at 1, but the fact that we do weight some votes at 0 and some at 1 is, so far as I know, completely unjustified. Perhaps the reader knows of some discussion of this point. Speaking personally, I would rather prefer that if we are going to weight people at different weights, we have more than two weightings. For example, a person who believed in very large transfers of income might argue that individual votes should be weighted inversely with income ($1/N$),[3] so that the poor have much higher voting power than the wealthy, and they can use this to extract additional transfers from the wealthy. Another method which is used in most corporations weights people's votes in terms of their economic interest in the matter at hand, with the result that large stockholders have many more votes than small stockholders. If we look around, we can find many other cases of differential weighting of votes which have used continuous variation, but the dominant one in the present-day world of politics is the 0,1 weighting.

With the demand-revealing process, different people's votes are weighted differently, depending on their demand for various government services – including transfers. The 0,1 dichotomy, however, is very easy to either implement in the demand-revealing process or to leave out.

Let us suppose, then, that we are in France where the poorest part of the population is Algerian immigrants. Suppose that the French citizens are interested in benefiting the Algerians who are, after all, very poor and live badly. Let us discuss how this should be done. For simplicity in diagrammatic exposition, I am going to assume that there are only two Frenchmen and one Algerian, but the demand-revealing process usually works much better with large numbers than it does with small numbers, so I trust the reader will accept this as merely a convention.

Consider Figure 3 which shows the demand for charitable transfer to the Algerian by two Frenchmen, *A* and *B*. The transfer itself is assumed to be done in franc units, and we will assume that the Algerian's demand for the transfer is simply 1 franc per unit, i.e. the horizontal cost line is his demand curve.[4] In a world of private charity, the situation is fairly simple: *B* would probably make a contribution to the Algerian, equivalent to the point where his demand curve crosses the cost curve; and *A*, observing that the Algerian has received a transfer larger than he wanted to pay, would pay nothing.

There is, clearly, a Pareto optimal move from this. We sum the two demand curves to get the line $A + B$, which is the social optimum. We then charge *B* a per-unit transfer, marked B', and charge *A* a per-unit transfer, marked A'. If we have presented their demands correctly, the Frenchmen will be better off, and the Algerian, who is now receiving more money, will be better off.[5] This amounts to using Lindahl taxes to pay for the transfer.

The demand-revealing process can very easily achieve this particular result – a result which I believe cannot be achieved by any other method. Note that, of course, there is the problem of approximating the Lindahl taxes, and it might turn out that we are rather bad at doing this with respect to transfers; but, once again, for the purpose of this

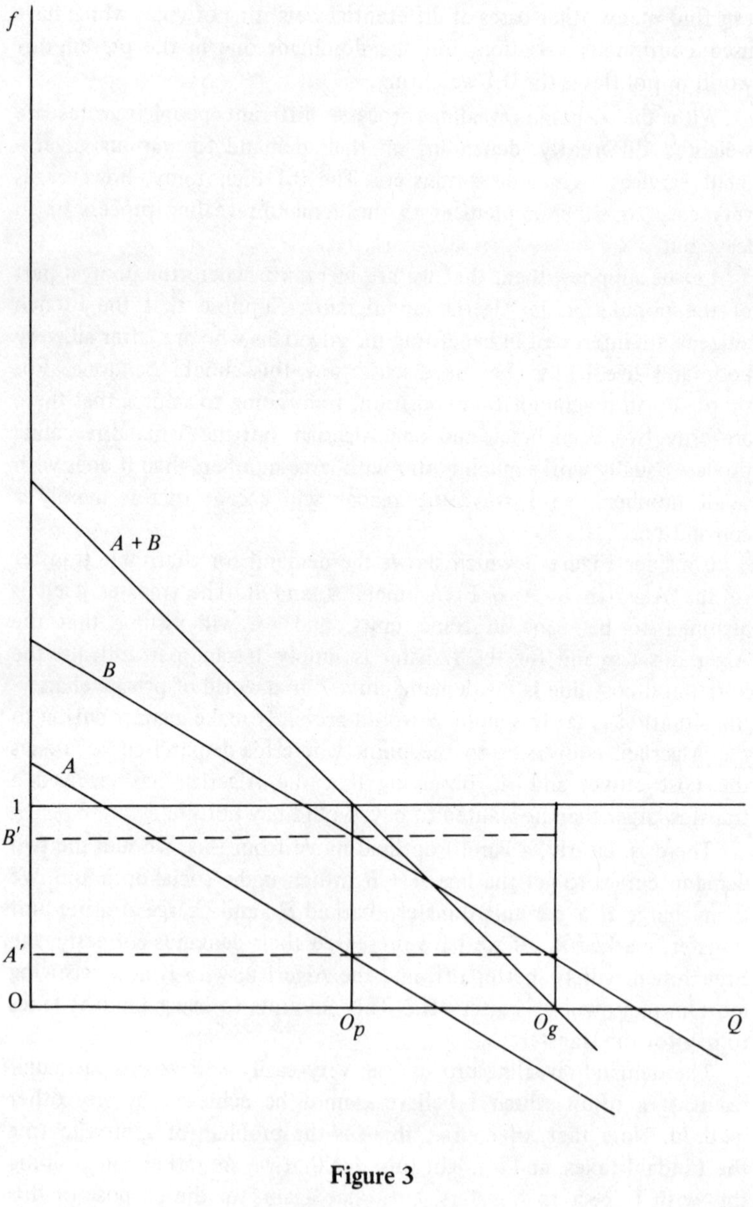

Figure 3

paper let me assume that we can do it very well. If it turns out that later experimentation indicates that we cannot, our results can be appropriately modified.

It is interesting that in this particular case, we have now generated the result that Milton Friedman uses to justify government coercion in the field of income transfer. He points out that income transfer does have neighbourhood effects, which show up in our diagram by the fact that the line $A + B$ lies above B at the point where it crosses the cost line. Thus, the demand-revealing process in this case achieves a goal which has the interesting characteristic that I cannot think of anyone really being opposed to it. One can argue that there should be more transfer than this, and I shall turn to such arguments in a moment, but surely it is hard to argue against this particular use of coercion which benefits everyone and injures no one.

This is the demand-revealing process equivalent to the way the French democracy currently treats the Algerians, i.e. the Algerians are not permitted to vote on various transfers given to them. It should be noted that the French are not unique in this. The guest workers, who are the poorest part of the population all over Europe, face the same situation. The United States, as it happens, does not have any guest workers, but it has illegal immigrants. The exact number is not known, of course, but it is thought to run into millions. They are treated this way, although, interestingly enough, they are frequently able to obtain full services of various government bureaus which deal with income transfers, because the bureau does not realize that they are illegal immigrants.

The problem is more significant in the world as a whole when it is realized that the nation-state itself is simply an artificial creation. There is, as far as I can see, no justification whatsoever – other than tradition[6] – why the citizens of India are not permitted to vote on transfers of funds from the United States and/or France to India. I am sure most 'egalitarians' would be horrified at any such proposal, but I have never read any egalitarian explanation as to why we should *not* do so that, quite frankly, does not abandon all egalitarianism. Limited egalitarianism within the group traditionally permitted to vote is what is normally aimed at, together with some modest income transfers to the really poor people who are not permitted to vote. For the modest transfer to the relatively poor people who are not permitted to vote, the demand-revealing process would obviously work very well.

It is notable that the present situation in which recipients of transfers within the society are permitted to vote is not universal and has not been historically universal. Until quite recently people who were on relief or receiving other kinds of public charity were automatically deprived of their vote. Furthermore, in many states government employees were deprived of the vote for the same basic reason.

I am not arguing for deprivation of the right to vote, but I am asking the people who favour income redistribution to explain to me who they think should be permitted to make decisions on income transfers, and I would also prefer that they tell me why. Perhaps they feel that the 'Wogs', 'Wops', and 'Chinks' – and other lesser breeds without the law – should not be permitted to interfere in the decision processes as to how much will be transferred to them.

But it is not necessary in the demand-revealing process to eliminate bureaucracies in this way. In democracy the actual situation we have is that some of the beneficiaries of charity are permitted to vote and some are not, and there is no reason why the demand-revealing process could not be adjusted to permit exactly the same people to vote or to permit all people to vote. Therefore, let us assume that France changes its constitution and permits Algerians to vote in French elections, and thereby to influence the transfers to them.

Turning once again to Figure 3, you will note that there is a portion of the diagram which is normally omitted, i.e. the part below the 0 line. Furthermore, the $A + B$ line crosses the B line instead of stopping at B in the traditional way. The explanation for this is simply that the demand, after a while, becomes negative. A regards transfers to the Algerian – even if they come from his own pocket – as worth more than their cost, left of the point where the A demand curve crosses the one unit cost line. He regards them as worth something, albeit less than a unit, to the point where his demand curve crosses the 0 line. For example, at O_p he regards the transfer of 1 franc to the Algerian as worth, let us say, 10 centimes.

Eventually, however, he gets to the point where he is positively annoyed by the transfer, and therefore he would be willing to pay something to bring the transfer to a halt. For example, suppose a government program were inaugurated to take \$100 from each person in this room and use it to make a nice gift to Nelson Rockefeller on his next birthday. I suspect that most of the people, if given their choice, would prefer to put up a sum of \$100.01 to avoid making this particular transfer which would be positively annoying to them. I may be wrong in this judgement. Perhaps people are nicer than I think they are, but I do think that there are many people who have positively negative feelings about some recipients of money drawn from their pockets. It is on the basis of this feeling that I have drawn Figure 3.

Thus, our donors at some point become positively annoyed by the transfer. If we are going to count the Algerian's preferences, however, his preference will, to at least some extent, counterbalance this annoyance. Using the demand-revealing process but including the Algerian's preferences, the amount transferred will be the amount O_g. Note that this is a case where the donors as a class cease to get any gain at all from the transfer, i.e. the annoyance of those who are annoyed by that size of transfer just exactly counterbalances the gain of *B* who is in favour, still, of transfers (although he regards them as worth less than their cost). He has squeezed out the entire social satisfaction from the transfer because, from this point on, although the Algerian will continue to gain 1 franc for every franc paid to him, the cost to *A* and *B* is greater than 1 franc.

The allocation of the tax cost between *A* and *B* can be carried out in such a way that they do not pay true Lindahl taxes but in such a way that the cost to them is equal, i.e. each one will be paying about 50 centimes more than his personal demand for the transfer, which in this case would mean that *A* was paying about 25 centimes and *B* about 75 centimes. This amounts to each one paying 50 centimes more than the gain he receives, which in *A*'s case is negative, which sums to 1 franc, exactly the gain which is being made by the Algerian.

There is a further difficulty here, if we include the Algerian's preferences in the system, then there is tax of some significance which must be collected and wasted in order to keep the incentives correct (Tideman and Tullock, 1976). Specifically, the amount wasted is exactly half of the amount which is added to the gift to the Algerian when we move from the first situation to the second. Suppose, for example, if only the two Frenchmen could vote, the Algerian would get 3 francs, and if he is permitted to vote, he will get 4 francs. The tax cost of transferring 4 francs to the Algerian will be 4.50 francs. This is not immense, but still is a defect of the system.

So far I have simply talked technically about the way of applying the demand-revealing process to either of the two possible vote-weighting systems now in use in democracy. The choice between them would, of necessity, mean that we would have to make up our minds on this issue and, as far as I can see, most intellectuals simply have not given the matter any thought. There are various possible reasons for this

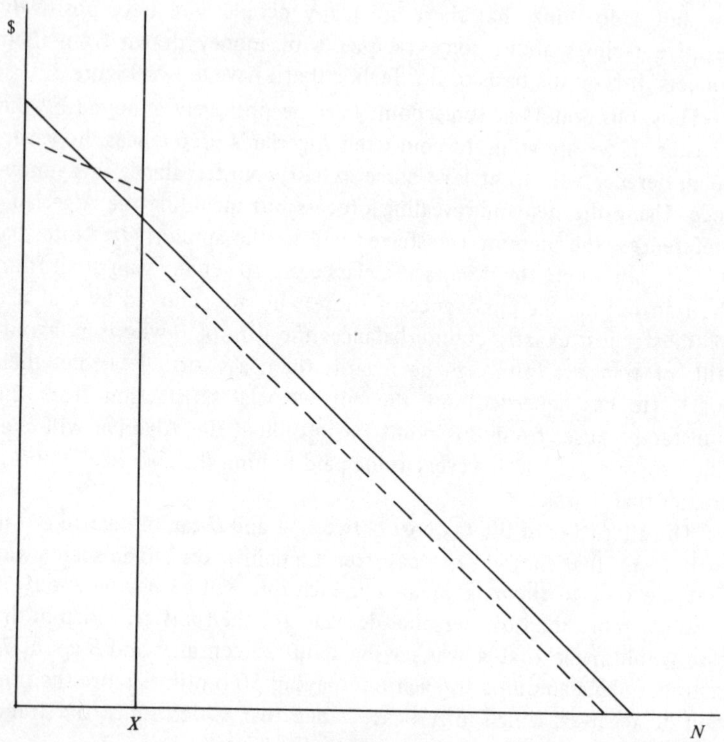

Figure 4

but, rather than looking into these issues, I would prefer simply to urge that some thought be given.

That it is an important matter can be seen from an examination of Figure 4 where I have put income on the left axis and all of the individuals in the world are ranged on the lower axis from left to right, with the wealthiest on the left. The down-slanting line, then, presents the distribution of income in the world. Suppose now that someone becomes disturbed by this distribution and decides to equalize incomes to the left of the line *X*, i.e. the higher incomes. Therefore, he changes the income between the vertical axis and *X* so that it follows the dotted line. As a result of the lowering of incentives from this equalization program, income throughout the entire world – perhaps by the foreign trade sector – falls, so that the dotted line to the right of line *X* is also the result of his activities. The actual reduction in income to the right of *X* is less than I have shown it in my diagram. The reason that the dotted line is well below the solid line is simply that I have to have it visible to the reader. Still, the reduction in the strength of incentives of the left of the line *X* would surely reduce total incomes to the right.

It is very difficult for me to regard this as an egalitarian change in society. Certainly it injures the poor, and the small group of people who do gain (i.e. those people to the left of *X* whose incomes are increased) are not markedly meritorious. This is, however, the kind of thing that we observe with most 'egalitarian' policies. National policies for some egalitarianism within boundaries are quite common at all income levels; but the ones we personally are apt to be concerned with are exclusively among the wealthier nations, and they do have the effects shown in Figure 4. A great many changes in government policy, which are described as 'egalitarian', simply make incomes more equal among upper-income groups within the country. For example, a program to equalize government support to college students would have this effect. The only government income equalization programs which do not have the kind of effects shown in Figure 4 are those rather rare direct transfers from the wealthy part of the world to the poor part of the world, which actually go to the poor in the poor part of the world rather than to upper-income groups there. These are not non-existent, but they are not gigantic. But perhaps I am being unjust. Perhaps there is some reason why income redistribution policies of the sort shown in Figure 4 are desirable.

I have read this paper in three Canadian and one American university as a sort of preparation for reading it here. In each case I asked the audience to vote on whether they think that recipients of transfers should be permitted to vote on the size of the transfers or whether they think they should not. The question is usually hard to put over, because most Canadians, let us say, think it perfectly obvious that all Canadians – whether they are recipients or not – should vote on income transfers, and that it is perfectly obvious that all non-Canadian citizens – whether recipients of transfer or even contributors to the Canadian tax base – should not. This is the traditional *legal* situation; but, so far, in the various discussions on this matter I have never encountered a single argument for it except that this is the way it has been done for some time.

Having gotten through this barrier, I find that the people voting on the issue do split roughly equally. About one-third are in favour of permitting the recipients to vote on transfers, about one-third are opposed, and about one-third 'don't know'. I take it that this is a reasonable indication that they had not given any great thought to it before the question was raised. I also take it that this would be true of the present readership, also. However, I believe it is an important question and suggest that it be given thought.

Indeed, it seems to me all three of the questions I have raised in this paper are important and that all three are cases where people interested in income redistribution *should* have an answer but apparently do not. The Chinese sage, Mencius, argued that before a person takes action, he should first clarify his thoughts. I would suggest that before proposing any income redistribution, its proponents first clarify their thoughts on these issues. Once they have done this, I think the demand-revealing process will reveal its superiority over ordinary voting in achieving whatever goal they have chosen. But in order to use the demand-revealing process, they first have to make up their minds on what will be the basic parameters of the redistribution they favour.

Notes

1. For a technical examination of the methods of using the demand-revealing process for income redistribution, see Tullock (1977).

2. Note, however, that although we wrote before the present surge of Rawlsianism, we were, at the time we wrote the book, familiar with Rawls's ideas from his previous work.

3. David Chapman has in fact so argued in an unpublished paper.

4. This is not a necessary assumption but, without it, things become quite complicated graphically.

5. Note that it is not really certain that A would be better off. If B is already making a gift to the Algerian out to the point where his demand curve crosses the one franc line, then A clearly can gain (as can B) from an agreement under which further payment out to the line O_p is made, with A paying the amount A' and B paying amount B' on the increment. It is possible, however, that movement to the line O_p, if it is accompanied by payment by A of A' for the entire range of payments, would be inferior from A's standpoint to leaving the situation as it was.

6. I realize, of course, that tradition in this case has been built into constitutions and laws.

References

BUCHANAN, J. M. and G. TULLOCK (1962) *The Calculus of Consent.* Ann Arbor: University of Michigan Press.

MENCIUS. *The Great Learning.*

Public Choice 29-2 (special supplement to Spring 1977).

TIDEMAN, T. N. and G. TULLOCK (1976) 'A New and Superior Process for Making Social Choices', *Journal of Political Economy* 84 (December).

TULLOCK, G. (1971) 'The Charity of the Uncharitable', *Western Economic Journal* 9 (December).

--, (1977) 'Revealing the Demand for Transfers', in: R. AUSTER and B. SEARS (eds.), *American Re-evolution: Papers and Proceedings.* Tucson: Department of Economics, University of Arizona.

WAGNER, R. E. (1974) 'Politics, Bureaucracy, and Budgetary Choice', *Journal of Money, Credit, and Banking* 8 (August).

• Comment

Jean-Claude Eicher

University of Dijon, France

Gordon Tullock presents a rather provocative paper which asks several deceptively naive questions. I am therefore not going to fall into the trap of attempting to answer them, at least directly. Instead, I shall explain why I am not entirely satisfied with the way those questions are presented while at the same time asking some of my own along the way.

Let me first state quite clearly that I have no quarrel with Tullock about the questions he asks. They are quite clearly interesting and important. Two of them, i.e. before redistributing, should one not decide what is to be redistributed and to whom? and why should the discussion be limited by national boundaries? must appear obvious to any intelligent outsider. But such is the state of affairs in the field of public finance that it is important that they should be asked.

The last one is stated in a less straightforward way, but it is the most fundamental. Why should we redistribute at all? Tullock tells us that he is in favour of 'a fairly low level of transfers' but he does not tell us why, and one cannot but be perplexed by this statement as the author's well known 'liberal philosophy' would lead us to expect him to favour situations with no transfers at all.

However, in a more general way, Tullock's paper raises questions on three different levels. The first is that of the demand-revealing process itself. Tullock argues that the demand-revealing process is the best procedure to adopt because 'it should be possible to achieve whatever goals are desired in the area of income distribution much more precisely with the demand-revealing process than with other methods' and because contrary to other methods, 'it does not permit transfers which are motivated *only* by the desire of the recipients to receive money'.

These statements may be challenged in a number of ways.

(1) One of the arguments is that it is possible to approximate Lindhal taxes for public goods by using the demand-revealing process. But the Lindhal tax itself can be shown to be optimal only if several highly unrealistic assumptions are fulfilled.

(2) Incentives to reveal one's preferences are very slight for most of the people who are not going to be very greatly affected, one way or the other, by a particular design. It is therefore to be presumed that some kind of administrative machinery will have to be set up to 'collect' statements of preferences. The cost of this administration might very well be far superior to the gain in efficiency.

(3) Fees have to be collected to compensate the losers. Here again we face the problem of the cost of implementing the system.

(4) Incentives will most probably be very unequal.

For any particular project which will benefit only a fairly small portion of the population,one might expect the members of the favoured group to express their preferences strongly, while the remaining members of the community 'who have a mild opposition' to the project will stay silent, which will bias the registration of so-called 'revealed' preferences. In any case, very rich people may have much more to gain than the poor from a given public action (for instance, if they believe they will be asked to produce part of the material necessary to the supply of the public good). They will then be ready to 'reveal' that they are ready to pay a large amount of money in order to have that good. One can even imagine them finding it profitable to bribe several poor people to fake strong preferences for that given good. One therefore feels inclined to conclude that the demand-revealing process is a smoothly working intellectual gadget, which could not be used in real life to apportion public goods.

The second level on which Tullock's paper raises important doubts in the reviewer's mind is that of the definition and treatment of individual preference. The author seems indeed to take a very narrow view of the determinants of individual preference. If I understand this paper correctly, he seems actually to assume that individuals are positively interested only in what happens to them personally, being either indifferent to whatever may befall others if it does not affect them, or opposed to more goods going to other people if they have to pay for them indirectly. The example of European farmers is very typical of this type of reasoning. Tullock assumes first that, if one decided to abolish the Common Agricultural Community 'clearly the benefit from this action would be much greater than the loss' and adds later that the Common Market agricultural policy is a clear example of 'transfer from party to party which is motivated entirely by the desire of the recipients, with the people who involuntarily make the contribution not having an interest in the matter at all or being opposed'. On the contrary, to the reviewer this is a clear case where non-farmers may very well draw some positive satisfaction out of policy measures meant to profit others, either out of a feeling of solidarity with a deserving but underprivileged group or, more selfishly, because they believe that if one does not at least partially compensate the farmers they will start blocking the roads and generally make a nuisance of themselves. It therefore seems rather surprising that this contribution runs counter to much of the current research on individual preferences, and especially to most of the papers presented at this seminar.

Finally, one is bound to question the underlying theory of the formation of preferences. Tullock's reasonsing seems in effect to assume that individuals not only know what they want but determine their preferences quite freely. What would be the use of using the preference-revealing process if one did not assume that the optimum is obtained when individual preferences thus revealed are best satisfied? But this means that one can only consider the demand-revealing process as optimal if one starts by assuming that the social structure is also optimal. In particular, there is no place here for situations in which the consumer's demand for a given good is in fact largely conditioned by the producer through advertising or other marketing activities. In an economy where the true characteristics of goods are seldom known to the consumer, where information is generally either biased or quite imperfect because of lack of time, and in a society where powerful groups are able to influence the preferences of others, it is difficult to assume that it will be enough to ask people to 'reveal' preferences they neither formulate clearly to themselves, nor control individually, to reach anything which one could call an optimum.

To end this review on a more positive note I should like to suggest that there is a criterion for redistribution which is at once logical and not new: that of commutative justice. If we agree with J. S. Mill that distribution is the result of conflicts and transactions between social groups and not the result of the action of some 'law of nature' which can be established scientifically, if we feel that in an ideal society everyone should be given according to his needs, the extent of redistribution and the identity of who should pay and who should receive follows immediately. But in such a society would economic activity still obey the same law of exchange value? This, however, is another story.

PART III

ORGANIZATIONS

7

The Economics of Conjugal Roles

Bertrand Lemennicier

University of Paris IX, France

How to interpret the variations observed in the way husbands and wives play a different role in the intrafamily allocation of time is one of the main problems in the sociology of the family. These variations are considerable. At one extreme there is a strict division of labour in the household. She has her tasks and he has his. In such a case we can clearly define the allocation of time between male and female tasks. This is what sociologists call a *segregated conjugal role-relationship*. At the other extreme is a family in which husband and wife share as many activities as possible. Husband and wife are interchangeable. In such cases we have what is termed a *joint conjugal role-relationship*. Between these two extremes there are many shades of difference. These differ-

I have benefited from the discussion of an earlier draft of this paper at the G. S. Becker Economics Workshop of the University of Chicago. I am indebted to G. S. Becker, M. J. Bowman, E. Lazear, T. W. Schultz and other participants for their valuable comments. I have gained much also from discussions with members of the Jean Baptiste Say Seminar at the University of Paris-Dauphine and particularly with M. Kemp when he was visiting Professor in Paris. I should like to extend my gratitude to R. Gronau for his extremely valuable comments and criticisms, and to G. Lassibille, Ph. Pleuvret, J. P. Vila for their excellent computational assistance. Any remaining errors are, of course, my sole responsibility.

ences in the degree of segregation of conjugal roles are the central theme of this paper and on these we want to test the economic approach.

The reason for applying the economic approach here is threefold.

First, through the works of Becker (1973), Gramm (1975), Gronau (1973), Leibowitz (1974), Willis (1973), and others on the intrafamily allocation of housewives' time and marriage, economists have produced some positive results in this field.

Secondly, we can use the analytical tools developed in international trade theory to handle this kind of problem as has been suggested by McKenzie and Tullock (1975).

Thirdly, we have access to an extensive survey covering 1,252 married women living in towns of over 10,000 inhabitants, which can be used to develop sociological as well as economic hypotheses.

Thus the first section will be devoted to a discussion of the pure economic theory of conjugal roles. The second section analyses this theory from an empirical point of view, comparing it with sociological theories.

1. The pure economic theory of conjugal roles

First, we shall briefly sketch the sociological hypotheses that the economic approach seeks to challenge.

1.1. An overview of sociological hypotheses

The conventional sociological analysis of conjugal roles in the family has centered around some basic models.

(i) *The 'culturalist' hypothesis* is based on the notion that each person has some cultural habits derived from his actual or inherited social environment. As culture is the total way of life of a group of people, we can divide up the population according to several criteria – age, race, social class, religious affiliation, occupational status, geographic location and so forth – some combination of them can then be used to classify the population into *segments* that differ in cultural habits. The fact that conjugal role relationships differ between families is 'explained' by differences between segments! Of course, any pattern of collective or individual human behaviour can be rationalized in this manner. There is little risk of this view being refuted as the question becomes: why are there segments or variability in cultural habits? Unfortunately, this is also one of the hardest questions which the sociologist has to answer.

(ii) The *'do-it-like-others' hypothesis* is based on the notion that each person behaves under the *pressure* of the cultural habits of his environment. But to behave like others necessitates being *exposed* to others' attitudes or pressures. Then again, one mechanism through which the social environment acts is the family's *immediate* environment, i.e. its actual relationships with parents, friends, neighbours or work colleagues. This is Bott's well-known hypothesis (Bott, 1955): 'The degree of segregation in the relationships of husband and wife varies directly with the *connectedness* of the family's social network.' Such a model leaves open the question of why there are differences in connectedness of social network to which the family is exposed. Bott suggests that these differences 'depend partly on the member's family and partly on a very complex combination of forces in the total social environment', which is an elegant way of avoiding having to pursue this analysis of the conjugal role relationship phenomenon. But this hypothesis has at least one testable implication: families with a low exposure to social environment have non-segregated attitudes towards their allocation of time and goods.

(iii) The *'nuclear family' hypothesis* of Parsons and Bales (1955) supposes that each family fills *the function* of a factory which produces personalities through the socialization of children and the stabilization of adults. As in any small group there is a tendency for a task-leader and a sociometric star to appear. The husband is the leader (or the head). The wife is the star (or the heart). This particular pattern of role differentiation is a condition of the nuclear family's existence and stability as a producer of children or adult personalities. Then, one of the main goals of this theory is to explore this existence and stability in relation to the segregation of conjugal roles. Parsons and Bales develop in detail the psychoanalytic or psychologic mechanisms of the organization of personality through the interaction of role differentiation. We shall put this last point on one side and retain from the above hypothesis the following strong empirical implication: segregated conjugal roles imply a high level of satisfaction between members of the family or non-segregated conjugal roles lead to a higher rate of role conflicts. Of course we assume a non-observable link between satisfaction and stability of the nuclear family.

(iv) The *'dual-career family' hypothesis* of Rapoport and Rapoport (1965) is based on the idea that a working career is the process through which husband and wife obtain maximum fulfilment. This is the opposite of Parsons' idea. A high level of satisfaction between members of the family is related to non-segregated conjugal roles. Then the question becomes: Why do women not enter the labour market? The answer is provided when we consider the balance between the expected benefits and costs of such a choice. A dual-career family has to assume: (1) an additional burden of roles; (2) conflicts with the norms and personal preferences of parents or husband; (3) deviations between role expectations and role performances; and (4) more connectedness in the social network, etc. The dual-career hypothesis is not devoid of empirically testable predictions: if quarrel frequency is a good sign of the family's instability when husband and wife both participate in the labour market, we will observe a lower rate of conflict between them.

(v) The *'Principle of least effort'* model of Blood and Wolfe (1960) is based on the idea that each person performs those tasks for which he has the greatest skill and other resources. This sounds very similar to the human capital approach to social phenomena: skill and time resources can be allocated to various activities in such a way as to increase the productivity of the family as a whole. This last hypothesis leads directly to the economic approach on which we shall now focus.

1.2. The economic approach to conjugal roles

The 'opportunity cost of time' hypothesis is a straightforward application of the classical theory of International Trade between two countries developed by Ricardo.

1.2.1. The framework of the model

According to the modern theory of household behaviour we assume each member of the family derives satisfaction from home-produced activities, H, and from income, I, which we have to consider as the real purchasing power in terms of market goods. Home activities and income are produced using only time inputs of spouses (TH_M, TW_M respectively for the male and TH_F, TW_F for the female).

$$I_M = w_M TW_M, \tag{1}$$

$$I_F = w_F TW_F, \tag{2}$$

$$H_M = TH_M / th_M, \tag{3}$$

$$H_F = TH_F / th_F. \tag{4}$$

Income and home activities are a constant proportion of time inputs.

Each member of the family faces a time budget constraint which states that the time spent producing income (working time in outside employment) and home activities must exhaust the length of time period arbitrarily set at T^0:

$$T^0 = TW_M + TH_M, \tag{5}$$

$$T^0 = TW_F + TH_F. \tag{6}$$

We can rewrite these two constraints as follows:

$$T^0 = I/w_M + th_M H, \tag{7}$$

$$T^0 = I/w_F + th_F H. \tag{8}$$

This will make it possible to deal with the *production-possibilities frontier* of the family as a whole, which will be helpful in simplifying the economic argument for sociologists and those economists who are not familiar with international trade theories. Equations (7) and (8) are linear and they are represented graphically by a straight line as shown in Figure 1. The I-axis intercept shows the maximum income that each member of the family can obtain from full-time outside employment. A similar interpretation holds for the H-axis intercept. Any point inside the production-possibilities frontier, such as M, implies that husband and wife are not making full use of their time resources. For $0A$ home-produced activities, wife as well as husband can increase their income of MN, MN', respectively. Now suppose that the wife (or husband) is located at point N (or N') and, as a result of an exogenous change in tastes in favour of home-produced activities, she (or he) moves to point P (or P'). There she (or he) has to reduce her (or his) income of $B'B$ (or $B''B$) units in order to increase home-produced commodities of AA' (or AA''). Therefore the absolute slope of the production-possibilities frontier of each member of the family has an

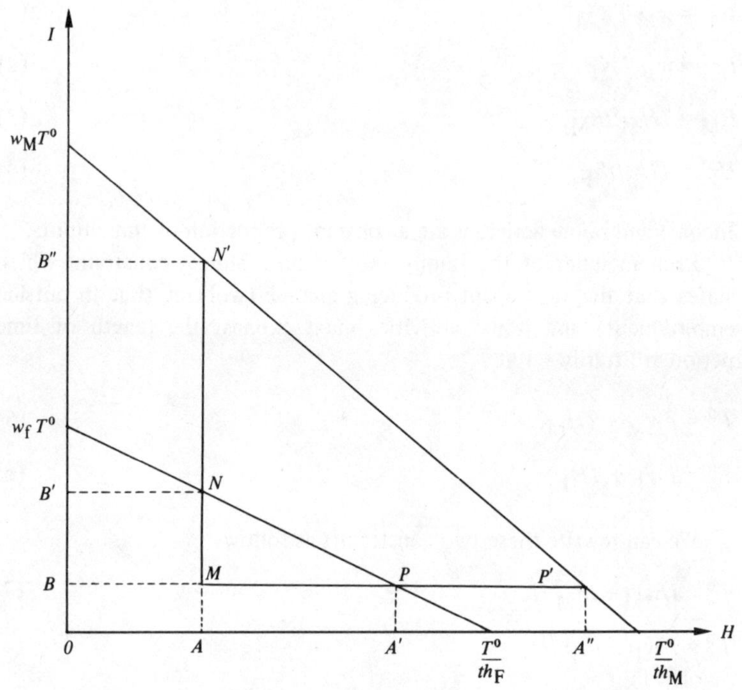

Figure 1

important meaning: it shows the opportunity cost of home-produced activities in terms of forgone income. This can be expressed as follows:

$$-\Delta I/\Delta H = w_s \, th_s, \quad \text{with } s = (\mathrm{M}, \mathrm{F}). \tag{9}$$

1.2.2. The production-possibilities frontier

Now we can use the family production-possibilities frontier to derive some conclusions about role differentiation based on the 'opportunity cost of time' hypothesis. Figure 2 shows the maximum amount of income that husband and wife together can produce for any given amount of home produced activities.Its construction is rather simple if we use Chacholiades' (1973) exposition. The triangle *hPA* represents the production-possibilities frontier of the husband, with *h* as its point of origin. The triangle *RPi* represents the wife's production-possibilities frontier with *R* as its point of origin. The intercept *R* of the family production-possibilities frontier with the *I*-axis is determined by the

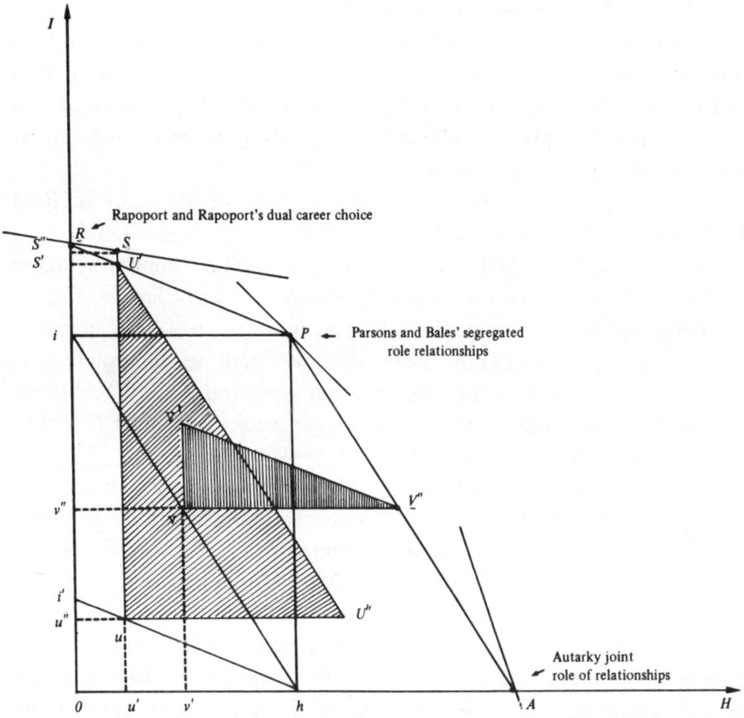

Figure 2

maximum sum of income that both husband and wife could obtain if they spent all their time in outside employment, i.e. $OR = Oi + Oi', = hP + iR$. Similarly, intercept A with the H-axis is determined by the maximum sum of home goods that the family could produce if they spent all their time at home, i.e. $OA = Oh + Oh = iP + hA$. Note that the wife's production-possibilities frontier has been assumed flatter than the husband's. The opportunity cost of time in producing home goods is lower for the woman. Suppose that we are at point u. The wife is working outside and gets Ou'' income, but she devotes some time to produce Ou' home goods. If the family as a whole uses all its time resources, the husband has to work in a full-time job and the family produce OS' income and Ou' home goods at point U'.

Suppose the family would like to produce an extra unit of H. Who of the wife or husband should undertake the production of home goods? Obviously the wife, because she has the lowest opportunity cost of time in producing these activities. Any other pattern of role differentiation would lead to a loss in income as well as in home goods, which is not sustainable in the long run for the family as a whole. From point v we can apply a similar reasoning, merely reversing the role of wife and husband.

One conclusion can be drawn at this stage in the analysis. Role differentiation has an important 'function': it leads the family as a whole to an efficient allocation of resources which implies a higher total amount of goods produced *without having to work harder.*

If the 'opportunity cost of time' is an incentive to role segregation in the family, it does not mean that we shall get complete role differentiation. Each point on the family production-possibilities frontier is an efficient pattern of role segregation. But along *RP*, only the husband performs a specific task.

The wife produces home goods as well as market goods via income. Along *PA*, the wife performs only home activities while the husband produces both market and home commodities. At point *P* we can recognize the *Parsonian* point of complete role segregation where the husband is the 'breadwinner' and the wife is 'in the home'. At point *R* we can recognize the Rapoport and Rapoport's point of double career choices. At point *A* husband and wife are in the home which is either an aristocratic way of life at the top of the social scale or a simple farmer's life at the bottom. The 'opportunity cost of time' theory leads to the strong conclusion that at least one member of the family is completely specialized either in producing income, or in producing home activities and goods depending on the comparative cost of the time of each of these. But it leaves open the question of why a family is located at the Parsonian point and not at the Rapoport and Rapoport's one. To answer such a question, we have to take our analysis further.

1.2.3. Allocation of conjugal roles

Let us assume that home-produced goods or activities have perfect substitutes in the market. Then the maximum amount of market goods that the family can consume is bound by the budget constraint:

$$C = I + pH, \tag{10}$$

where I is the real income used to purchase market goods other than those produced at home and pH are real expenditures on market substitutes for home goods; p is the relative market price of H and is assumed given.

Equation (10) is a straight line showing us the maximum combination of I and H that the family can consume from the commodity market as illustrated in Figure 2. This is the consumption-possibilities frontier. Observe that this particular line must necessarily pass through the production-possibilities frontier since the maximum amount of income is obtained on this dotted line.

The determination of this consumption-possibilities frontier answers the question raised earlier.

A relative market price of home goods less than the woman's opportunity cost of time encourages the wife to work outside – home-produced goods cost more in terms of forgone income than it costs to purchase them on the commodity market. At point U' it costs RS' of income to produce and consume Ou' home goods; by contrast, at point S the income forgone to consume the same amount Ou' of H is RS'', which is less than RS'. Then the family as a whole chooses the dual-career way of life. In the particular case where the consumption line coincides with the production-possibilities frontier, i.e. the relative market price of home goods is equal to the woman's (or husband's) opportunity cost of time, the role differentiation inside the family is indeterminate.

Now we can write the condition of some segregation within the home as follows:

$$w_F \, th_F \leqslant p \leqslant w_M \, th_M.$$

If this equation holds, i.e. if the relative market price of home-produced goods lies between the husband's and wife's opportunity costs, the result is the traditional pattern of conjugal roles.

Valuable insights into conjugal role behaviour can be gained by analysing the problem via an economic approach. Note that the sociological approaches are not free from value judgement, e.g. both the Parsonian or 'conservative' view and the Rapoport and Rapoport or 'radical' view are neither right nor wrong, they are not *positive* statements. Husband and wife do not change their patterns of behaviour because the double-career family choice is the *best* way of life, but because relative costs and prices of home-produced activities are changing. To prove this point we can now turn to the analysis of the effects of an increase in: (1) unearned income; (2) the wife's wage rate; (3) the husband's wage rate; (4) the price of market substitutes for home-produced goods; and (5) productivity at home through human ability.

1.2.4. Wage and ability effects

(1) An increase in non-wage income raises the family as a whole to a higher consumption level and degree of welfare. But as the differences between the husband's and wife's wages remain the same, no specialization effect is, in fact, induced. If more home goods are consumed, they are bought in the market place.

(2) An increase in the wife's wage rate gives rise to an 'income effect' and a 'specialization effect'. A rise in the average wage rate for married women increases the income of the family as a whole and results in a higher consumption level. This is the income effect. But it

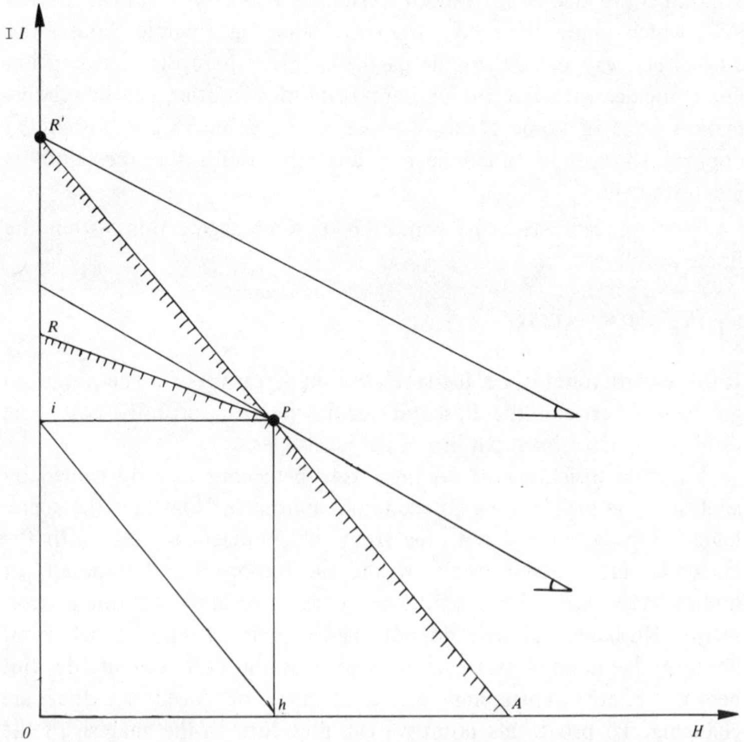

Figure 3

tends to raise their opportunity cost of time in producing home goods and induces them to work outside the home. This is shown in Figure 3. This specialization effect, through the increment of the woman's wage rate, explains why the traditional pattern of role differentiation has begun to break down in favour of Rapoport and Rapoport's double-career choice.

(3) An increase in the husband's wage rate induces an income effect but does not induce a specialization effect if the husband is working in the labour market. This increment plays a role only when both spouses produce at home by encouraging the member of the family with the highest opportunity cost to work outside. Figure 4 illustrates the point.

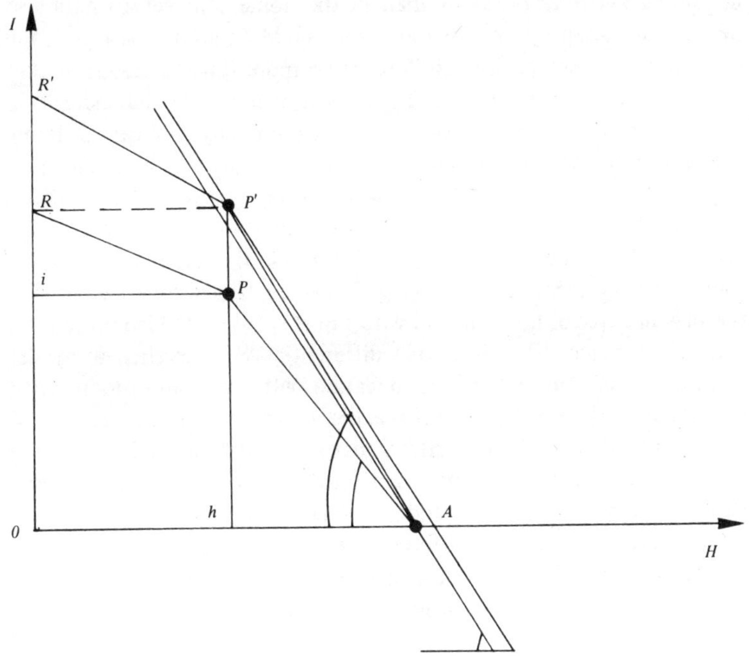

Figure 4

(4) An increase (or a decrease) in the prices of market substitutes for home goods induces a 'substitution effect' and a 'specialization effect'. The former concerns spending decisions between market and

home goods, but the latter involves allocation of the roles or time resources of each spouse.

(5) One of the factors raising the wage rate is the better educational standard of women. We can expect that more educated women are present in the labour force. But as stated by Michael (1972), there is no reason to suppose that education raises the productivity of labour market time only. Human capital also has some effect on productivity in other activities. It seems reasonable to expect, therefore, that education increases the productivity of time spent in home production. As noticed by Leibowitz (1974), census data confirm the fact that more better-educated women are present in the labour market.

Hence, education has the non-neutral effect of raising productivity in production outside rather than in the home. But census data also indicate an exception to this rule: when children are in the home, the more highly educated woman devotes no more time to labour market activities than other women. Thus, we can conclude that education raises the productivity of mother-time in producing childcare at home in the same manner as the time in the labour market. This is shown in Figure 5; for this group of women a traditional pattern of role differentiation follows. The opportunity-cost-of-time theory shows how the economic approach to role relationships within the family is a powerful tool of analysis. 'Static' role segregation is 'explained' by differences in the productivity of husband and wife's time spent on the labour market and in the home. 'Dynamic' role differentiation is 'explained' by the neutral or non-neutral effect of education on the woman's productivity of time at work or at home. But this theory leaves open the question of why productivity of time differs between husband and wife. One answer to this question is provided by the human capital hypothesis. Differences in wage rates and non-market productivities between spouses are governed by differences in educational attainments. Of course, other explanations are available such as pure discrimination on grounds of sex or simply a difference in innate abilities between males and females.

We have presented one view on the economics of conjugal roles within the framework of international trade theory, but surely many sociologists and psychologists will think we have solved conjugal role segregation 'by systematically destroying the idea of a family' as Rider's comment (1973) on Willis's (1973) paper suggests. Until now, we have deliberately avoided any reference to the interaction between spouses as a result of the satisfaction and dissatisfaction of husband and wife in

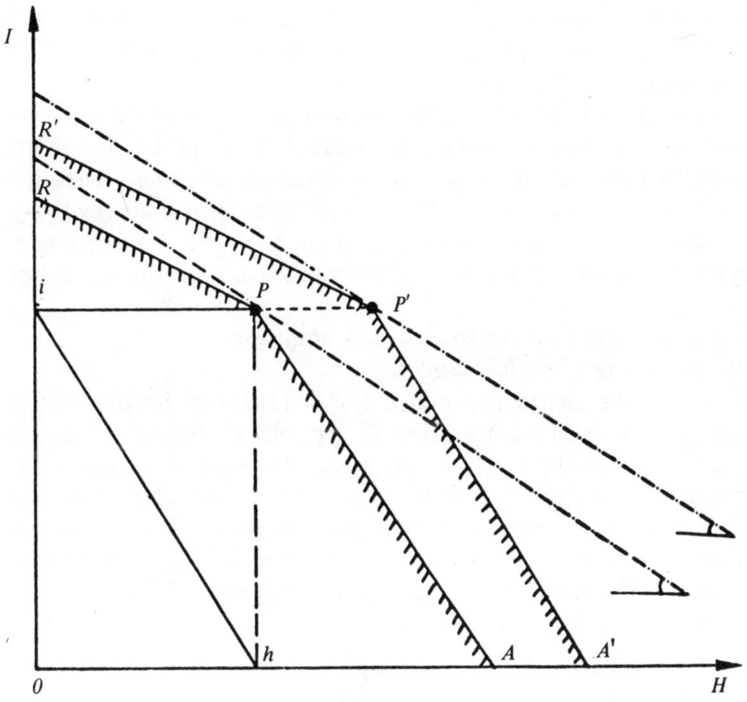

Figure 5

performing their respective roles, a question which is central to the sociological literature.

To fill this gap we can assume that husband and wife derive satisfaction from time spent at home or outside. Time enters the utility function like home or market goods. In so doing, the opportunity cost of time of an activity contains some positive and negative utility returns. These new elements modify the production possibilities frontier in the output space and thus the pattern of conjugal roles.

To give one specific example, refer back to Figure 3 where we assume only one factor of production: time. Assume that *RPA* is the production-possibilities frontier when the spouses disregard that they derive satisfaction from time spent in performing their respective roles, then the wife is 'in the home'; but assume now that the 'true' opportunity cost of time spent at home is higher for the wife because she likes time spent outside the home and dislikes the time spent in home production of goods. Then the 'true' production-possibilities frontier is $R'PA$. Hence, we observe a 'modern way of life' for the wife, i.e. both spouses are working in the market.

But this way of thinking suffers from one major weakness: it is a post facto explanation as long as we lack a theory of the mechanisms whereby tastes for time spent at home or outside are formed. Thus, this interaction between spouses has to be worked out in a different way. To do so, let us turn to the benefit from marriage and segregation of roles. This issue will link conjugal role behaviour to marital instability.

1.2.5. The gain from marriage and specialization: the perspective of marital dissolution

Following the pioneering work of Becker (1973) on marriage, let us assume that single persons marry if, and only if, the share of market and home goods they receive from the married consumption-possibilities frontier exceeds that obtained from their single consumption line. This is a crude hypothesis, but nevertheless some predictions about marital dissolution can be drawn from it. Referring back to equation (10), the consumption-possibilities frontier of the family as a whole can be rewritten as follows:

$$C = I_M + I_F + p(H_M + H_F) = C_M + C_F. \tag{11}$$

The combination of equations (7), (8) and (11) gives:

$$C_M + C_F = w_M T^0 - (w_M\, th_M - p)\, H_M + w_F T^0 - (w_F\, th_F - p)\, H_F\,. \tag{12}$$

Let us assume that each member of the family receives an equal share of the consumption bundle produced. Then a single person is encouraged to marry, from the economic point of view, if, and only if:

$$\frac{C_M + C_F}{2} \geqslant C_M \text{ for M}; \qquad \frac{C_M + C_F}{2} \geqslant C_F \text{ for F}. \tag{13}$$

Let us take as an example a family where the husband is more productive than his wife on the labour market and equally productive at home:

$$w_M = w_F + z, \qquad th_M = th_F = th, \quad \text{with } z \geqslant 0.$$

Does the husband benefit from marriage when his market productive capacities are higher than those of his wife? Replacing in equation (13)

w_M by $w_F + z$ and then th_M by th_F we get the benefit from marriage for the wife:

$$B_F = \frac{C_M + C_F}{2} - C_F. \tag{14}$$

A similar equation holds true for the husband replacing w_F by $w_M - z$ and th_F by th_M:

$$B_M = \frac{C_M + C_F}{2} - C_M. \tag{15}$$

First, when the market price, p, of substitutes for home-produced goods is less than the opportunity cost of time of both husband and wife, the family follows a double-career way of life. Consequently, the benefits from marriage resulting from such a conjugal role allocation within the household are found by substituting the values of H_M or H_F which are equal, respectively, to TH_M/th_M, TH_F/th_F in equations (12), (14) and (15). When p is less than $w_M th_M$ and $w_F th_F$, $TH_M = TH_F = 0$.

In such a case the gains from marriage for the wife are positive:

$$\frac{C_M + C_F}{2} = \left(w_F + \frac{z}{2}\right) T^0 > C_F = w_F T^0, \tag{16}$$

that is

$$B_F = \frac{C_M + C_F}{2} - C_F = \frac{3}{2} T^0.$$

By contrast, the husband suffers a loss:

$$\frac{C_M + C_F}{2} = \left(w_M - \frac{z}{2}\right) T^0 < C_M = w_M T^0, \tag{17}$$

that is

$$B_M = \frac{C_M + C_F}{2} - C_M - \frac{3}{2} T^0$$

Secondly, when the market price, p, of substitutes for home-produced goods lies between the husband's and wife's opportunity costs, the family follows a traditional pattern of conjugal roles: $TH_M = 0$, $TH_F = T^0$.

In such a case the gains from marriage for the wife are still positive but less so than in the double-career way of life:

$$\frac{C_M + C_F}{2} = \frac{1}{2}\left[w_F + z + \frac{p}{th}\right] T^o > C_F = \frac{p}{th} T^o, \tag{18}$$

as $p/th > w_F$. Then

$$B_F = \frac{C_M + C_F}{2} - C_F = \frac{1}{2}\left[w_F + z - \frac{p}{th}\right] T^o,$$

which is less than $\frac{1}{2} z T^o$.

The husband loses from marriage as his benefits are negative, but the losses are less than in the double-career way of life:

$$\frac{C_M + C_F}{2} = \frac{1}{2}\left[w_M + \frac{p}{th}\right] T^o < C_M = w_M T^o, \tag{19}$$

as $w_M > p/th$ and $w_M = w_F + z$. Then

$$B_M = \frac{C_M + C_F}{2} - C_M = -\frac{1}{2}\left[w_F + z - \frac{p}{th}\right] T^o,$$

which is less than $-\frac{1}{2} z T^o$.

Thirdly, when the market price of substitutes for home goods exceeds both the husband and wife's opportunity costs, the members of the family stay at home: $TH_M = TH_F = T^o$.

In such a case neither the husband nor the wife gain from marriage:

$$\frac{C_M + C_F}{2} = \frac{pT^o}{th} = C_F, \tag{20}$$

then $B_F = 0$;

$$\frac{C_M + C_F}{2} = \frac{pT^o}{th} = C_M, \tag{21}$$

then $B_M = 0$.

A single person who marries a more market-productive partner gets positive benefit from marriage (i.e. in this case the wife gains from marriage).

By contrast the more productive person suffers a loss from marriage. The loss and gain become nil when both spouses stay at home (if $p > w_M th > w_F th$) and maximum when both husband and wife work outside (if $w_M th > w_F th > p$). Specialization within the home when p lies between $w_M th$ and $w_F th$ decreases the wife's gain but reduces the husband's loss comparatively to a double-career way of life.

Starting from the Parsonian point of complete specialization and assuming that the woman's wage rate rises until the relative price of the market substitutes for home goods is less than this opportunity cost, what happens to the gain from marriage? If the wife stays at home the benefits from marriage are unchanged for both spouses, but the family as a whole suffers a loss in their consumption possibilities, as a result of the absence of an efficient allocation of conjugal roles (both spouses have to work on the labour market to avoid this loss in consumption). If the wife moves to the Rapoport and Rapoport point, the gains from marriage increase for the wife but the husband suffers a maximum amount of loss as a result of his marriage with a less productive partner. Then we can expect conflict between husband and wife. Quarrels and marital dissolution can be expected to occur more often in couples engaged in a double-career way of life. From this theory we can predict that couples with similar productive capacities have no economic incentive to get married since the benefit or loss from marriage are nil for both partners.

Now let us proceed to test the relative strength of the different hypotheses reviewed in this section.

2. Empirical analysis

The data are drawn from a survey conducted by Tabard in 1971. This study (see Tabard, 1974) covers a sample of 1,256 women living in towns of more than 10,000 inhabitants. Ninety-five percent of these women have at least one child and receive family allowances from the government. A time-budget was compiled, together with many other facts on socio-economic background and family members' attitudes toward satisfaction and socialization. The background information for each respondent includes age, education, occupation, income, work status, family composition, residence, etc. Time data are expressed as average time per day measured in hours limited by the time constraint of 24 hours a day.

Unfortunately, the sample's unit of enquiry for time-budget data was the wife. Thus, our information on time-use does not include the husband's allocation of time. We hope that this deficiency will not limit the analysis too much. This survey concentrates on married women with at least ,one child so we can expect that the results will be probably biased in comparison with the standard population.

The economic approach tells us that segregated or joint conjugal roles result from an efficient allocation of resources within the home, which implies a higher amount of both income and home goods without having to work harder. One hypothesis governs this allocation: the difference in human capital endowments of each spouse. This difference alters the ratio of opportunity costs of time as well as the ratio of the home productivity of husband and wife, and induces a re-allocation of roles within the family, which affects benefits and losses from marriage. Our aim is to test this theory against those of the sociologists.

We first calculated the opportunity cost of time for women who do not work at a full-time job, taking into account the wage rate that they could have received on the labour market with their specific characteristics (age, education and so forth). The husband's wage rate is known directly from the survey, hence we can get the ratio of wage rates of husband and wife even for women who stay at home. The ratio of human capital endowments is derived from the survey as we know the educational level or the number of school years invested by each respondent. Marital conflicts is a dummy variable which takes value 1 if the wife mentions a lot of quarrels with her husband each week and value 0 if this is not the case. This is a crude measure of the Parsonian theory. When the wives are working on the labour market they increase the losses from marriage borne by their more productive husbands. Hence, there is greater probability of more frequent quarrels. Conflicts within the home alter the allocation of time and reduce the stability of the 'nuclear' family. If we observe, by contrast, that quarrels increase the participation of women in the labour force in order to escape from tension in conjugal role relationships, we would expect the Rapoport and Rapoport hypothesis to be better suited to the facts. Family relations, participation in religious activities or membership of associations and the socio-economic status of the husband are one way of taking into account Bott's argument about the pressure of the social environment. The more a wife is seeing her kin or participates in religious or other social activities, the more we can expect her to be sensitive to the opinions and values to which she is exposed. To these variables we add the woman's age and the size of the urban area where the respondent is living.

Table 1 indicates means and standard deviations for this set of variables drawn from Tabard's survey. Housework is the broad home-produced activity we have chosen to deal with. Housework includes cleaning, cooking, and laundry. Thus, from Table 1 we observe that

TABLE 1

Means and Standard Deviations of Selected Variables Used in the Study and Drawn from Tabard's Survey

Variables	Unit of measure	Total women sample	Women at work sample	Test* of differences in means: *Z* score
Number of children		2.70 (1.23)**	2.60 (0.86)	−1.72
Age of wife	number of years	33.4 (7.6)	33.6 (7.0)	−0.47
Age of husband	number of years	35.8 (7.6)	36.4 (7.8)	0.44
Size of urban area	polychotomous variable rated from 1 to 5 by decreasing size	3.2 (1.2)	3.1 (1.3)	−1.35
Relationships with kin and friends	dichotomous variable which is given value 1 if the wife is seeing her parent(s) at least once a week and 0 if this is not the case	0.57 (0.49)	0.59 (0.49)	0.71
Membership of associations	dichotomous variable which is given value 1 if the wife is a member of an assocation and 0 if this is not the case	0.15 (0.35)	0.21 (0.41)	2.6
Participation in religious activities	dichotomous variable which is given value 1 if the wife is a member of an association and 0 if this is not the case	0.39 (0.49)	0.32 (0.46)	−2.59
White-collar husband	dichotomous variable of the husband's socio-economic status	0.38 (0.48)	0.41 (0.49)	1.07
Blue-collar husband	dichotomous variable of the husband's socio-economic status	0.56 (0.49)	0.51 (0.50)	−1.72
Ratio of opportunity costs of time	ratio of the husband's wage rate to the wife's opportunity cost of time	1.70 (1.15)	1.60 (1.22)	−1.42
Ratio of human capital endowments	ratio of the number of school years of husband to those of his wife	1.08 (0.34)	0.99 (0.27)	−2.83
Time input to household tasks (wife)	hours per day	5.53 (2.22)	2.9 (1.62)	−24.5
Time input to labour market (wife)	hours per day	1.72 (3.42)	7.44 (2.9)	24.2
Quarrels	dichotomous variable which is given value 1 if the wife has a lot of quarrels each week and 0 otherwise	0.16 (0.36)	0.23 (0.42)	3.3
Expected dissolution of marriage	dichotomous variable which is given value 1 if the wife anticipates a divorce and 0 if this is not the case	0.062 (0.24)	0.085 (0.27)	1.49
Sample size		958	409	

* To be significant at the 95% level *Z* has to be outside the range of −1.96 to 1.96.

** Standard deviations in parentheses

women who participate in the labour force drastically reduce the time input to home-produced goods like household tasks. The difference in means is highly significant between the total women sample and the employed women sample. Consequently, a crucial question can be raised: what are the economic or social forces which explain women's participation in the labour market? A crude and partial answer to this question can be found in Table 1. The ratio of human capital endowments differs significantly between the two samples. This ratio is lower for employed women. A decrease in this ratio, i.e. a more equal productive capacity between husband and wife, increases the participation of women in the labour market because the value of time is higher for the wife and higher than the relative price of market substitutes for home goods. Marital conflicts are significantly higher in the women at work sample. This does not invalidate our hypothesis about the increasing loss from marriage suffered by high potential-earning husbands when there is no specialization within the home. To isolate the effect of the different economic and sociological variables on the allocation of conjugal roles and on the benefit from marriage, we have to run a regression analysis.

First, we will show that the French pattern of conjugal role allocation is consistent with our theoretical analysis. Secondly, we will try to compare the value of the economic versus the sociological approaches as an explanation of this. For the first objective we need only qualitative effects, i.e. the sign of the effect: negative or positive; for the second objective we need to measure the individual contribution of each variable to the calculated value of the dependent variables. 'Beta' coefficients are an objective measure which satisfy both objectives, although they are rarely used in econometrics (see Goldberger, 1964). The beta coefficient for an independent variable is defined as the regression coefficient for that variable multiplied by the standard deviation of the variable and divided by the standard deviation of the dependent variable.

One of the fundamental problems in estimating the effects of education (or other variables) on the specialization within the home is that of establishing the causality among the different variables. We will assume that the variables operate independently of one another with respect to home or outside activities and marital conflicts. The coefficients derived from this estimation by ordinary least squares will provide a measure of the direct effect of each independent variable.

In what follows we therefore focus on two issues:

(1) the allocation of conjugal roles, and
(2) the probability of marital dissolution.

2.1. The allocation of conjugal roles

The basic theoretical framework used to explain labour supply is that of an application of the traditional consumer theory to the income-leisure choice. This approach yields the following general labour supply of husband or wife:

$$TW_{M,F} = TW(w_{M,F}, p, Y), \tag{22}$$

where $TW_{M,F}$ is hours work and $w_{M,F}$ is wage rate of husband or wife, p is the price of market goods, and Y is non-labour income.

Within the context of a two-person model of the household whose goal is to maximize labour income earnings and home-produced goods for the family as a whole, we formulate a rather different labour supply function:

$$TW_{M,F} = TW(w_M/\hat{w}_F, p, SES, A), \tag{23}$$

where $w_M/\hat{w}_F$ is the ratio of opportunity costs between husband and wife, *SES* is a set of sociological variables, and A combines woman's age and city size. For simplicity's sake we ignore p, since each household faces the same set of market prices. We will test a linear approximation of this last equation.

Table 2 contains ordinary least squares (OLS) estimates of time input to the labour market and to home tasks. The difference between the two sets of regressions lies in the fact that the ratio of human capital endowments is omitted in the first set. The empirical results reflected by the first set of regressions of Table 2 show that the existence of a child under three years is the major determinant of the women's labour supply. Quarrels, decreasing size of urban area and ratio of opportunity costs of time are the other variables which are t-statistically significant. As expected, an increasing difference in wage rates of both husband and wife decreases time input to the labour market. Less opportunities to find a job in the area where the respondent is living explain why decreasing city size has a similar impact. By contrast, quarrels increase time input to outside employment. The major determinants of time to home tasks are the age of the

TABLE 2

Ordinary Least Squares Regression Estimates of Beta Coefficient for Time Inputs to Home Tasks and the Labour Market

Explanatory variable \ Individual contributions to the explanation of:	I		II	
	Time input to the labour market	Time input to home tasks	Time input to the labour market	Time input to home tasks
Number of children	−0.039 (1.1)	0.146 (4.3)	−0.028 (0.8)	0.133 (3.9)
Age of wife	−0.048 (1.1)	0.159 (3.8)	−0.045 (1.0)	0.155 (3.9)
Child under three years	−0.098 (2.5)	−0.011 (0.3)	−0.095 (2.4)	−0.014 (0.3)
Decreasing size of urban area	−0.071 (2.2)	0.123 (3.9)	−0.077 (2.4)	0.132 (4.4)
Quarrels	0.082 (2.5)	−0.051 (1.6)	0.089 (2.8)	−0.059 (2.0)
Parental relationships	0.048 (1.4)	−0.051 (1.6)	0.041 (1.2)	−0.043 (1.3)
Membership of associations	0.053 (1.6)	−0.068 (2.1)	0.042 (1.2)	−0.051 (1.6)
White-collar husband	0.055 (1.5)	–	0.063 (1.5)	−0.013 (0.3)
Blue-collar husband	–	0.104 (3.2)	−0.009 (0.0)	0.112 (3.1)
Ratio of opportunity costs of time	−0.075 (2.2)	0.044 (1.4)	−0.058 (1.7)	0.024 (0.7)
Ratio of human capital endowments	–	–	−0.135 (4.2)	0.164 (5.4)
Constant	3.52	2.38	4.86	1.34
R^2	0.032	0.115	0.050	0.140
F	3.5	13.8	4.54	14.2
Sample size	958	958	958	958

t – values in parentheses.

wife, the number of children, the decreasing city size, and a low social status of the husband. All these variables increase time input to home-produced goods.

Differences in wage rates and non-market productivities between spouses are governed by differences in school years invested. Then a better proxy for the difference in human abilities is the ratio of human capital endowments or educational attainments. The second set of regressions shows the results when this variable is not omitted.

As expected, the ratio of human capital endowments is negatively correlated to the supply of women's labour. Its contribution in explaining the time input to the labour market is significantly the highest. A pronounced difference of productivity between husband and wife tends to lower the opportunity cost of home-produced goods for the wife and induces her to work at home. Household tasks appear to be positively affected by women's age and a decreasing city size as well as by a low social status of the husband. But clearly the ratio of human capital endowments is positively correlated to work in the household and its contribution is significantly the highest.

The individual contribution of the ratio of time values or of school years for husband and wife are significant and higher than other variables. Thus, we cannot reject the economic point of view (and more specifically the human capital point of view) with regard to the allocation of conjugal roles.

2.2. The probability of marital dissolution

Referring back to the Parsons and Bales' theory, and to the Rapoport and Rapoport argument, can we settle out of hand the conflict between these two views?

We have suggested in the theoretical part that marital instability would be greater in the case of couples engaged in a double-career way of life because of the diminishing benefits from marriage for the husband. We have argued that the member of the family with the highest productive capacity loses more from marriage if specialization at home of the less productive member of the family does not occur. As a consequence, quarrels or marital conflicts with husbands are likely to occur more often when wives are working on the labour market. The economic approach and the Parsonian view of the stability of the family are quite in harmony. To test this argument we first established the link between quarrels and the likelihood of an anticipated marital dissolution. The eventual marital break-up is a dummy variable which takes value 1 if the woman respondent anticipates a divorce as a solution to her dissension with her husband and value 0 otherwise. As we use unity to indicate the occurrence of the event and zero its non-occurrence, we may interpret the coefficients as an estimate of the conditional probability of an eventual divorce. Table 3 shows the results of an estimated linear probability function on the total women sample and on the employed women sample for this dependent variable, with quarrels, decreasing city size, participation in religious activities, etc. as independent variables. As expected, quarrels with husband increase the probability of an anticipated eventual divorce. The fraction of explained variance, a measure of closeness of fit, is weak (around 12 percent), but a similar regression on the women at work sample has, by

TABLE 3

Ordinary Least Squares and Logistic Approaches to the Probability of an Expected Divorce

Explanatory variable	Coefficients			
	Total women sample		Women at work	
	OLS	Logistic function	OLS	Logistic function
Decreasing city size	0.029 (6.3)	–0.421 (5.3)	0.031 (4.4)	–0.446 (5.9)
Quarrels	0.111 (4.1)	0.676 (2.2)	0.230 (6.1)	1.840 (4.1)
Parental relationships	–0.035 (1.8)	–1.052 (3.2)	–0.083 (2.9)	–1.743 (4.6)
Participation in religious activities (catholic)	–0.061 (2.9)	–1.245 (3.8)	–0.075 (2.4)	–1.609 (2.8)
Membership of associations	0.019 (0.7)	–0.161 (0.4)	0.039 (1.0)	0.09 (0.1)
R^2	0.12	–	0.23	–
$-\ln(\hat{L})$		214	–	80.1
Sample size	680	680	294	294

t – values in parentheses.

contrast, a higher explained variance (23 percent). Quarrels become the most determinant variable for the probability of anticipating a divorce. The link between quarrels and expectation of marital dissolution seems to be established. As Goldberger (1964) has shown, a dichotomous dependent variable results in a heteroskedastic error term. Then ordinary least squares regression leads to inefficient (non-minimum variance) estimates of the regression coefficients. Rather than fitting a linear function with OLS, it is possible to estimate a logistic function by non-linear estimation techniques.

Refer back to Table 3. Maximum likelihood estimates of a logistic function show us that we have *underestimated* the explanatory power of quarrels, decreasing city size, parental relationships and participation in religious activities. Decreasing city size and social pressure lower the probability of an expected divorce, but quarrels between spouses, as we have already suggested, increase the probability of an anticipated marital dissolution. The link between quarrels and expected marital dissolution is not refuted by the logistic approach, and so we are more inclined to use quarrels as proxy for marital dissatisfaction between spouses.

As quarrels are a good predictor for anticipation of marital dissolution, a crucial question can be raised: does lack of specialization within the home or lack of segregation of roles increase the quarrel frequency and marital instability, as the economic theory and the Parsonian view suggest? To test this argument we again ran a regression with marital conflict as the dependent variable. As it is a dummy variable we got an estimate of the conditional probability of quarrels between spouses. Table 4 shows the results obtained. The number of children, the ratio of time values, participation in religious activities and lack of outside employment significantly decrease this probability. The ratio of opportunity costs of time seems to contribute most (*t* value) to quarrelling.

This suggests that the working time of women is a major factor in explaining quarrels within the home.

The results obtained with the OLS technique illustrate how the linear probability approach leads to wrong results. The coefficient of the number of children shows an erratic pattern, statistically significant with both techniques if its sign is reversed. The ratio of time values and the fact that the woman stays at home are not significant with the OLS technique, but perform well with the logistic function approach.

To escape from the multicolinearity between women at home and

TABLE 4

Estimates of the Effect of Some Variables on the Probability of Quarrels between Husband and Wife

	Coefficients			
Explanatory variable	**OLS**	**Logistic function**	**OLS**	**Logistic function**
Number of children	0.046 (6.5)	−0.128 (3.7)	0.047 (6.8)	−0.096 (2.0)
Relationships with kin and friends	0.065 (2.5)	−0.218 (1.5)	0.069 (2.6)	−0.155 (0.9)
Participation in religious activities (catholic)	0.047 (1.6)	−0.600 (3.0)	−0.051 (1.7)	−0.612 (3.3)
Membership of associations	−0.052 (1.3)	−0.629 (2.0)	– –	– –
Ratio of opportunity costs of time	−0.001 (0.2)	−0.410 (6.0)	−0.001 (0.1)	−0.359 (4.5)
Women at home	–	–	−0.025 (0.9)	−0.578 (2.9)
R^2	0.17	–	0.17	–
$-\ln(\hat{L})$	–	318	–	315.5
Sample size	680	680	680	680

t-values in parentheses

the ratio of time values, we ran a regression between quarrels and the ratio of opportunity costs, holding constant the number of children, participation in religious activities, parental relationships, and membership of associations. Table 4 shows the results obtained. The ratio of time values is highly significant with the ML method while with the OLS technique only children and parental relationships are significant. When we focus on the logistic function approach, we observe that the ratio of time values has a direct effect on the probability of quarrels between spouses and an indirect effect through the women labour supply. Refer back to Table 4 and assume first of all that the Parsons and Bales' as well as the Rapoport and Rapoport theories are false, i.e. women in the home are quarrelling as much as those who are employed outside the home. In this case the estimated coefficient will be zero.

This assumption is seen to be false. Now assume that the Parsons and Bales' view is false and Rapoport and Rapoport's view true, i.e. women at home quarrel more than those at work, where they get their greatest fulfillment. In this case the estimated coefficient will be positive. This assumption is also seen to be false.

This empirical result supports the Parsonian view but not that of Rapoport and Rapoport about the double-career way of life as the best means of fulfillment for both spouses. It also supports the economic argument concerning the benefits and losses from marriage that husband and wife redistribute between themselves. Note that differences in time value have a negative effect on quarrels: we have seen above that the woman benefits from such a difference when her husband spends all his time on the labour market and the husband suffers losses when the wife spends all her time at home or at work. When the ratio of time value increases, specialization occurs and the husband is made better off. Then we can expect that he is less disposed to quarrel with his partner.

We have formulated an economic approach to conjugal roles where the ratio of opportunity costs of time and human capital endowments become the key variables in the allocation of roles between husband and wife and the distribution of benefits and losses from marriage. This approach does not invalidate other approaches such as Bott's hypothesis or Parsons and Bales' theory, but it competes with them.

Since women have acquired education, the differences in opportunity costs of time or human capital endowments between spouses have diminished. So, as the production of family income is more human capital-intensive than home production of goods, the traditional pattern of role differentiation has begun to break down. Couples with more equal endowments in skill resources will increase the wife's participation in the labour market. As time is more restricted, men are called upon to help out with household tasks. The burden of roles and the losses from marriage increase for the husband and this induces tension in conjugal relationships and consequently quarrels occur more frequently. These quarrels curb the husband's assistance to his wife. The wife re-allocates her time to activities which do not involve relationships with family members (household chores or outside work). A further increase in conflicts results from this redistribution of the woman's time. A cumulative and destabilizing process is generated within the household.

3. Conclusion

Economics has been defined in terms of both its method and field. Over the last decade however its subject matter has expanded enormously. That is to say, some economists think that economic reasoning and models, verified by statistical tests, can throw light on more social phenomena than those traditionally dealt with in economic text-books. This paper is an attempt to apply economic methods to conjugal role relationships and marital dissolution.

We set out to achieve two objectives: on the one hand to convince sociologists as well as economists that analytical tools developed by international trade theorists are relevant to the study of the variations observed in conjugal roles within the household; and, on the other hand, to measure the respective contribution of the economic as well as the sociological hypotheses advanced in this area.

With regard to the first objective, it follows that women perform (give up) those tasks which use intensively their abundant (scarce) factors relative to their husbands. Thus, families with a wider difference between spouses in opportunity costs of time or in the number of school years specialize women with low formal education or opportunity cost of time in the production of home goods.

With respect to the second objective, it follows that the economic hypotheses (stated in terms of the ratio of opportunity costs of time or of the ratio of educational attainments between spouses) disclose key variables for a middle-range theory like those developed by orthodox economists or sociologists. Hence we cannot reject them. On the other hand, their performance when confronted with the same data does not justify the economist's ignorance of the adjustment mechanism suggested in this connection by sociologists of the family. We have shown that Bott's hypothesis concerning the cultural traits of the husband or participation in religious or social activities is a determining factor in the role performed by the wife. And lastly, quarrels and dissension within the household seem to corroborate the statements of the economic theory and Parsons and Bales' hypothesis about the destabilizing role played by the woman's choice of an outside employment. We believe that a theory, the aim of which is to explain segregated or joint conjugal role relationships as well as marital dissolution, cannot avoid applying analytical tools developed in international economic theory to the interaction between spouses within the family.

References

BECKER, G. S. (1973) 'A Theory of Marriage', *Journal of Political Economy* 81 (July-August).

BLOOD, R. O. and D. M. WOLFE (1960) *Husbands and Wives: The Dynamics of Family Living* London: Free Press and Collier, Macmillan.

BOTT, E. (1955) 'Urban Families: Conjugal Roles and Social Network', *Human Relations* 8.

CHACHOLIADES, M. (1973) *The Pure Theory of International Trade* London: Macmillan.

GOLDBERGER, A. S. (1964) *Econometric Theory* New York: John Wiley & Sons.

GRAMM, W. L. (1975) 'Household Utility Maximisation and the Working Wife', *American Economic Review* 65 (March).

GRONAU, R. (1973) 'The Intra-Family Allocation of Time: The Value of the Housewife's Time', *American Economic Review* 63 (September).

LEIBOWITZ, A. (1974) 'Education and Home Production', *American Economic Review* 64 (May).

MICHAEL, R. T. (1972) *The Effects of Education on Efficiency in Consumption* New York: NBER, Columbia University Press.

McKENZIE, R. and G. TULLOCK (1975) *The New World of Economics* Homewood, Illinois: Richard D. Irwin Inc.

PARSONS, T. and R. BALES (1955) *Family, Socialisation and Interaction Process* New York: Free Press, Routledge & Kegan.

RAPOPORT, R. and R. RAPOPORT (1965) 'Work and Family in Contemporary Society', *American Sociological Review* 30 (June).

RIDER, N. (1973) 'Comment', *Journal of Political Economy* 81 (January-February).

TABARD, N. (1974) *Besoins et Aspirations des Familles et des Jeunes* Paris: éd. CAF.

WILLIS, R. J. (1973) 'A New Approach to the Economic Theory of Fertility Behavior', *Journal of Political Economy* 81 (January-February).

• Comment

Reuben Gronau

Hebrew University, Jerusalem, Israel

In this paper the author undertakes an ambitious project – the confrontation of two disciplines. In the first part of his paper Lemennicier examines the explanations offered by sociologists for the differentiation of conjugal roles and confronts them with those of economists who have recently ventured into the field. In the second part of the paper the author takes the further step of confronting the various theories with data in order to see what can be gained by closer cooperation between the economists and sociologists analysing household behaviour. Given the inherent difficulties, Lemennicier does a good job. Still, I would like to point out some shortcomings and lines for future research.

In the theoretical part of the paper, the author adopts, for the sake of simplicity, the traditional version of the Ricardian international trade model. It is assumed that a person's marginal productivities in the production of market and home goods are constant and hence that the transformation curve between home and market goods is linear. Given this oversimplified assumption, the model can generate only corner solutions, i.e. in these circumstances a person spends his whole time in either market work or work at home. According to the model, a two-person household has only three alternatives to choose from: both persons devote the whole of their time to work in the market; both devote their whole time to work at home; or one works in the market and the other works at home. Needless to say, this model provides only a very crude description of reality. Single persons and even married ones engage in both activities (for example, employed married women in the United States spend as much time working at home as in the market). In its present form the model cannot capture this phenomenon. In order to allow for partial specialization one has to assume that the transformation curve is concave (e.g. by assuming that marginal productivity at home diminishes as the number of hours worked at home increases).

Lemennicier assumes that the optimum allocation of time is determined solely by a person's productive capacity (in the market and at home) and by the relative price of home goods, tastes having no effect on the time budget. But this is not a very satisfactory analysis, since it ignores the three-way division of time between work in the market, work at home, and leisure. Tastes affect the amount of time spent at home and in the market by affecting the amount of time spent at leisure. The analysis of the effects of changes in the economic parameters (such as income, wages, the price of market substitutes for home goods, productivity at home) on the allocation of time will inevitably be incomplete if the effect of these parameters on leisure is not taken into account.

Furthermore, the paper ignores the asymmetry of the market for home goods: people are ready to buy home goods (or home good substitutes) in the market but they are reluctant to sell such services as child care, and housework. Thus, p can be regarded as a buying but not as a selling price.

Consider my Figure 1. Let *EBC* be the family's transformation curve and let $P'P$ be the price line. If the household wants to consume more than *OA* units of home goods it can obtain them in the market by working OF/W units of time in the market and using the income generated to buy the market goods and the additional home goods. However, if the household wants to consume less than *OA* home-good units, the price line $P'P$ becomes irrelevant. In this case the optimum point is on segment *EB* of the transformation curve, and the exact allocation of time depends on the household's tastes and market goods (i.e. it is at the tangency point of the indifference and the transformation curves). Thus, one cannot dispense with tastes when analysing the allocation of time and differentiation of conjugal roles.

Tastes play an even more important role when one discusses the gains from marriage. Economic theory tells us that trade benefits at

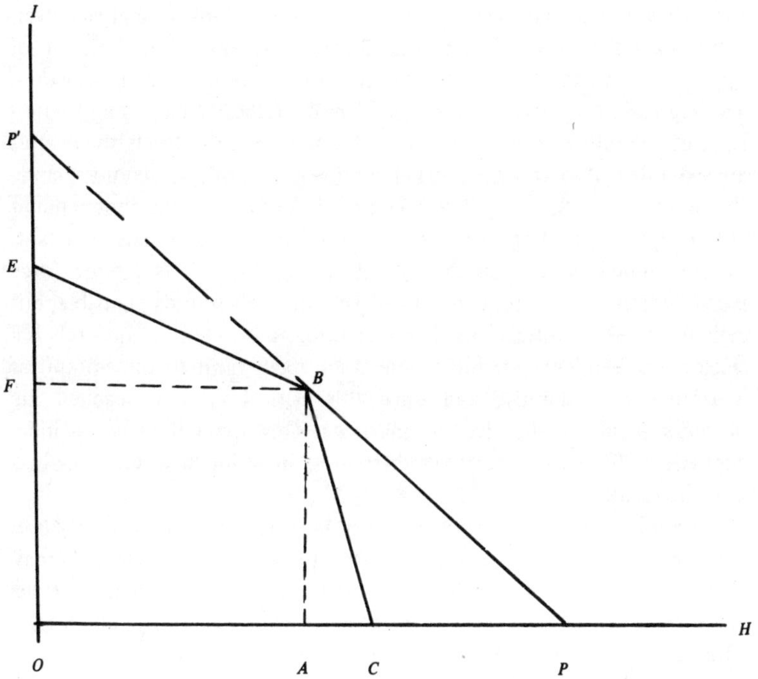

Figure 1

least one trading partner and that neither partner will end up worse off (because he would not participate in the exchange otherwise). The terms of trade are determined by the production capabilities of the two partners and their tastes. In Lemennicier's model the terms of trade are determined exogenously (in his example both members share the family's resources equally) and consequently marriage may result in a loss to one of the partners. This pitfall could have been avoided by allowing for the endogenous determination of the terms on which home goods and market goods are exchanged within the family. Once again, one cannot analyse the determination of the terms of trade without allowing for tastes.

In the empirical part of the paper the author examines two aspects of role differentiation within the family: the effect of educational levels (i.e. the endowment of human capital) on the supply of labour to the market and on work at home, and the effect of the woman's work in the market on marriage stability. The time budget analysis overemphasizes the ratio of human-capital endowments (and the ratio of opportunity costs of time) at the expense of more traditional measures. The regression equations contain the *ratio* of the husband's and wife's level of schooling as an explanatory variable, but the levels themselves are excluded. A better test of Lemennicier's hypothesis would include the latter as well, since it would permit examining the independent effect of the schooling ratio with the level of schooling held constant.

Lemennicier's analysis of the effect of the wife's labour force participation on the frequency of marital quarrels sounds plausible, but calls for some qualifications. For one thing, the extent of quarrels is a censored dependent variable. There is an upper limit to the amount of quarreling in a family, and once this critical value is reached the partners decide to dissolve the marriage. This upper limit is not independent of the explanatory variables, thus introducing a censoring bias into the results.

Secondly, the direction of causality between marital instability (i.e. quarrels) and the wife's labour force participation is not clear. It may be that the woman's working leads to increase tensions and quarrels, but it may just as well be that increased marital instability induces the wife to look for escape in a market career. Either way, Lemennicier's conclusion that 'the working time of women is a major factor in explaining quarrels within the home' seems to be somewhat premature.

These comments are not intended to detract from the importance of Lemennicier's work, but to suggest how much work still lies ahead.

8

Determinants of divorce

Robert Michael

Stanford University, Palo Alto, USA

Economists have only recently joined sociologists and psychologists in studying the determinants of divorce. The contributions of sociologists are best known. They are exemplified by the works of Jacobson (1959) and Carter and Glick (1970) and are surveyed by Levinger (1965) and Hicks and Platt (1970). Less well known are attemps by psychologists in the 1930s to construct prediction equations for marital success. These efforts were inspired by previous successes in predicting school achievement by means of an IQ test. Psychologists reasoned that the construction of an analogous marital-success quotient and an estimating equation for marital success based on personal and family background, economic and attitudinal variables should be as useful a tool for marriage counselors as IQ tests were for school guidance counselors.[1]

The author wishes to thank the Alfred P. Sloan Foundation and the Lilly Endowment for financial support through NBER. This is not an official NBER publication as it has not been reviewed by the NBER Board of Directors. My debt to my collaborators on another paper on divorce – Gary Becker and Lis Landes – is apparent; neither should be thought responsible for flaws in the present paper. Barbara Andrews has provided excellent research assistance on this project.

Economists' recent interest in divorce has been prompted by several factors.

(1) Divorce affects several, more traditional concerns of economists including the labour force participation rates of women, housing demand, tax revenues, measures of the distribution of income, and fertility (and hence population growth). Thus, the doubling of divorce rates in the past decade in the US and several Western European countries has generated considerable new interest in better understanding the determinants of divorce.

(2) The growing concern in recent years for welfare reform in the US has prompted interest in understanding the impact of a change in the structure of the welfare program on the stability of families and the nature of personal living arrangements. Several of the recent studies of determinants of divorce have focused on this particular issue.

(3) The development of a body of theory and applications in the 'new home economics' or 'family economics' has also contributed to the interest in divorce by economists. This research, growing out of work in the early 1960s by, for example, Becker (1965) and Mincer (1963), has addressed a set of interrelated topics including family formation, fertility, family labour supply, family migration, schooling, etc. to which the study of divorce is a natural extension.

(4) A fourth reason for growth in interest in studying divorce is the recent availability of several longitudinal data sets that have considerable information on household characteristics in successive years. With these data insight about the dynamics of divorce decisions can in principle be obtained.

The purpose of this paper is to acquaint participants of an international, interdisciplinary conference with some of the contributions of these recent studies of determinants of divorce. The paper contains an appendix which presents new results from a regression analysis of divorce among a small but very unique sample of American women. These results are incorporated in the summary which discusses both theoretical contributions and empirical findings.

Analytical issues

One cannot very well think of a theory of divorce without considering why people marry in the first place.[2] To incorporate marriage and divorce decisions into an economic framework we might assume that an individual has a utility function in which a 'companion' is one of the arguments. In such a model of marriage and divorce the individual would have a demand for a companion which would be affected by income and prices in the usual way – the demand for a spouse or companion would be roughly analogous to the demand for a car or any other durable good, and the supply of spouses to a given individual would be the demand by others for this individual as their spouse.

The actual approach taken in the recent economic literature on marriage (see Becker, 1974) captures the essence of that demand model, but goes behind its initial, rather sterile assumption that a companion yields utility. The fundamental notion used instead is that productive activities are undertaken in the home or nonmarket sector and that by pooling together their resources through living arrangements such as marriage, one may achieve production gains accruing from (a) technical production efficiencies (i.e. from economies of scale, specialization in the division of labour, and technical complementarity in the use of family members' time) and from (b) joint consumption of public goods within the household (e.g. all family members can enjoy the same work of art and share the same electric light without one person's enjoyment restricting the access of other family members).

A second important notion in this analytical framework of marriage and divorce is that people choose their marital status on the basis of what seems most beneficial. So the most persuasive evidence that there are substantial gains from marriage is that the overwhelming majority of men and women do in fact choose to marry – by one set of estimates, for men and women in the US in the 1960s, well over 90 percent eventually married (see Schoen and Nelson, 1974: 281).

These gains from marriage presumably vary among couples and are expected (see Becker, 1974) to be greater the greater the level of the couple's resources, the greater their ability to capitalize on the division of labour – i.e. by having different skills which can be substituted for each other – and the greater the similarity or complementarity between spouses in traits used jointly in productive activities. Individuals presumably search for a best possible mate and are constrained in their selection by their own limited set of abilities, traits or endowments through competition from others. Since this search is costly (partly in terms of forgone gains from marrying the best available spouse), many marriages which take place may be less than ideal, although 'optimal' in the light of these costs.

Regarding divorce, the analysis again assumes that individuals divorce when doing so is expected to increase their income, broadly defined. Since the individual is assumed to marry when that action maximizes his or her expected real income, the analysis of divorce focuses on why the individual's expectation may change sufficiently to induce or justify divorce.

Let M_t be the expected *net* present value at time t of the person's real income over the rest of his or her life when married to a particular spouse. That is, M_t is a measure of the attractiveness of being married to that spouse compared to any other attainable marital circumstance. Aside from the costs of marrying, a person marries when $M_t > 0$. Likewise, aside from the costs of divorce, one would chose to divorce if M at some later time, say M_{t+k}, becomes negative.

The question then becomes: if $M_t > 0$ (inducing marriage), why might $M_{t+k} < 0$ (inducing divorce)? One answer could be that the individual's expectations about this marriage turned out to be incorrect because either the benefits were not as great as expected (e.g. he is not what she thought he would be or *she* is not what he expected her to be) or the alternatives available turn out to be better than expected (e.g. he finds a preferred, available spouse). Hence, M might change signs as time passes as new information is acquired. Alternatively, even if expectations are borne out perfectly, it is possible that when evaluated at one age, say 22, M_{22} is positive, but that after living out a few years of marriage, the remaining streams yield a negative M say $M_{30} < 0$. In this latter case, but not in the former, divorce might have been fully anticipated, and planned for, at the outset of marriage. Based on evidence that most divorces occur within the first few years of marriage (the median duration of marriage prior to divorce in the 1960s in the US was about six years according to Plateris (1973: 49)). Becker, Landes and Michael (BLM) (1977) contend that most divorces result from uncertainty and are not anticipated at the outset of marriage. In this view unexpected events are likely to be the causes of divorce.

Divorce does not automatically occur, of course, when $M < 0$. One reason is the cost of divorce. If C represents the many kinds of costs incurred in divorcing, then the individual chooses divorce when $M + C < 0$. These costs include not only the direct dollar and time costs involved in effecting the divorce, but also the pecuniary and non-pecuniary losses in property and human capital.

The discussion has not introduced the complication of which spouse calculates these M's and C's, or what happens if $M + C$ is negative for one spouse and positive for the other. BLM discuss this issue at length and argue that *if* the costs of negotiating, redistributing and policing are sufficiently small, then in principle the two parties can reach agreement. The partner for which $M + C > 0$ may have sufficient gains to be able to transfer enough real income to the other spouse so that after the transfer, $M + C > 0$ for both. If so, they can agree to remain married; if not, there is some transfer which might leave $M + C < 0$ for both and they could agree to end the marriage. The disagreements which frequently accompany a couple's discussion of whether or not to divorce is evidence that these costs of negotiating, transferring and policing are generally not small!

What causes divorce, therefore, is whatever causes $(M + C)$ to be negative. Taxonomically, this includes (a) factors that cause the positive gains from marriage to be small; (b) factors that cause the gains to vary considerably over the lifetime (either anticipated volatility in the M series or unanticipated, stochastic fluctuations in M); and (c) factors that cause C to be small. The likelihood of divorce for a couple in some interval of time can be viewed as the probability that $(M + C)$ is negative in that period. The research design in many empirical studies is to estimate a relationship between variables that affect M or C and a measure of the probability of divorce.

Regarding the factors that may cause the gains from marriage to be small, Becker's analysis of marriage (1974) has shown that the gains from marriage are greater the higher the level of income of the primary earner, the more similar the traits of spouses with respect to characteristics used jointly in their nonmarket activities, and the more dissimilar the spouses' traits with respect to characteristics that can be substituted for each other in market activities. Thus, one expects several relations to appear in empirical analysis: (a) the level of income of the primary earner, typically the husband, should be negatively related to the likelihood of divorce; (b) variables reflecting similarity of background characteristics such as age, intelligence, race, religion, and so forth should be negatively related to divorce; and (c) the level of earnings of the secondary worker should be positively related to divorce.[3] The gains from marriage can also be affected by governmental tax and transfer schemes that alter the resources available in or outside of marriage.

More indirectly, as searching for a mate is a costly activity, individuals with high search costs are expected to search less before marrying and thus to settle for a somewhat less-suitable match. Hence, those who search less before marriage are expected to have a higher likelihood of divorce. Marriages at young ages are notoriously less stable than other marriages, a phenomenon that can be understood in the context of a marital search model.

Regarding the factors that cause the gains from marriage to vary over the lifetime, consider a marriage contract as a long-term agreement. Unforeseen changes in circumstances that occur as time passes may affect the suitability of the contract to one or both spouses, may make renegotiation of the contract necessary, and thus raise the likelihood that a dissolution of the contract – a divorce – will take place. Therefore, unexpected events are likely to be maritally destabilizing whether they represent unexpectedly good or bad news. If misfortune befalls one spouse – say his earning power is impaired by an accident or say she is found to be infertile – the other spouse may find that marriage to someone else if relatively more attractive than initially expected. If good fortune comes to one spouse – say his career succeeds far beyond their initial expectations or she unexpectedly establishes a successful and demanding career – then that spouse may feel his or her mate is no longer an acceptable one. Under any circumstances other than the one anticipated when the marriage was formed, the actual marriage partnership may not be the preferred one.

Another change that may affect the gains from marriage over time is not directly related to the occurrence of unforeseen events. Individuals make decisions in one time period that affect their opportunities and well-being in subsequent periods. Just as the traits and endowments of a couple at the time of marriage affect gains from their marriage, their decisions after marriage about the acquisition of types of physical and human capital, the development of skills and interests, etc. affect subsequent gains from their marriage. As some forms of assets are more valuable in the current marriage than elsewhere (i.e. 'spouse-specific capital' such as knowledge of one's mate), the incentive to acquire this type of capital is affected by the couple's assessment of the likelihood of their marital success. The less likely a divorce, the more spouse-specific capital they will choose to obtain. And, conversely, the more of such capital they have, the greater the 'capital loss' from divorcing. The widely observed decline in the probability of divorce with increased duration of marriage can be explained by this phenomenon – as the years pass, more and more spouse-specific capital is acquired which inhibits divorce.[4] The most obvious form of this kind of capital is children born and raised by the couple.

Regarding the third set of factors causing divorce, the determinants of the cost of divorce, some have already been mentioned. Spouse-specific capital is by definition capital on which a loss is incurred by divorcing; so the greater the amount of this capital the couple has, the greater the costs of divorcing. One of the important costs which varies among states in the US as well as among countries is the legal cost of divorce. In some circumstances a divorce may be obtained by simply indicating that a divorce is desired – sometimes this requires agreement between the spouses, as in many states with 'no-fault' divorce laws, and sometimes it is the prerogative of the male spouse only, as in certain Middle-Eastern societies. Elsewhere, more elaborate and costly procedures are required and presumably this difference in cost affects the likelihood of divorce (residence requirements in states with easier divorce laws help maintain these cost differentials among states). Religious strictures against divorce vary considerably as well. Presumably one of the primary reasons one sees so little divorce in Catholic countries such as Guatemala and Venezuela is the added costs of divorce among Catholics.

Empirical formulation

Empirically, the research strategy followed by most recent studies of the causes of divorce involves estimating the partial effects of a set of variables such as those just discussed on the probability of divorce. The underlying logic is this: the probability of a couple's divorcing in period t given that they had not been divorced in an earlier period is equal to the probability that $(M + C)$ becomes negative in time interval t. Symbolically,

$$P_t = P((M + C)_t < 0). \qquad (1)$$

$(M + C)$ is related to a set of exogenous variables, $Y_1, Y_2, \ldots,$ such as husband's income, age at marriage etc. so that

$$(M + C)_t = \phi_t(Y_1, Y_2, \ldots, Y_n) + e_t. \qquad (2)$$

The probability of divorce can then be expressed as a function of this set of Y's:

$$P_t = P(\phi_t(Y_1, Y_2, \ldots, Y_n) < - e_t). \qquad (3)$$

If $\phi_i \equiv (\partial\phi/\partial Y_i) > 0$, then $(\partial P/\partial Y_i) < 0$: a variable which raises the net gain from remaining married lowers the probability of divorce. Writing equation (3) as a linear function of Y_i,

$$P_t = a_t + \sum_i b_{ti} Y_i + e_t, \tag{4}$$

has the convenient property that b_{ti} can be interpreted as the partial effect of variable Y_i on the probability of divorce.[5]

Equation (4) has been used in one of two ways in recent empirical studies. In both P is defined as the probability of divorce in a fixed period of n years.

(1) In one set of studies couples are selected at various durations of marriage and P is defined as the probability of divorcing over the next n years. The Ross-Sawhill (RS) (1975) study, for example, examined the determinants of divorce over a four-year period from 1968 to 1972 for a sample of 1,900 couples whose marriages were intact at the beginning of the period. Some of the couples were in their second or third year of marriage in 1968, others were in their twenty-second or twenty-third year of marriage; the mean duration of marriage for the couples was about fourteen years. So, on average RS studied how a set of explanatory variables affected the probability of divorce over a four-year period starting in the fourteenth year of marriage. Likewise, Sawhill, Peabody, Jones and Caldwell (SPJC) (1975) analysed further the same group of 1,900 couples from the Michigan Panel on Income Dynamics survey and, in addition, analysed a sample of about 1,000 couples over a three-year period beginning in 1970 drawn from the New Jersey Income Maintenance Experiment (NJIME). The approach by Tuma, Groeneveld and Hannan (TGH) (1976) has been to transform the probability of divorce over a two-year time span into a 'continuous rate of divorce'[6] and to regress this 'continuous rate' on a set of Y-variables as suggested in equation (4); again, the observations contain both couples recently married and couples married as long as twenty years prior to the beginning of the two-year interval investigated.

(2) In another set of studies, P is defined for specified durations of marriage. Becker, Landes and Michael (BLM) (1977), for example, define P over five-year intervals of time for each successive five years of marriage duration. They first regress the probability of divorce by the fifth anniversary of the marriage on the set of Y_i. In a separate equation they regress the probability of divorce by the tenth anniversary (conditional upon the marriage being intact at the fifth anniversary) on the set

of Y_i, and so on for successive five-year intervals. BLM use retrospective information covering approximately a twenty-five year period from the 1967 Survey of Economic Opportunity data for about 4,500 white men and 5,500 white women separately for the bulk of their analysis. In the appendix to the present paper the 'Terman data' are used to investigate determinants of P over three different lengths of time covering nearly thirty years, all beginning with the date of marriage which occurred in the 1930s. The following section discusses empirical findings pertaining to the stability of marriages from these five separate studies.

Empirical findings

All five of the studies summarized here – the book by RS, the published reports by SPJC and TGH, the article by BLM and the Terman data discussed in the appendix – pertain to recent US divorce behavior using cross-sectional data. The first three examine divorce behavior in the late 1960s or early 1970s, assume no interactions of background variables with duration of marriage (i.e. the studies hold duration of marriage constant as a single variable in a linear, multivariate regression), and emphasize the importance of the source or type of income (especially the role of welfare income) in determining divorce. The latter two studies cover a wider time span (from the 1930s to the 1960s), place some emphasis on interactions of exogenous variables with duration of marriage, and generally employ fewer explanatory variables. Results from even so small a set of studies are not easily summarized; the major consensuses and differences are discussed below.

Age at marriage

The finding of a negative relation between age at first marriage and the probability of divorce pervades the sociological literature on divorce. The contribution of the recent studies is in estimating more accurately the size and functional form of this relation, holding constant other factors which also influence divorce. RS estimate a linear relationship between husband's age at first marriage and the four-year probability of divorce: a five-year increase in age at marriage lowers the probability by two percentage points. (The sample's mean four-year probability of divorce is 7.6 percent.) The Terman data suggest the effect is much stronger at shorter durations of marriage: an estimate comparable to RS's estimate (2 percent) based on the twenty-four year behavior of the Terman sample is a four percentage-point reduction while the comparable estimate based on the behavior in the first four years of marriage is an 8.5 percentage-point reduction.[7] (The difference between RS's 2 percent and the Terman data's 4 percent is not especially interesting because of lack of comparability in the two data sets, the decades to which they pertain, and the differences in variable definitions; the difference between the 4 percent and 8.5 percent is far more informative.)

Results from BLM's analysis confirm the evidence that age at marriage has a far stronger impact on the likelihood of divorce at shorter durations of marriage. They estimate, for example, that a five-year increase in age at marriage of husbands (from age 20 to 25) lowers the probability of divorce by 2.1 percentage points during the first five years of marriage, but by only 0.7 percentage point during the third five years of marriage.

The BLM study presents another important fact – the impact of age at first marriage on divorce is nonlinear and appears to be 'U-shaped'. The impact is strongest for ages at marriage in the teens, still negative but much weaker in the twenties, and is actually slightly positive over the age of thirty! (An interpretation of this phenomenon is presented by BLM.)

These results regarding age at marriage illustrate two more general points. Both the nonlinearity and the interaction of age at marriage with duration of marriage suggest that age at marriage is properly viewed as a proxy for the amount of marital search that preceded the marriage. So the functional form can in general shed light on the appropriate interpretation of why a variable operates as it does. Secondly, the results suggest that even this well-established negative relationship is not an easy one with which to build demographic predictions. A one-year change over time in the average age at marriage has a quite complicated influence on the stability of marriages over time. Therefore, social policy decisions predicted on the expected repercussions of one or another structural change may be even more hazardous than one might have thought previously.

Income of husbands

The results in these five studies provide strong evidence confirming the maritally stabilizing effect of husband's income. SPJC, for example, find in the New Jersey IME data that a $1,000 increase in earnings lowers the three-year probability of divorce by about 4.6 percentage points. RS and SPJC also report a negative effect from the Michigan Income Dynamics data, and TGH results from the Denver-Seattle IME imply that white couples having low husband's income (e.g. $3,000) have well over twice as high a likelihood of divorce as white couples with high husband's income (e.g. $10,000).[8]

The Terman data do not contain a direct measure of husband's earnings, but husband's schooling level, which is a good proxy for earnings, does show a generally significant negative effect of income on the probability of divorce (e.g. four years more schooling lowers the probability of divorce by ten percentage points in a fourteen-year period for a sample whose mean probability of divorce was 12.3 percent).

The BLM results for the SEO data are again revealing. They suggest that a $4,000 rise in husband's earnings (e.g. from $7,000 to $11,000) is associated with about a one-percentage-point reduction in the five-year probability of divorce in the first five years of marriage, only about a one-half percentage-point reduction from the tenth to the fifteenth year of marriage and a stronger effect of nearly one percentage point again in subsequent five-year intervals. Here again significant nonlinearity is found in several marriage duration intervals. It appears that increases in income at low levels of income substantially lower the likelihood of divorce, but the effect weakens and even turns positive above income levels of about $40,000 (in 1967 dollars). BLM argues that this upturn suggests unexpectedly high income is as maritally destabilizing as unexpectedly low income is; they have further evidence on this point which is discussed below.

Income of wives

It may be only moderately inappropriate in studying the impact of husband's income on divorce to assume no causal influence of marital status on hourly earnings, but in studying the effects of the wife's income the problem of simultaneity seems much more severe. Hence, estimates of the wife's income on the couple's probability of divorce are more likely to be biased by this simultaneity. The evidence-available suggests that wife's income is maritally destabilizing. RS, for example, find that a $1,000 increase in the earnings of the wife raises the four-year probability of divorce by about one percentage point, and TGH conclude from a regression which includes husband's and wife's hourly wages and education levels as well as 'normal income', that 'higher-wage women . . . have a higher rate of marital dissolution' (p. 49).[9]

A less endogenous proxy for the wife's earnings potential is the wife's schooling level. The Terman data indicate a persistent positive, although not always statistically significant, effect of wife's schooling on the likelihood of divorce. The destabilizing effect appears to be stronger at later durations of marriage than in the first few years, in contrast with the effect of age at marriage (see Michael, 1976: 25). The BLM study also included wife's schooling level, but they found no significant effects at any duration of marriage. The difference here between the Terman result and the BLM result may be attributable to the inclusion of variables capturing the effects of children in the BLM equations. With a negative correlation between wife's schooling level and number of children, the positive effect of schooling on divorce present in the Terman data may have been captured by the negative coefficients on children in the SEO data. That is, more educated women have both higher market opportunities and fewer children; both phenomena are associated with higher probabilities of divorce.

As one compares several different sets of regression results it becomes clear that there are consistent associations between the likelihood of divorce and various measures of the wife's market opportunities, such as her education level or her fertility. But there is not yet enough precision or control in the available studies to distinguish hypotheses regarding these persistent broad findings. Multiple regression analyses in which several proxies for these factors are all included may not be the most fruitful approach in trying to sort out these channels of influence. Longitudinal observations may provide the key, but the promise of such data lies in the future.

Transfer income

As mentioned at the beginning of this paper, one of the motivations for much of the recent divorce analysis has been concern about the impact on family stability of reforms in the welfare system in the US. The studies by SPJC and by TGH address this issue in detail. RS find 'no evidence of a welfare effect in these (Michigan Income Dynamics) data' (p. 58), but emphasize the difficulties in determining that effect with their data. By contrast, SPJC do find a substantially higher rate of dissolution for families involved in the New Jersey IME than for the comparable control families. Moreover, SPJC emphasize that the effect seems more related to being a part of the experiment than to the level of payments received. They contend that there is 'some feature of the experiment other than the level of payments or guarantee that is responsible for the higher dissolution rate among families receiving payments' (p. 70). They suggest greater sampling attrition by unstable families in the control group as an explanation. Another explanation is the unexpected nature of the experiment itself. The experiment was not anticipated by the couples, presumably, when they married. When they were brought into this several-year experiment, that event itself represented an unexpected change in their financial circumstance, and as discussed in the preceding section, any such change can be expected to be maritally destabilizing.

The work of TGH represents the most thorough study of the relation of income maintenance programs to marital stability. Using the first two years of data from the continuing Seattle – Denver IME, they conclude that 'Income maintenance raises rates of marital dissolution' (p. 9). They find the effects are largest for couples on the lower support programs. White couples receiving maintenance payments had over twice as high dissolution rates as the control couples; black couples had about 75 percent higher dissolution rates. TGH explore interactions between income maintenance support levels and several other variables and find, for whites, no interactions with wife's education or wage rate, but significant interactions with duration of marriage and family's normal income level. The destabilizing effects are greater for couples with lower levels of normal income and for couples already married a relatively longer time at the beginning of the experiment.[10]

Unexpected events

One of the more important products of the recent studies of causes of divorce has been the emphasis on the maritally destabilizing effects of unforeseen events, as discussed above. The empirical applications are abundant. BLM cite several examples including evidence that women with stillbirths or with child deaths as well as women with what appears to be exceptionally high rates of fertility have relatively high divorce rates. They suggest that the couple's fecundity or fertility capacity is hard to predict prior to marriage, so both sub-fecundity and excess-fecundity may be viewed as unforeseen and hence maritally destabilizing influences. Likewise, they indicate that men whose health status changes appreciably over time are more likely to be divorced, both for men whose health improves as well as for those whose health deteriorates.

Using the SEO data, BLM attempted to estimate the impact on the likelihood of divorce of unexpectedly high and unexpectedly low levels of earnings, for white men. First, an estimate was computed of what each man in the sample might have guessed his earnings at age 45 to be. Then that estimate was compared to his actual earnings at age 45. When the deviation between the two figures was used in the divorce equation, results suggested that both unexpectedly high earnings and unexpectedly low earnings increased the man's likelihood of divorce. (Of course, increases in the value of his expected earnings had the usual maritally stabilizing effect.)

RS used a different procedure but found the same qualitative effect. Men whose earnings are substantially (50 percent) higher or lower than they might have expected had *higher* rates of divorce than men whose actual earnings were similar to the earnings they might have expected.

RS studies the impact of an episode of serious unemployment on the likelihood of divorce and found a sizable effect: men who had experienced serious unemployment had a seven-percentage-point higher probability of divorce in the four-year period studied.

As suggested earlier, the substantially higher rates of divorce among couples participating in the income maintenance experiments might in part be caused by the fact that the experiment per se was an unforeseen event in their married lives. Any event which alters the circumstances on which the present marriage was judged relatively attractive may be expected to raise the likelihood of divorce.

Children

There is considerable disagreement among the five papers in their statements about the impact of children on the likelihood of divorce;

there is much less actual contradiction in the reported results. The impact of children on divorce appears to be a generally negative one (more children associated with lower likelihood of divorce), but the relationship is complex. RS and SPJC use a dummy variable reflecting the presence of children under age 18 in the home and conclude that the presence of children did not have a statistically significant effect of marital stability in the Michigan data; similarly in the New Jersey IME data a linear relationship between number of children and divorce was insignificant. TGH found a sizable but insignificant negative relation between the number of children and the likelihood of divorce.

BLM, on the other hand, investigated the relationship with children more thoroughly and found a quite strong although complicated one. Using the number and ages of children present at, say, the fifth anniversary of intact marriages, BLM observed a sizable, nonlinear effect of these children on the probability of divorce over the subsequent five years. The presence of one young child was associated with a two-percentage-point decline in the five-year probability of divorce; the presence of a second young child further lowered the probability by 1.2 percentage points; the third young child lowered it additionally by a tiny amount and the fourth young child actually *raised* the probability by a tiny amount; and more than four young children by the fifth year of marriage had a sizable postive effect on the prospect of divorce over the next five years. So the effect of children was found to be nonlinear and related to the ages of the children. (Children over age six had a much smaller deterrent effect.) The effect of children was also found to vary with the duration of marriage. No wonder a simple dichotomous variable or a single linear variable does not capture the apparent effects of children on the likelihood of divorce!

Other factors

Even within the small number of studies summarized here, there were several other factors identified as influencing the likelihood of divorce. In this regard the RS study is most fruitful, revealing evidence through multiple regressions of several partial effects that have in the past been frequently observed as simple correlations. For example, RS find that whites in the Western region of the country face a probability of divorcing over a four-year period that is six percentage points higher than that for whites in the Eastern region.[11] Couples living in dense central cities also have about six percentage points higher probabilities of divorcing over the four-year period studied. Greater likelihood of meeting a preferred prospective spouse, greater anonymity and hence lower cost of divorce, and greater market career opportunities for women in large cities probably explain this latter finding. RS also find that in the Northeast, nonwhites have substantially higher rates of divorce (about ten percentage points higher) than whites; in the West this racial differential is even larger but is in the opposite direction.[12] The typical simple relationship with race suggests that marital instability is higher for nonwhites, especially if separation as well as formal divorce is considered instability.

The Terman data in the appendix indicate that spouses of the same religion are considerably more maritally stable than couples who have intermarried. Apparently this effect is the same across religions, at least for the first few years of marriage (see Table A4). RS also find a measure of religious activity affecting stability: families that attend church at least once a week have a four-percentage-point lower probability of divorce over the four-year period studied. It is not clear if the RS finding reflects an impact of intensity of religious attitude, similarity of religious affiliation of members of the family, or perhaps a Catholic religion influence (since the Catholic church seems to promote church attendance relatively effectively and to discourage divorce relatively strongly). Evidence that Catholics do in fact divorce less frequently is seen from the Terman data (see Tables A2 and A4 and the discussion associated with them). The suggestive evidence that, other things held constant, Catholic women are maritally less happy is consistent with the notion that their costs of divorcing are relatively high, causing them to remain married at higher levels of dissatisfaction than non Catholics would tolerate.

A final intriguing finding related to the likelihood of divorce in first marriages is BLM's evidence that a premarital pregnancy raises the likelihood of divorce. (This finding is also reported in sociological studies.) BLM suggests two reasons for this effect: (1) an accidental premarital pregnancy cuts short the marital search and hence is likely to be associated with a less-than-optimal match; and (2) if the child's father is not the husband, then that child is a maritally destabilizing influence for the same reason children from first marriages are destabilizing in remarriages (BLM find this to be the case in their study of the stability of remarriages); that is, the child represents 'spouse-specific' capital from another 'marriage' and that capital may have an adverse effect on the gains from subsequent marriages.

The foregoing discussion of factors influencing the likelihood of divorce, based on several recent research projects, has referred to numerous factors. A few generalizations emerge.

(1) The source, level, and predictability of income all appear to be important determinants of marital stability. The larger the percentage of family income earned by the primary earner and the higher the level of family income, regardless of composition, the lower the probability of dissolution. Also, the less volatile the income and the more accurately it can be predicted, the lower the probability of divorce.

(2) The better informed the partners are about themselves and their spouse at the time of marriage the more stable the marriage.

(3) As a corollary to (2), the circumstances unforeseen at the time of marriage are maritally destabilizing. This generalization applies to circumstances internal to the family such as changes in the health or labor-marketability of one of the spouses and to external circumstances such as changes in the social services provided the family by governments.

Other studies

While the studies summarized here all pertain to recent cross-sectional US data on marital instability, there are many other research projects in related areas under way. For example, the studies by Sawhill, Peabody, Jones and Caldwell; by Tuma, Groeneveld and Hannan; and by Becker, Landes and Michael, all also address the question of determinants of remarriage. A large percentage of divorced persons eventually do remarry and the study of factors affecting the speed and likelihood of remarriage provides additional information about the underlying influences on marital stability.

Another area of research is the analysis of the time series of divorce rates. In the US since, say, 1900, the annual probability of divorce has risen more or less steadily with major deviations from that upward trend in the period 1943-47 and in the most recent few years. The positive simple relationship between the probability of divorce and the level of income in this long time series is one of the apparent contradictions between the time series and the cross-sectional findings. A line of argument suggested by BLM may prove to be an important element in reconciling these findings: as real wages rise for men and women, the degree of division of labor between spouses diminishes and the resulting increase in women's labor market attachment lowers the gains from marriage thus leading to increased divorce. But a lower overall gain from marriage should also be reflected by a decline in the probability of marrying in the first place and in the probability of remarriage, and at least until the most recent few years no such indication in the national statistics was present.

The decline in fertility over time does appear broadly consistent with the cross-sectional evidence of a negative relationship with divorce, but as emphasized earlier, the cross-sectional relationship does not appear to be a simple one; so here, too, further reconciliation of the time series and cross-sectional relationships is needed.

The growth in divorce may build upon itself in several respects: a rise in divorce increases the pool of nonmarried people from whom one might find a preferred spouse and with whom one might associate without social stigmas if divorced. Also, as the number of divorced persons increases, the general social acceptance of divorce and its codification in laws governing divorce would be expected to be modified toward a more tolerant position.

Regarding the two major disruptions from the upward trend in US divorce rates,[13] the higher levels of divorce during and immediately following World War II can be viewed as reflecting several of the cross-sectional results. The war was an event unforeseen in the case of many older marriages and an event which precipitated more hastily arranged marriages (hence marriages among less-well-informed couples). Furthermore, as a result of the forced separations between spouses and the dislocating effects of the war, probably the amount of 'spouse-specific' capital was reduced in many marriages. All of these forces would be expected, on the basis of the cross-sectional results, to lead to higher divorce rates.

A small portion of the recent precipitous rise in divorce rates can be attributed to the age structure of the population. Owing to the fluctuation in births over the preceding decades, a larger-than-usual portion of the married population is young and hence in the early years of marriage when rates of divorce are normally high. However, most of the increase in divorce rates in recent years is attributable to a rise in age-specific divorce rates for women in their twenties. Michael (1977) contends that one of the major explanations of the rise in divorce in the late 1960s and the 1970s has been improved birth control technology including oral contraception and the introduction of intrauterine devices in the US market in the early 1960s and the subsequent technological improvement in sterilization and legalization of elective abortion. These technological changes create marital instability because they were unanticipated by couples marrying prior to the availability of these improved techniques and also because the repercussions of effective, inexpensive fertility controls on such long-term decisions as women's market career choices required several years to become clear. Hence, the influences of the 'contraceptive revolution' have been in evidence throughout the past decade.

One of the most difficult issues in the time series studies as well as in cross-sectional analyses is the direction of causation of effects such as the negative relationship between fertility and divorce or the positive relationship of women's labor force participation rates and divorce rates. The time series as well as longitudinal cross-sectional data may prove useful in identifying directions of causation in future research.

In addition to questions about post-divorce marital behavior and time series studies, there are important issues regarding marriage and divorce laws, international comparisons, the implications of migration patterns on divorce, etc. Beyond these and other topics dealing with the causes of marital instability, a whole host of questions about the consequences of this instability for the family members, the economy and the society have not been systematically addressed. Perhaps enough has been said here to not only acquaint the reader with some of the recent contributions, remaining puzzles, and inconsistencies of the study of causes of divorce, but also to convince the reader that there is much in this dimension of sociological economics that constitutes a challenging body of material for further research.

Appendix: The Terman sample

This appendix describes an analysis of determinants of divorce at specific lengths of marriage duration for a very unrepresentative sample of American women – a group of geniuses.[14] The data are from the Terman Sample of persons selected for study in 1921 by psychologist Lewis M. Terman. The sample was chosen from children enrolled in

California schools in urban areas and included children whose measured IQ was 135 or above. The sample thus represented students in the highest 1 percent of the school population in general intelligence. In addition to information obtained in the early 1920s from the children, their parents and their teachers, the subjects were resurveyed in 1927-28 and again in 1936, 1940, 1950-52, 1955, and 1960.[15] The available data file includes information on each individual's marital history and marital status in 1940, 1950, and 1960. That information is the basis of the study reported here.

This sample differs in many respects from those more often analysed. Several features of the sample are especially advantageous, including: (a) the high IQ of the subjects provides the opportunity to study the marital behavior of women with a unique characteristic; (b) the longitudinal (not retrospective) nature of the data permits study of the impact of certain variables on marital stability through time; and (c) the availability of information on characteristics of both subject and spouse makes the sample relatively well-suited for a study of marital stability.

The disadvantages in analysing the Terman sample include the following: (a) the sample is, by conventional standards, quite small; (b) the sample is also quite homogeneous with respect to many of the characteristics of interest, thus one cannot parcel out separate effects of variables as easily as in more diffused, broadly based samples; (c) despite the abundance of some kinds of information, especially psychological and social variables, there is relatively little useful information on economic variables; and (d) since the sample was selected from California schools, comparisons between the sample and a population at large are made more difficult by the differences in marital behavior between Californians and residents of other states.

The results reported below estimate the impact of a small set of variables on the probability of dissolution of the first marriage. These variables are the level of schooling of the wife and the husband, the wife's age at first marriage, and two dummy variables, one reflecting whether either the husband or wife was Catholic (defined as one if so) and one reflecting whether the wife and husband had the same religious affiliation (defined as one if so). The explanatory variables represent characteristics of the individuals or the marriage partnership at the time of marriage. Thus, they are not themselves affected by the success of the marriage but are parametric to the couple by the time the marriage takes place.[16] Their impact on the stability by 1940, by 1950, and by

1960, of first marriages formed 1-4 years before 1940 and 5-8 years before 1940 is studied. Because of the nature of the available information, the two groups of women analysed (114 women married in 1936-39, and 97 women married in 1932-35) exclude those who were first married by age 20.

TABLE A1

Means and Standard Deviations of Selected Variables for Terman Women First Married 1-4 Years Before 1940 and 5-8 Years Before 1940

	Women first married			
	1-4 years before 1940		5-8 years before 1940	
	mean	s.d.	mean	s.d.
DIVORCED 1940	0.044	(0.21)	0.093	(0.29)
DIVORCED 1950	0.123	(0.33)	0.175	(0.38)
DIVORCED 1960	0.158	(0.37)	0.196	(0.40)
SCHOOL, WIFE	15.658	(1.86)	15.763	(1.91)
SCHOOL, HUSBAND	15.193	(2.48)	14.979	(2.59)
AGE MARRIED	24.465	(2.32)	23.381	(1.94)
CATHOLIC	0.079	(0.27)	0.062	(0.24)
SAME RELIGION	0.842	(0.37)	0.887	(0.32)
IQ	149.877	(12.84)	148.557	(10.14)
AGE, WIFE	27.316	(2.42)	29.876	(2.06)
AGE HIGH SCHOOL (WIFE)	16.538	(0.73)	16.592	(0.85)
AGE, HUSBAND	31.825	(4.75)	34.216	(4.79)
AGE MARRIED, HUSBAND	28.079	(4.33)	26.980	(4.71)
YEARS SINCE MARRIAGE 1940	2.851	(1.07)	6.495	(1.20)
BOTH CATHOLIC	0.026	(0.16)		
BOTH JEWISH	0.026	(0.16)		
BOTH PROTESTANT	0.544	(0.50)		
BOTH NO RELIGION	0.167	(0.37)		
BOTH OTHER RELIGION	0.044	(0.21)		
CATHOLIC, WIFE	0.044	(0.21)		
CATHOLIC, HUSBAND	0.061	(0.24)		
Sample size	114		97	

Table A1 indicates means and standard deviations of a set of variables for these two groups of women. The variable DIVORCED 1940 is defined as one if the woman's first marriage had ended by divorce or separation by the time of the 1940 survey, and is defined as zero otherwise. The table indicates that about 4 percent of these 114 women were divorced or separated by 1940. The variable DIVORCED 1950 indicates that among the same set of 114 women, by the 1950 survey approximately 12 percent had been divorced (that 12 percent includes the 4 percent already divorced by 1940). Similarly, DIVORCED 1960 indicates that about 16 percent had been divorced by 1960. These three variables have each been used as dependent variables in estimating linear and logistic relationships with the five variables SCHOOL WIFE, SCHOOL HUSBAND, AGE MARRIED, SAME RELIGION, and CATHOLIC. Table A2, Panel A, contains the estimated coefficients for each of the two groups of women.

The qualitative effects of these five variables are, generally, as expected: the probability of divorce appears to be lower for couples with both spouses sharing the same religious affiliation, with at least one of the spouses Catholic, with the wife's age at first marriage relatively high, with the husband's schooling level relatively high, and with the wife's schooling level relatively low.

The effect is quite strong for the SAME RELIGION variable. This coefficient can be interpreted as indicating that where spouses share the same religion, other things the same, the couple's probability of divorce within the first four years of marriage is twenty percentage points lower than if they had different religious affiliations. (The logistic estimates suggest a reduction of thirteen percentage points.) That effect is quantitatively quite large, persists over time, and is observed in both the samples reported in Panel A and in Panel B. The CATHOLIC variable also has a quite large coefficient throughout these estimates, but its statistical significance is lower, especially in the logistic estimates where the coefficients are also erratic.

The wife's age at marriage seems to have a small but persistent negative effect on the probability of divorce. The variable shows considerable statistical significance in the 1950 and 1960 regressions, but only in Panel A. Using the coefficient from the first column of Panel A for illustration, an increase in the age at marriage from one standard deviation below the sample mean to one standard deviation above the sample mean (i.e. from age 22.2 to age 26.8) would be associated with a five percentage point reduction in the probability of divorce by 1940 and a seventeen percentage point reduction in the probability of divorce by 1960.

We might ask how well these equations distinguish the maritally

TABLE A2

OLS Regression and Logistic Estimates of Effects of Five Variables on the Probability of Divorce by Duration of Time Since First Marriage

Explanatory variables	OLS regressions by 1940	OLS regressions by 1950	OLS regressions by 1960	Logistic functions by 1940	Logistic functions by 1950	Logistic functions by 1960
Panel A Women First Married 1-4 Years Prior to 1940 (114 Observations)						
SCHOOL, WIFE	0.0032	0.0346	0.0321	0.0040	0.0472	0.0408
	(0.29)[a]	(1.99)	(1.63)	(0.30)	(2.02)	(1.67)
SCHOOL, HUSBAND	0.0037	−0.0250	−0.0264	0.0056	−0.0299	−0.0297
	(0.47)	(−0.198)	(−1.85)	(0.59)	(−2.02)	(−1.88)
AGE, MARRIED	−0.0110	−0.0360	−0.0379	−0.0122	−0.0507	−0.0493
	(−1.34)	(−2.77)	(−2.58)	(−1.09)	(−2.50)	(−2.41)
SAME RELIGION	−0.2063	−0.2546	−0.2173	−0.1315	−0.2090	−0.1838
	(−3.64)	(−2.85)	(−2.15)	(−2.92)	(−2.45)	(−1.90)
CATHOLIC	−0.1533	−0.1246	−0.1462	−0.4552	−0.0967	−0.1344
	(−2.02)	(−1.04)	(−1.08)	(−0.11)	(−0.70)	(−0.82)
CONSTANT	0.3940	1.0648	1.1792	0.1108	0.8635	0.9166
				(0.36)	(1.62)	(1.63)
Adjusted R^2	0.086	0.116	0.082			
F	2.91	3.74	2.80			
Panel B Women First Married 5-8 Years Prior to 1940 (97 Observations)						
SCHOOL, WIFE	0.0260	0.0442	0.0563	0.0276	0.0483	0.0622
	(1.52)[a]	(1.98)	(2.39)	(1.46)	(1.88)	(2.25)
SCHOOL, HUSBAND	−0.0351	−0.0513	−0.0459	−0.0384	−0.0545	−0.0484
	(−2.84)	(−3.18)	(−2.69)	(−2.55)	(−2.92)	(−2.56)
AGE MARRIED	−0.0110	−0.0125	−0.0127	−0.0088	−0.0101	−0.0109
	(−0.73)	(−0.63)	(−0.61)	(−0.48)	(−0.44)	(−0.46)
SAME RELIGION	−0.2526	−0.3198	−0.3077	−0.2110	−0.3058	−0.3042
	(−2.50)	(−2.42)	(−2.21)	(−2.34)	(−2.33)	(−2.16)
CATHOLIC	−0.0968	−0.2321	−0.2295	−0.1036	−0.1704	−0.2680
	(−0.73)	(−1.34)	(−1.26)	(−0.78)	(−1.22)	(−1.17)
CONSTANT	0.6967	0.8390	0.5816	0.2952	0.3104	0.0245
				(0.64)	(0.53)	(0.04)
Adjusted R^2	0.097	0.107	0.084			
F	2.83	3.07	2.53			

[a] t–values in parentheses.

unstable from the maritally stable. The adjusted R^2 in the OLS regressions range between 8 and 12 percent, so one answer is that about 10 percent of the observed variation in the dependent variable is correlated with these five variables. That level of explained variance is surely not overwhelming, but neither is it exceptionally low when compared to other regression results with micro data pertaining to demographic phenomena.

To obtain an intuitive sense of the equation's ability to predict marital dissolution, the probability of divorce has been calculated using the estimating equations in Table A2 for each observation. The observations were grouped into three subgroups from each of the two samples of married women: subgroup A included only those women who had been divorced by 1940; subgroup B included those women who were maritally stable in 1940 but who were divorced by 1960; and subgroup C included those women whose first marriage had not ended in divorce or separation by 1960.

Table A3 indicates the average probability of divorce calculated from the linear and logistic functions for the women in each of these

TABLE A3

Probability of Divorce
Estimated from the OLS Regression and Logistic Estimates in Table A2, by 1940 and by 1960, for Three Groups

Group	Women married			
	1-4 years prior to 1940		5-8 years prior to 1940	
	OLS estimate	Logit estimate	OLS estimate	Logit estimate
	Using 1940 equation			
A	15.7%	22.3%	21.5%	21.1%
B	5.2	3.3	11.5	11.8
C	3.7	3.6	7.6	7.6
	Using 1960 equation			
A	29.1	30.1	34.3	34.7
B	24.0	25.7	25.1	25.5
A+B	25.4	26.9	29.4	29.9
C	14.0	13.7	17.2	17.1

Group A: those divorced by 1940.
Group B: those stable in 1940 but divorced by 1960.
Group C: those stable in 1960.

three groups. The 1940 equation from Panel A, for example, discriminated between the maritally unstable by 1940 and the maritally stable by yielding a predicted probability of dissolution of 15.7 percent for the former group and 3.7 percent for the latter. More interesting is the fact that the same equation (which was itself estimated for a dummy variable defined as one for the observations in group A and zero for the observations in groups B and C) discriminated with some success between those who were stable in 1940 but did not remain stable by 1960 (group B) and those who were stable in 1940 and who remained stable until 1960 (group C). It yielded estimated probabilities of divorce which were appreciably higher for group B in the OLS estimates, but did so for the logistic estimates only in the case of those married 5-8 years prior to 1940. Using the 1960 estimating equations from Table A2, again the unstable (A's and B's) were successfully discriminated from the stable (the C's), and here, too, the equation yielded a higher estimated probability of divorce for those who had been divorced relatively early (i.e. compare the predictions for the A's with the predictions for the B's). Here the OLS and logistic estimates yielded remarkably similar results. Lest the reader be more optimistic about the usefulness of these prediction equations than is justified, it should be noted that these estimates have quite large standard errors. We have not as yet produced a tool with which to equip marriage counselors or judges!

Several additional regressions were estimated using other information about the couples; a few of these modifications deserve mention (others are described in Michael, 1976). For the sample of women first married 1-4 years prior to 1940, the dummy variable SAME RELIGION was decomposed into five dummy variables defined as one if the spouses were BOTH CATHOLIC, BOTH JEWISH, BOTH PROTESTANT, BOTH NONE, or BOTH OTHER RELIGION. These OLS regressions are shown in Table A4 and are comparable to those in Panel A, Table A2.

A comparison of the results in Tables A4 and A2 reveals that the effects of the non-religion variables are not greatly affected by the changes in the religion variables. The religion variables themselves showed several interesting results. The magnitude of the effect of both spouses having the same religious affiliation is remarkably similar across religions in the first few years of marriage. The particular religion does not seem to matter. This result is quite understandable if the variable reflects one dimension of complementarity between spouses in a rele-

TABLE A4

OLS Regression Estimates of the Probability of Divorce by 1940 and by 1960 for Women Married 1-4 Years Prior to 1940

Explanatory variable	Probability of divorce by 1940		by 1960	
SCHOOL, WIFE	0.0090	0.0076	0.0409	0.0398
	(0.83)	(0.72)	(2.02)	(1.94)
SCHOOL, HUSBAND	0.0054	0.0071	−0.0284	−0.0274
	(0.69)	(0.95)	(−1.97)	(−1.87)
AGE MARRIED	−0.0133	−0.0111	−0.0408	−0.0392
	(−1.65)	(−1.42)	(−2.74)	(−2.56)
BOTH CATHOLIC	−0.2407	0.2827	−0.3870	−0.1157
	(−2.03)	(1.43)	(−1.76)	(−0.30)
BOTH JEWISH	−0.2254	−0.3090	0.0291	−0.0110
	(−1.94)	(−2.72)	(0.13)	(−0.04)
BOTH PROTESTANT	−0.2453	−0.3282	−0.2515	−0.2909
	(−5.09)	(−6.38)	(−2.82)	(−2.89)
BOTH NO RELIGION	−0.2505	−0.3349	−0.1582	−0.1986
	(−4.13)	(−5.35)	(−1.41)	(−1.62)
BOTH OTHER RELIGION	−0.2746	−0.3513	−0.2680	−0.3030
	(−2.82)	(−3.69)	(−1.49)	(−1.63)
CATHOLIC, WIFE		−0.2839		−0.1749
		(−2.05)		(−0.65)
CATHOLIC, HUSBAND		−0.3178		−0.1330
		(−3.17)		(−0.68)
CONSTANT	0.3457	0.3707	1.1318	1.1329
Adjusted R^2	0.170	0.246	0.104	0.093
F	3.73	4.55	2.49	2.04

vant nonmarket trait. However, while the effect of the SAME RELIGION in the regressions in Table A2 suggests a relatively constant partial effect as time passes, a comparison of columns 1 and 3 in Table A4 reveals that, in this sample at least, the stabilising influence differs considerably among religions over time. In particular, the Catholic couples are persistently more stable while the stabilising effect of religion for Jewish couples especially is not evidenced at all over the entire 21-24 year period. The result for Catholics is explained, I think, by the effect of the Catholic religion on the costs of dissolution. If the full cost of marital dissolution is higher for couples of the Catholic faith, that higher cost probably does not decline appreciably over the lifetime. So the cost of divorcing imposed by Catholicism presumably persists over time, while the similarity in interests or the absence of conflict present in other marriages of like-religion spouses might deteriorate over time.

The second and fourth columns of Table A4 decompose the Catholic-religion effect into the partial effect on stability of each spouse's being Catholic. The results indicate that there is very little difference in terms of the probability of divorce whether the wife or the husband is Catholic – the partial effects in the first four years of marriage are -0.28 and -0.32, respectively. Results for 1940 imply the somewhat surprising conclusion that there is no additional effect of both spouses' being Catholic – the partial effect of *both* spouses being Catholic given that one spouse is Catholic is approximately zero.[17] In the 1960 regression the effects of the three Catholic variables are considerably weaker.

An additional, closely related regression might be mentioned here. Terman gave a 'marital happiness' test to the subjects in 1940, based on his own extensive research on marriage. For the 109 maritally-stable couples in 1940 from the sub-group of women married one to four years before 1940, the same five variables used in Table A2 were regressed on the marital happiness scores of the subjects.[18] The regression results were:

$$\begin{aligned}\text{Marital happiness score} = {} & 84.5 \underset{(-2.8)}{-\ 2.6\ (\text{SCHOOL, WIFE})} \underset{(1.4)}{+\ 0.9\ (\text{SCHOOL, HUSBAND})} \\ & \underset{(0.6)}{+0.5\ (\text{AGE MARRIED})} \underset{-(0.7)}{-\ 3.5\ (\text{SAME RELIGION})} \\ & \underset{(-3.5)}{-22.5\ (\text{CATHOLIC})} \quad \bar{R}^2 = 0.12 \quad F = 3.71. \\ & \qquad (t \text{ in parentheses})\end{aligned}$$

The Catholic variable was very strongly negatively related to the marital happiness score. That is what one might have expected. Other variables which adversely affect the success of the marriage, e.g. AGE MARRIED, would presumably lead to divorce and among those still married one would not expect a strong relationship with a true 'marital happiness' score. But the Catholic vaiiable is related to the *cost* of divorce. At a given level of marital dissatisfaction, a Catholic couple would not be expected to divorce as readily as a non-Catholic couple. So among those still married one would expect a lower average score for Catholics on a marital happiness scale. That phenomenon is very much in evidence here.

Notes

1. Constructing the marital success index proved a manageable task, but the subsequent lack of attention paid to the predicting equations is testimony to their very limited usefulness. These studies include Terman's (1938) study of some 400 variables affecting the marital happiness of a group of 800 married couples surveyed in the mid-1930s; Burgess and Cottrell's (1939) sociological study of some 500 couples surveyed in 1931-33; and a study of several hundred married and divorced couples surveyed between 1938 and 1944 by Locke (1951). Also see Terman and Wallin (1949).

2. This section draws heavily on the analytical section of Becker, Landes and Michael (1977).

3. Notice that schooling level is not included in this list of potential variables. The reason is that schooling has two offsetting effects yielding no clear implication for marriage stability. An increase in the schooling levels of the husband and wife raises their income thus *raising* the gains from marriage, but it also reduces one of the important divisions of labor between spouses (by increasing the likelihood that both spouses are employed in the market) thus *lowering* the gains from marriage.

4. Another obvious reason for the observed decline in the probability of divorce with marriage duration is cohort attrition – if couples initially differ in their likelihood of divorce, those with the highest probability will tend to divorce in the early years leaving a pool of married couples with a lower and lower average probability of divorce.

5. This linear probability model also has the well-known inconvenient property that the predicted linear relationship is not bounded at probabilities between zero and one. An often-used traansformation which converts the continuous variable bounded by 0 and 1.0 into a continuous, unbounded variable is $\ln(P_t/1 - P_t)$ and frequently equation (4) is formulated as

$$\ln\left(\frac{P_t}{1-P_t}\right) = \alpha + \sum_i \beta_{ti} Y_i + u_t,$$

where the estimated coefficients β_{ti} can be used to calculate the intuitively interpretable b_{ti}.

6. With N_0 the number of couples at risk of divorce at the beginning of the period and N_t the number still married at the end of the period, we can define r as the 'continuous rate of divorce' in

$$N_t = N_0 e^{-rt}.$$

If the probability of divorce in the two-year period $P = (N_0 - N_t)/N_0$, then $P = 1 - e^{-rt}$ and $r = (\partial P/\partial t)/((1 - P)$. Whereas equation (4) puts P on the left-hand side of the equation, TGH put r on the left-hand side.

7. These estimates require several assumptions in transforming the regression coefficient shown in Table A2 to the number in the text. Let p be the yearly

probability of divorce, and assume it constant from year to year with behavior represented by a Bernoulli process. Then, the probability of divorce in n years, P_n, is

$$P_n = 1 - (1-p)^n \tag{F1}$$

and

$$\frac{\partial P_n}{\partial AM} = n(1-p)^{n-1} \frac{\partial p}{\partial AM}, \tag{F2}$$

where the left-hand side derivative is estimated by the age-at-marriage (AM) coefficient in the divorce regression on the probability of divorce over an n-year period. Thus, for the coefficient in Table A2, column 1, $\partial P_n / \partial AM = -0.0110$ for $n = 2.5$ years and mean $\bar{P}_n = 0.044$. So $\bar{p} = 0.01784$ $(= 1 - (1-P)^{1/n})$, and substituting into (F2) for n, for $\partial P_n / \partial AM$ and for $\bar{p}$ implies $\partial p / \partial AM = -0.0045$, the estimate of a one-year increase in AM on the fixed annual probability of divorce. Then substituting into

$$\frac{\partial P_n}{\partial AM} (dAM) = n(1-\bar{p})^{n-1} \frac{\partial p}{\partial AM} (dAM) \tag{F3}$$

for $n = 4$ and $dAM = 5$ years yields -0.085, the estimate of the effect over a four-year period. Similarly, the coefficient for the period $n = 22.5$ in column 3 of Table A2 is -0.0379 with $\bar{P}_n = 0.158$, hence $\bar{p} = 0.0076$ and $\partial p / \partial AM = -0.0020$; so for $n = 4$ and $dAM = 5$ years the estimated effect over a four-year period from this regression is -0.039, or about a 4.0 percentage-point reduction.

8. All three of these summary statements require amplification. Regarding the New Jersey IME effect, I calculated (\$20) (–0.0023) from p. 68 assuming \$20 per week to reflect an annual \$1.000. The RS result is very small and insignificant, but their regression has many other income measures included as well; moreover, an index of the family's asset position did show a significant negative effect. The TGH result is reflected in their Table A–1 (p. 46).

9. It is difficult at best to interpret the separate effects of as many closely related variables as were used by TGH. None of their wage or schooling effects for whites is statistically significant. The New Jersey IME results in SPJC's study showed a stabilizing effect of wife's earnings on the likelihood of divorce, but here, too, the effect was not robust.

10. This latter effect holds for two of the three levels of support for which it was tested. Incidentally, the TGH paper reports all results in percentage terms and, so far as I can see, nowhere indicates any results (even the mean level of divorce for the reference group) in actual levels.

11. This partial effect of region is observed holding the head of household's age at first marriage constant. Another recent study of cross-state differences in rates of divorce attributed much of the higher divorce rate in the West to the lower age at first marriage in the West (see Weed, 1974). Michael (1977) has suggested that the fact that the West has nearly twice as large a percentage of second marriages as the East can explain much of the observed difference in

regional divorce rates; this factor might explain the RS result as well. RS include second as well as first marriages in their sample, but define 'duration of marriage' as the time lapsed since the beginning of the first marriage. Thus, the Western region dummy variable is a proxy both for living in the West and being much more likely to be in a second marriage at a considerably shorter duration of current marriage. Therefore, the five-percentage-point higher probability of divorce in the West may in large part simply reflect the shorter average duration of the marriages under observation in the West.

12. I have no simple explanation for the reversed racial differential in the East and in the West. There is some recent evidence in McCarthy (1977) that the marriage duration-specific divorce rates for blacks decline with marriage order while rising for whites (i.e. for whites the probability of divorce is higher in the third year of the second marriage than in the third year of the first marriage, but the opposite is true for blacks). If that finding is accurate, then the higher proportion of second marriages in the West would have different effects for blacks than whites and may help explain this interaction of race and region in RS's data.

Incidentally, in an earlier, interim report Hannan, Tuma and Groeneveld (1976) indicated considerably higher (40 percent higher) unadjusted rates of divorce for blacks than for whites (Table 6–1, p. 60 of their report).

13. Michael (1977) investigates the US time series divorce rate. The following paragraphs rely heavily on that study. An additional recent analysis of US time series divorce rates is a cohort analysis over nearly 100 years by Preston and McDonald (1976).

14. This appendix is a condensation of much of the material in an unpublished NBER Working Paper, no. 147, August 1976. A copy of that working paper is available upon request.

15. The analysis of these data by Professor Terman and his associates is reported in a several-volume study entitled *Genetic Studies of Genius,* edited by Lewis M. Terman (1925-1959). Incidentally, this is a wholly independent sample from the one used in Terman's study of *Psychological Factors in Marital Success* (Terman, 1938).

16. This is strictly true of the age at marriage variable only, but religious affiliation is not likely to be altered by experience in marriage. The schooling levels are somewhat more troublesome since marriage prior to the completion of formal schooling is not unusual. We will assume that the level of schooling attained by 1940 for couples wo married in the eight years prior to 1940 was determined prior to marriage. A recent study by Davis and Bumpass (1976) indicates the extent of post-marriage schooling from the 1970 NFS data. They found that about 20 percent of white women married since 1950 had attended school since marriage for an average of about one year.

17. The total effect of both spouses being Catholic is the sum of the three coefficients on the Catholic dummy variables. The partial effect of the wife's being Catholic given that the other spouse is Catholic is the sum of the two coefficients on CATHOLIC, WIFE and BOTH CATHOLIC.

18. The scores were scaled from 0 to 100 and for these 109 observations the mean and standard deviation were 64.2 and 17.5. The correlation between the subjects' 1940 marital happiness score and marital dissolution was quite high: –0.26 and –0.25 for divorce dummies for 1950 and 1960, respectively.

References

BECKER, G. S. (1965) 'A Theory of the Allocation of Time', *Economic Journal* 73 (September)

––, (1974) 'A Theory of Marriage', in: T. W.. SCHULTZ (ed.), *Economics of the Family*. Chicago: University of Chicago Press.

––, E. H. LANDES and R. T. MICHAEL (1977) 'Economics of Marital Instability', *Journal of Political Economy* 83 (December).

BURGESS, E. W. and L. S. COTTRELL, Jr. (1939) *Predicting Success or Failure in Marriage*, New York: Prentice-Hall, Inc.

CARTER, H. and P. C. GLICK (1970) *Marriage and Divorce: A Social Economic Study*. Vital and Health Statistics Monographs, American Public Health Association, Cambridge, MA: Harvard University Press.

DAVIS, N. J. and L. BUMPASS (1976) 'The Continuation of Education after Marriage among Women in the United States: 1970', *Demography* 13 (May).

HANNAN, M., N. TUMA and L. P. GROENEVELD (1976) 'The Impact of Income Maintenance on the Making and Breaking of Marital Unions: An Interim Report on the First Eighteen Months of the Seattle and Denver Income Maintenance Experiment', Center for the Study of Welfare Policy, Stanford Research Institute, Research Memorandum 28 (June).

HICKS, M. W. and M. PLATT (1970) 'Marital Happiness and Stability: A Review of the Research in the Sixties', *Journal of Marriage and the Family* 32 (November).

JACOBSON, P. H. (1959) *American Marriage and Divorce*. New York: Rinehart and Co.

LEVINGER, G. (1965) 'Marital Cohesiveness and Dissolution: An Integrative Review', *Journal of Marriage and the Family* 27 (February).

LOCKE, H. J. (1951) *Predicting Adjustment in Marriage: A Comparison of a Divorced and a Happily Married Group*. New York: Henry Holt and Company.

McCARTHY, J. F. (1977) 'A Comparison of Dissolution of First and Second Marriages', mimeo. Office of Population Research, Princeton University (presented at the 1977 Annual Meetings of the Population Association).

MICHAEL, R. T. (1976) 'Factors Affecting Divorce: A Study of the Terman Sample', NBER Working Paper 147 (August).

––, (1977) 'Why Has the Divorce Rate Doubled Within the Decade?', mimeo National Bureau of Economic Research (June).

MINCER, J. (1963) 'Market Prices, Opportunity Costs, and Income Effects', in: C. CHRIST (ed.), *Measurement in Economics*. Stanford, California: Stanford University Press.

PLATERIS, A. A. (1973) *100 Years of Marriage and Divorce Statistics*, Series 21, no. 24. National Center for Health Statistics, Washington D.C.: Government Printing Office.

PRESTON, S. H. and J. McDONALD (1976) 'The Incidence of Divorce Within Cohorts of American Marriages Contracted Since the Civil War', mimeo. Center for Studies in Demography and Ecology, University of Washington.

ROSS, H. L. and I. V. SAWHILL (1975) *Time of Transition, the Growth of Families Headed by Women.* Washington,D.C.: The Urban Institute.

SAWHILL, I. V., G. E. PEABODY, C. A. JONES and S. B. CALDWELL (1975) *Income Transfers in Family Structure.* Washington, D.C.: The Urban Institute.

SCHOEN, R. and V. E. NELSON (1974) 'Marriage, Divorce, and Mortality: A Life Table Analysis', *Demography* 11 (May).

TERMAN, L. M. (1925-59) *Genetic Studies of Genius,* Volumes I-V. Stanford: Stanford University Press, 1925, 1926, 1930, 1947, and 1959, respectively.

--, (1938) *Psychological Factors in Marital Happiness.* New York: McGraw-Hill Book Company, Inc.

--, and P. WALLIN (1949) 'The Validity of Marriage Prediction and Marriage Adjustment Tests', *American Sociological Review* 14.

TUMA, N. B., L. P. GROENEVELD and M. HANNAN (1976) 'First Dissolutions and Marriages: Impacts in 24 months of the Seattle and Denver Income Maintenance Experiments', Center for the Study of Welfare Policy, Stanford Research Institute, Research Memorandum 35 (August).

WEED, J. A. (1974) 'Age at Marriage as a Factor in State Divorce Rate Differentials', *Demography* 11 (August).

• Comment

Reuben Gronau

Hebrew University, Jerusalem, Israel

I fully share Robert Michael's belief in the importance of the economic analysis of marital instability. Indeed, one can only deplore the fact that economists have not done more to analyse the mechanisms of divorce. The purpose of Michael's paper is not to propound a detailed economic theory of divorce (something he has already attempted elsewhere) but rather to report on some recent findings on the factors affecting divorce. However, it is difficult to judge these findings without having a solid theory in the background.

Inherent in Michael's brief analytical discussions is the notion that divorce should be regarded as the reverse of marriage. Thus, factors that affect gains from marriage favorably should have a deterrent effect on divorce. To use an analogy from the labor market, if marriage corresponds to entry into the labor force, divorce corresponds to exit from it. However, this approach ignores the fact that about half the divorced remarry. The decision involved in divorce is not whether to be married, but whether to stay married to a certain person. To return to our analogy, divorce must be discussed in terms of labor turnover rather than in terms of exit from the labor force.

The timing of divorce depends on changes in the gains from marriage over time (i.e. with age and duration of marriage). Let it be assumed that gains from marriage vary with age, a, and duration of marriage m. Let $X(a, m)$ and $Y(a, m)$ denote the gains from being married to persons X (say, the present spouse) and Y, respectively. Let $C(a)$ denote the cost of divorce at age a (I assume that this cost is independent of the duration of marriage).

The present value gains from marrying person X now (call it age 0), divorcing him at age t and marrying person Y is

$$V(t) = \sum_{k=0}^{t-1} q^k X(k, k) + q^t \left[\sum_{k=0}^{T-t} q^k Y(k+t, k) - C(t) \right],$$

where q is the discount factor and T is the person's horizon. The benefits from divorcing person X at age t rather than at age $t+1$ are

$$V(t) - V(t+1) = q^t \left\{ -X(t, t) + \left[\sum_{k=0}^{T-t} q^k Y(k+t, k) - \sum_{k=1}^{T-t} q^k Y(k+t, k-1) \right] + [qC(t+1) - C(t)] \right\}.$$

The decision whether to postpone the divorce by one year depends on the gains (positive or negative) from the current marriage, the loss from postponing the future marriage, and the effect of postponement on the cost of divorce.

If the gains are independent of the duration of marriage and depend only on age,

$$V(t) - V(t+1) = q^t \left\{ [Y(t) - X(t)] + [qC(t+1) - C(t)] \right\},$$

i.e. the person takes into account only the gains from being married to person Y (rather than X) in period t and the cost of postponing his divorce by one year. If the gains from marriage depend solely on its duration,

$$V(t) - V(t+1) = q^t \left\{ \left[-(q-1) \sum_{k=0}^{T-t-1} q^k Y(k) + q^{T-t} Y(T-t) - X(t) \right] + [qC(t+1) - C(t)] \right\},$$

i.e. the person takes into account both the postponement of costs and gains and the curtailment of the gains from his future marriage.

Let t be the optimum date of divorce [i.e. $V(t) > V(k)$ for any $0 < k \leqslant T$] then the person will opt for divorce only if

$$\sum_{k=0}^{T-t} q^k \left[Y(t+k, k) - X(t+k, t+k)\right] - C(t) > 0.$$

In his paper, Robert Michael defines the necessary condition for divorce but not its optimum timing (to use his notation, $M_{t+k} < 0$ does not imply that the person will divorce in period $t + k$). Furthermore, factors which have a negative effect on the gains from marriage will be conducive to divorce only if the person expects that they will not interfere with his next marriage. For example, if the husband has low earnings (and therefore gets less benefits from marriage) there is nothing to assure him of greater benefits from his future marriage, unless he expects to become rich. For similar reasons it is not clear why women with high earnings or people who are hasty searchers should be more prone to divorce than others.

In summary, Robert Michael's paper fulfils an important purpose in reporting on recent research on the determinants of divorce. One would wish, however, that this important empirical work were accompanied by theoretical work of the same quality. It seems to me that economic theory has yet to perfect the tools for the analysis of marital instability.

• Comment

Bertrand Lemennicier

University of Paris IX, France

Robert Michael's paper provides a very useful summary of the economists' recent interest in the determinants of divorce both from the theoretical and empirical point of view. As I have no disagreement with the underlying theory, my discussion will be centered around the following question: to what extent does the economic approach of marital dissolution fit the French data on divorce?

First, I shall sketch the basic framework of the economic theory of marital dissolution through a graphical analysis. This will be helpful in understanding the prediction drawn from it. Figure 1 illustrates the economic argument on divorce. The horizontal axis and the vertical axis show respectively the number of marital dissolutions and the marginal gains or costs of divorce. The MGD line shows the marginal gain from divorce. It is the difference between the future expected net benefit from a marriage, $E(BM_f)$, and the net benefit from the present marital status (single or married), BM_p. This difference decreases with the number of divorces. The more a person experiments with new mates over his life cycle the higher is his net benefit from the last marriage and the less is the marginal gain from a new divorce. The MCD line shows the marginal costs of marital dissolution. These costs are assumed independent of the number of divorces. Hence, a person will marry and remarry (or divorce) as long as the marginal gains of divorce exceed marginal costs. Consequently what causes divorces is whatever causes:

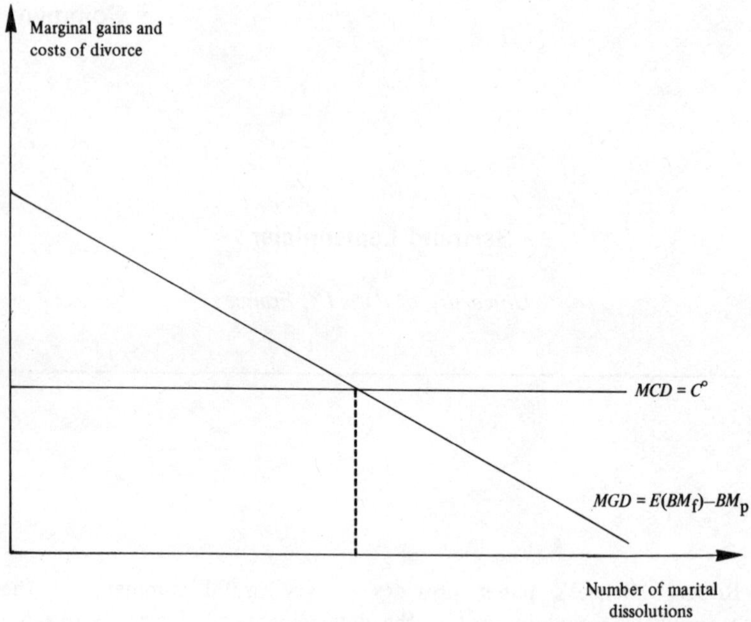

Figure 1

(1) an increase in the future expected net benefit from a marriage with a new mate; and (2) a decrease in the net benefit from the present marital status or in the costs of divorce. Now let me comment on the empirical findings raised by Michael and present some French data drawn from a survey conducted at INED by Boigeol, Commaille, Lamy, Monnier and Roussel (1974) (see also Roussel, 1975).

Age at marriage

Figure 2 shows a negative relationship between the probability of divorce and age at marriage holding constant the duration of marriage. Refer back to Figure 1. A simple explanation can be found to this negative relation. At younger ages net benefits from marriage are low

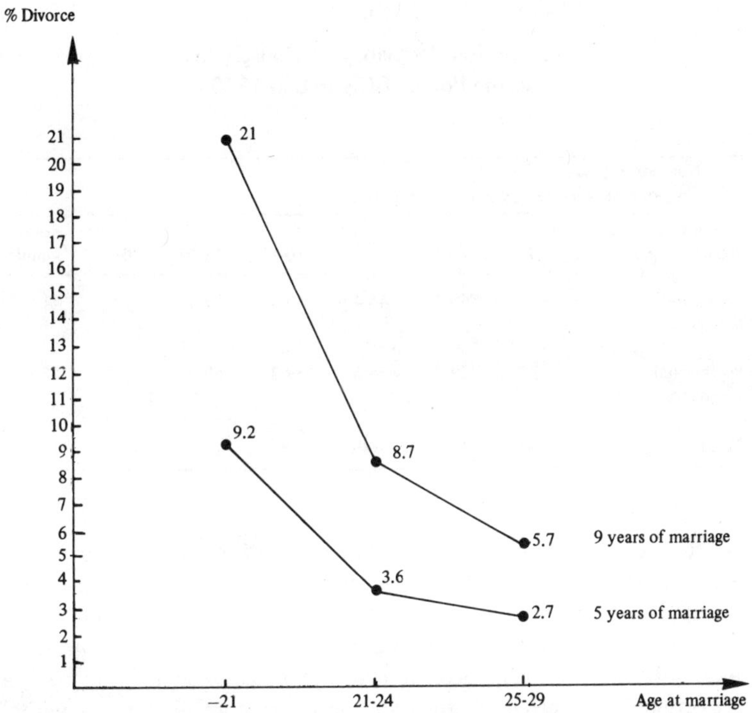

Figure 2. Divorce and age at Marriage – Paris, 1960

because of the low market productivity of spouses. By contrast, the expected net benefits from another potential mate are higher. Then the marginal gain from divorce is higher for young persons than for old ones. The MGD line shifts to the right and the probability of marital dissolution increases. This is why Becker, Landes and Michael (1977) argue that 'the young are less informed about themselves, their mates and the marriage market'. At younger ages the amount of search is less than optimal. This is one reason for the negative relationship. Another is the lack of human capital investment in market productivity at young ages which reduces the gain from marriage. But an interesting argument is put forward by Roussel (1975). Table 1 shows premarital pregnancy by duration of marriage.

TABLE 1
Pre-Marital Pregnancy of Households on the Point of Divorce in 1970

Number of years of marriage / Pre- or post-marital pregnancy	Duration of marriage (years) 0-1	2-4	5-9	10-14	15-19	20+	Total sample
Premarital pregnancy	87.3	60.3	45.4	40.3	39.6	27.5	44.2
Postmarital pregnancy	12.7	39.7	54.6	59.7	60.8	72.5	55.8
Total	100	100	100	100	100	100	100

A correlation between age at marriage and premarital pregnancy appears. The negative relationship observed in Figure 2 would reflect 'compulsory' marriage. Then the net benefit from marital union becomes negative and increases the marginal gain of divorce. The MGD line shifts to the right. Age at marriage is, consequently, in part, a reflection of another factor. We have to control for premarital pregnancy to test the effect of the age at marriage. This is done in the BLM study. The result shows that age at marriage has a negative effect for which the *t* statistic is significant.

Income of wives

An increase in the wife's income leads to a decline in the husband's gains from marriage as there is less specialization. Consequently, the gains from the present marital status fall. At the same time the gains from divorce and remarriage increase because the wife's labor force participation raises the opportunities to find potential mates. The MGD line shifts to the right. The evidence available shows that an increase in the labor supply of wives is maritally destabilizing. Table 2 gives the labor force participation rates for divorced women in 1970 and for married women in 1968: 68.3 percent of divorced women were engaged in market activities, as against 34 percent for married women.

TABLE 2

Rates of Labor Force Participation

Population \ Age	−20	20–24	25–29	30–34	35–39	40–44	45–49	50–59	60+	Total
Divorced women 1970	57.9	71.6	71.3	69	64.8	63.2	61.6	55.3	37.6	68.3
Married women 1968		51.2	43.1	37	35.6	37.4	39	36.6		34

This is a well-known result. But its interpretation is not so easy. The supply of female labor reduces the gains from specialization in conjugal roles and increases the opportunity for divorce through access to a market of potential mates. This is the argument that economists favor. In contrast, sociologists argue that women who are engaged in market activities are freer to choose divorce than women at home. The costs of divorce are lower for women at work than for those at home. The MCD line shifts downwards. Such an argument is confirmed by Table 3. It shows which of husband and wife seek the divorce. We observe that among couples engaged in a double career 70.5 percent of wives seek a divorce as against only 58 percent of women at home.

TABLE 3

Spouse Decision to Divorce

Who decides	Wife at work	Wife at home	Wives
Husband	29.5	41.7	33
Wife	70.5	58.3	67
Total	100	100	100

Number of children

The impact of the number of children appears to be negative. Figure 3 illustrates this relation. Holding the duration of marriage constant, Roussel (1975) found a difference between the standard population and the divorced one. An increase in the number of children increases the benefit from present marital status (through the production of specific human capital in the household). The MGD line shifts to the left. Consequently the probability of divorce is lower.

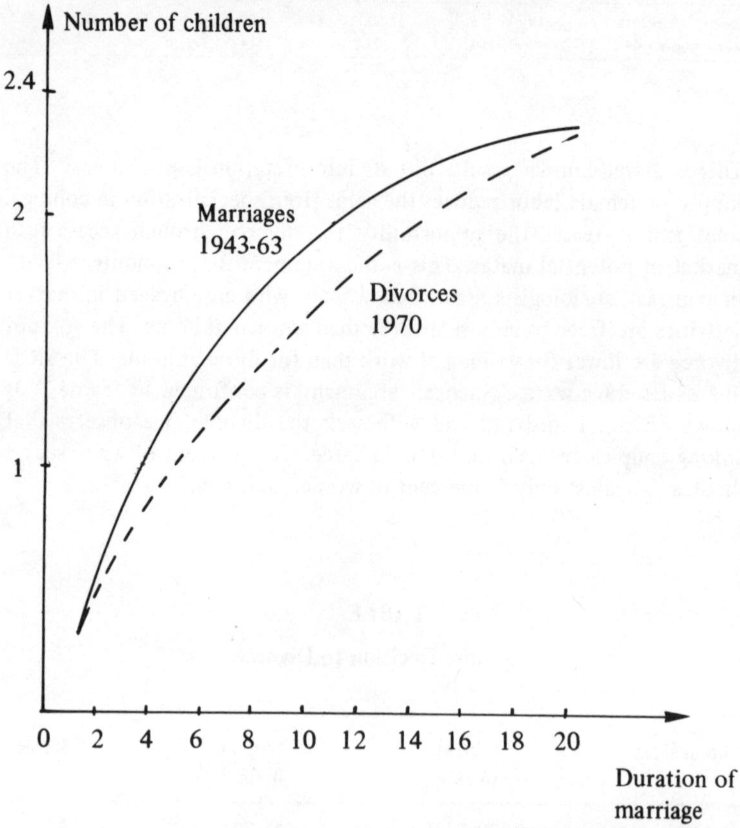

Figure 3. Cumulative number of children associated with the divorced population in 1970 and the married population from 1943 to 1963 (means per 100 women).

Other factors

Couples living in densely populated city centers have a higher probability of divorce. Of the people who divorced in 1970, 21.8 percent were living in Paris. The lower cost of divorce, and the higher opportunity of finding a better mate explain the difference between Paris and the rest of France. But this finding also reflects the correlation between rates of labor force participation of women and rates of divorce as in large cities greater market career opportunities are available. In 1968 the labor force participation rate of married women was 34 percent for the whole of France while for Paris it was 45 percent.

TABLE 4

Participation in Religious Activities

Religious activities \ Population	Divorced (%)	Standard population (%)
Without religion	9	12
No participation	51	37
Occasional participation	25	29
Participate *regularly*	15	22

The negative relationship between participation in religious activities (Catholic) and divorce is well known in the sociological literature. Table 4 shows that there is a higher proportion of people who do not participate in religious activities and a lower proportion of people who participate regularly in the divorced population than in the standard one. The Catholic religion lowers the expectation of net benefits from a new marriage with a potential mate. The MGD line shifts to the left and the probability of dissolving a marriage is drastically reduced.

An increase in education has an ambiguous effect. It is positively correlated with the family income which lowers the probability of divorce. But it is also positively correlated with the labor force participation rate of women and negatively correlated with the number of children, which would increase the probability of divorce. The data for France show that we find a lower proportion of persons who have a high level of education in the divorced population than in the standard one (see Table 5, the difference in proportion is not very strong). On the one hand, education reduces the net gain from marriage as it involves less specialization and less investment in spouse-specific capital like children. On the other hand, the level of education increases the net gain from marriage through an increase in income. Education has two countervailing influences on the probability of divorce.

TABLE 5

Educational Level

Population / Education	Divorced (%)	Standard population (%)
Low level	74	70
High level	26	30
Total	100	100

We have no empirical evidence on the effects of unforeseen events (except premarital pregnancy in Table 1) – one of the most important predictions of the marital search economic model – but we do have some data on remarriage. Figure 4 (a)-(c) shows the percentage of remarriages among the divorced population associated with age at divorce (a), the level of schooling (c) and the number of children (b).

The probability of remarriage depends directly on the expected net gains from marriage with a new mate. As the net gains of marriage are greater when the differential between male and female earnings is greater, the probability of remarriage is postively correlated with male earnings and negatively correlated with female earnings (see Becker, 1973). As schooling levels are a good proxy for earnings, Figure 4 (c) corroborates this argument. The probability of remarriage decreases with the educational level of women, while it increases for men. Children increase the net gain of the present marital status as they

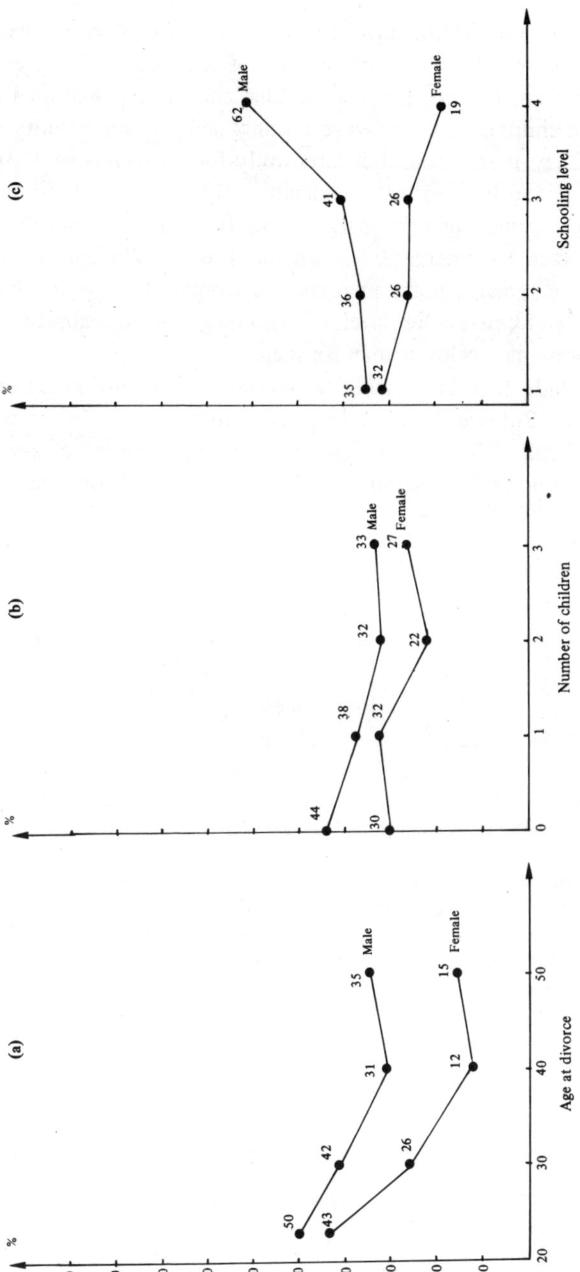

Figure 4. Number of remarriages per 100 divorced persons

represent a spouse-specific investment in human capital. We expect, then, that children lower the probability of remarriage. This seems to be true for men, but not for women. One current explanation is that women with children have low wage earnings and low opportunity costs of search. They therefore search intensively for a new husband. Age at divorce is obviously negatively associated with the probability of remarriage. At younger ages the marginal gain from marriage is higher. An interesting fact to emerge from Figure 4 is the difference in the probability of remarriage for men and for women. For age at divorce, number of children or for level of schooling, the probability of remarriage for women is lower than for men.

We conclude that the marital search model 'explains' much of the French data. But we have to be very cautions with the empirical evidence presented here, as we face the difficult problem of assessing the effect of one variable without holding 'other things' constant.

References

BECKER, G. S. (1973) 'A Theory of Marriage' *Journal of Political Economy* 81 (July-August) and 82 (March-April 1974).

––, E. LANDES, and R. T. MICHAEL (1977) 'The Economics of Marital Instability', *Journal of Political Economy* 85 (November-December).

BOIGEL, A., J. COMMAILLE, M. L. LAMY, A. MONNIER and L. ROUSSEL (1974) *Le Divorce et les Français* INED, no. 71-72, Paris: Presses Universitaires de France.

ROUSSEL, L. (1975) *Le Mariage dans la Société Française* INED, no. 73, Paris: Presses Universitaires de France.

9

Profits, Optimality, and the Social Division of Labor in the Firm

Herbert Gintis and Donald W. Katzner

University of Massachusetts, USA

Neoclassical theory has traditionally taken the production function as an exogenous datum reflecting the technical structure of production (Samuelson, 1947: 57; Ferguson, 1971: 7). Hence, little effort has been expended on the analysis of the production process itself.[1] Yet surprisingly powerful theorems follow from this hypothesis according to the microeconomic logic of profit maximization. Certainly the most central of these theorems is that the profit-maximizing firm will choose Pareto-optimal production under normal conditions.

But in general, there is no reason to suppose that a profit-maximizing entrepreneur will make profit-maximizing decisions which are also in the best interests of his workers. In any given circumstance, therefore, it may be possible to make workers better off without reducing profits. Such a situation can not be Pareto optimal. Nor is there an obvious mechanism, such as competition, operating within the firm which automatically leads it to optimality. Indeed, by modeling the firm as a complex collection of social relationships, we shall suggest that the neoclassical assertions concerning optimality in the firm hold only under restrictive and highly unrealistic assumptions. Specifically, profit-maximization need not always result in the optimal allocation of human resources.

This observation calls into question a number of derivative but socially critical propositions often expressed as follows. First, the structure of authoritarian relations in the firm will be Pareto optimal. Secondly, wage differentials will reflect differences in the marginal productivity of workers in specified jobs. Thirdly, worker sovereignty will obtain in the same sense, and under the same conditions, as the more traditional consumer sovereignty (Gintis, 1972). That is, the overall constellation of jobs in the economy will reflect the trade-off of workers between wages and job satisfaction, given an initial distribution of talents, skills, and material wealth. From these propositions arise some of the most fundamental perspectives on modern society gleaned from neoclassical economics. The first implies that production is socially neutral, in the sense that it is independent of property relations, class structure, and the mode of social control of economic life. The social relations of the enterprise are technologically determinate and ensure high productivity. From the second, it is deduced that wage inequality results from the differences in technically-relevant attributes of individuals. In particular, capitalism exhibits a strong tendency toward 'meritocracy', whereby individuals attain economic positions based on their 'achievements' alone independently of such ascriptive characteristics as race, sex, social class background and ethnic origin. Thus, persistent differences in economic outcomes across ascriptively distinct groups are imputed to differences in tastes, abilities, or opportunities of skill-acquisition. The third implies that the historical development of work corresponds, within the limits imposed by science and technology, to the preferences of workers. If work is less than satisfying, it is because most workers prefer higher incomes to more satisfying jobs. These views are not part of the picture emerging below.

We start by supposing that the firm relies on authoritative rather than market allocations of human activity. Coase (1937) and Simon (1957b) also introduce authority into the operation of the firm but argue that optimality would result provided that the entrepeneur (a) lets the market allocate those elements which it does so efficiently, and (b) allocates through entrepreneurial authority those which it cannot. This approach, however, assumes that once the contract between entrepreneur and worker is settled, the latter tells the former exactly what to do. The worker either does it or finds another job. But contracts are not explicit enough, nor are capitalists' powers sufficiently encompassing to dictate a worker's attitudes, his values, his relations with his superiors, subordinates and co-workers, the manner in which he discharges his responsibilities, and so on. Yet all of these factors influence the output and hence profits of the firm. Thus, our analysis differs from Coase and Simon in that the worker is permitted to choose these factors for himself subject to the constraints imposed by authority. Market allocations are not considered.

More precisely, this paper develops an alternative model of the hierarchical division of labor within the firm. At its heart is the commitment to treat all actors in the enterprise, not only the capitalist, as maximizing an objective function subject to constraints. The model is then used to investigate the conditions under which profit maximization leads to Pareto optimality. Theorems also are developed relating profit levels to preference orderings and skills among workers. The beginnings of a mathematical theory of organizational structure in the firm are obtained thereby.[2]

It is clear that many of the questions to be addressed below cannot be discussed in a totally quantifiable setting. Variables such as human attitudes and human values seem to defy numerical representation. Values of these variables, i.e. realizations of specific human attitudes and human values which might arise, have to be handled in abstract set-theoretic terms. Furthermore, we must be sure that, even in the absence of measurement, the structure relations of the model are internally consistent and determinant. Previous methodological investigations by Katzner (1973, 1976) have pointed the way towards handling these kinds of technical problems and our analysis rests squarely on them.

A model of the production process

We define the *job set* of the firm as $J = \{1, \ldots, n\}$ for a specified integer $n \geqslant 1$. The *job structure* of the firm represents the organizational hierarchy of authority within the firm, and will be described in terms of a relation ρ on J where $j_1 \rho j_2$ for j_1, j_2 in J should be interpreted as j_1 lies not below j_2 in authority. The job set and the job structure are taken as given. We also require ρ to be reflexive and transitive, and to possess the pyramidal property: For any j_1, j_2, j_3 in J, if $j_2 \rho j_1$ and $j_3 \rho j_1$, and if it is not the case that $j_1 \rho j_2$ and $j_1 \rho j_3$ then either (a) $j_2 \rho j_3$ and not $j_3 \rho j_2$, or (b) $j_3 \rho j_2$ and not $j_2 \rho j_3$.

Consider a collection of *workers* $W = \{1, \ldots, n\}$. An *assignment function* $K{:}J \rightarrow W$, one-to-one and order preserving, is assumed as given.

K then associates each worker with a particular job and induces a hierarchical relation $\geqslant$ on W such that $K(j_1) \geqslant K(j_2)$ if and only if $j_1 \rho j_2$. If w and z are in W and $w \geqslant z$ but $z \not\geqslant w$, we write $w > z$. If $w > z$, we say *w is (directly or indirectly) superior to z in authority*, and *z is (directly or indirectly) subordinate to w*. If $w \geqslant z$ and $w > z$, we write $w \sim z$ and say *w and z are co-workers.*.

Let w be in W. Define

$$\underline{S}_w = z \text{ in } W : w > z\} ,$$

and

$$\overline{S}^w = \{ z \text{ in } W : z > w \} .$$

Let S_w be the set of maximal elements of $\underline{S}_w$ and S^w the minimal elements of $\overline{S}^w$. Thus, S_w is the set of immediate subordinates of w, and S^w is the set of immediate superiors of w. Now set

$$C_w = \{ z \text{ in } W : z \sim w \} ,$$

that is, C_w is the set of co-workers of w. It is clear that while every worker has at most a single immediate superior, he may have more than one immediate subordinate.

Assume each worker w possesses a non-empty act set A_w contained in an act space $\mathscr{A}$, such that for any a_w in A_w, w is capable of performing act a_w and performance falls within the terms of the worker's contract with the employer. We do not require the elements of A_w to be in any way quantifiable. Define $A = \underset{w \text{ in } W}{\times} A_w$ and assume a *production function* f such that $q = f(a)$ when output q results from each worker w choosing a_w in A_w, and $a = (a_1, \ldots, a_n)$.[3]

With the choice of a in A unknown, output will be indeterminate since A_w will not normally reduce to a single element for all w in W. Indeed, a broad range of behaviors are available to the worker at any time, all of which are legitimate in terms of the employment contract. Within this range we view the worker as acting to pursue his own goals subject only to the direct and indirect constraints the capitalist can place on the worker's choices, and the 'moral influence' he can exercise over these choices within the constraint set. To formalize the notion of 'constraint' we define *rules* of the organization as restrictions on A_w

imposed upon workers by their superiors. Thus, for any z in $\bar{S}^w$, suppose z is capable of imposing a *rule-set* $R_{wz} \subset A_w$ on w. Let

$$R_w = \bigcap_{z \text{ in } \bar{S}^w} R_{wz}.$$

Thus, R_w is a collection of restrictions imposed on w by all of his superiors.

Note we are not assuming that a superior can choose the rule-set R_{wz} at will. While in principle z's choices may vary over the power set of A_w, in fact z may be restricted contractually or legally to some subset of this power set. The subset to which z is so restricted is called the collection of *w-admissible rules*. In addition, z must also take into account the possibility that different rule sets may incur different costs to the firm in implementation.

Not all workers necessarily have superiors. If w in W has no superior in the sense defined above, the *director* of the firm (the capitalist or top management) is taken as his superior. For any worker w, the rule-set imposed by the director is written $R_{w*} \subset A_w$. Let $R_* = \underset{w \text{ in } W}{\times} R_{w*}$ and take R_* as given by the director. For any worker w with $\bar{S}^w \neq \phi$, set $R_w^* = R_w \cap R_{w*}$. If $\bar{S}^w = \phi$ so that the only superior is the director, set $R_w^* = R_{w*}$.

Now consider any worker w. Let $\mathcal{R}_z^w$ be the collection of z-admissible rule-sets R_{zw} that w can impose on z in $\underline{S}_w$ and write

$$\mathcal{R}^w = \underset{z \text{ in } \underline{S}_w}{\times} \mathcal{R}_z^w.$$

Denote the elements of $\mathcal{R}^w$ by r^w. If $\underline{S}_w = \phi$, set $\mathcal{R}^w = \phi$. We take $\mathcal{R}^w$ as given for our purposes. In a larger model $\mathcal{R}^w$ would depend on legality, as well as feasibility and cost of formulation and enforcement (Simon, 1957b; Barnard, 1966; Gintis, 1976). We assume for the time being that workers obey all rules. The contingent status of this assumption will be discussed later.

We are now in a position to define a *decision* of an individual w in the organization. This will consist of two components: an act and a

z-admissible rule for each subordinate z in S_w. Formally, we define the *decision space* of w as $D_w = A_w \times \mathcal{R}^{\overline{w}}$, and call elements of D_w, namely, $d_w = (a_w, r^w)$ *decisions of* w. Let $D = \underset{w \text{ in } W}{\times} D_w$ and denote the elements or decisions of D by $d = (d_1, \ldots, d_n)$. Since output depends only on the acts of each worker and since $d_w = (a_w, r^w)$, for $w = 1, \ldots, n$, and $a = (a_1, \ldots, a_n)$, we write $f(d) = f(a)$.

It is assumed that workers base their choices of decisions on a real valued utility function $p_w = P_w(d_w, \alpha_w)$ defined on D_w for each vector of parameters α_w. The nature of these parameters, as well as their ability to be altered through the actions of the entrepreneur, affect the worker's decisions within the rule restrictions imposed on him. We shall specify four components of α_w in ways which reflect the major lines of influence of members of the organization on the choices of a particular worker. First, the director may provide monetary incentives for worker performance. More precisely, for each w in W there is a non-negative real-valued *incentive function* $y_w = Y_w(d_w)$ defined over D_w, where y_w is interpreted as the income w receives upon taking decision d_w. Subject to certain admissibility constraints which will not be specified, Y_w is chosen by the director.

According to the Weberian model of bureaucracy, no further elements are necessary to explain organizational behavior. The incentive structure will induce workers to obey rules, and adhering to rules is sufficient to ensure adequate worker performance. But there are at least two difficulties with this perspective. On the one hand, whether rules are obeyed depends not only on their substance, but also on the perceived authority of the superior (Barnard, 1966: 168). A superior appearing to be weak may obtain relatively less cooperation from his subordinates in following the rules he issues, and may also be reluctant to prescribe certain rules which are in the interests of the firm if they might tend to decrease cooperation still further. On the other hand, even finely articulated rules are insufficient to provide for all possible contingencies arising in production. Thus, unless supported by other forms of influence, authority is not enough to ensure that the worker will always make the 'correct' decisions in unforeseen circumstances (Simon, 1957a: 227). To avoid these pitfalls we follow Simon in supposing that a worker's immediate superior not only imposes rules upon him, but also provides *goals and premises* to guide the worker's choices. In other words, for each w in W whose immediate superior is z in $\overline{S}^w$, there is a real-valued *premise function* $g_w = G_w(d_w)$ defined over

D_w. We take G_w as an attribute of z, in the sense that it reflects a property of the behavior of z, but G_w is given and not chosen through utility maximization. In case w has no superior, G_w is an attribute of the director. Of course, not all real-valued functions on D_w can serve as premise functions. But the characteristics such functions should possess are not discussed here.

Once it is acknowledged that workers are influenced by their superiors, it should also be admitted that they are influenced by their co-workers as well (Gintis, 1976). Like the former, the latter too may have a significant impact on worker behavior. We capture the influence of co-workers on their mutual performance by assuming each worker has a set of *value orientations* arising from the decisions of his co-workers and these, in turn, affect the actions of each. Thus, let V be the class of all possible value-orientations. For any co-worker z (in C_w) of w let V_{wz} be a function transforming decisions of z into value-orientations v_{wz} (in V) of w, where $z \neq w$. Thus,

$$v_{wz} = V_{wz}(d_z).$$

Enumerating the elements of C_w distinct from w as $k_1, \ldots, k_{n_w}$, there are n_w such functions. These are abbreviated as

$$V^w(d_{k_1}, \ldots, d_{k_w}) = (V_{wk_1}(d_{k_1}), \ldots, V_{wk_w}(d_{k_w})).$$

As with incentive and premise functions, we note but do not dwell on the presence of admissibility requirements for the V^w.

The fourth and last component of α_w is based on the observation that decision-making in the organization depends on the types of information at hand. Following Hurwicz (1960), we introduce communications among individuals consisting of (possibly empty) strings of alpha-numeric characters, blueprints, etc. Let $*$ represent the profit-maximizing director, and define $W^* = W \cup \{*\}$. The space of all possible communications among individuals is written M. For w, z in W^*, and $z \neq w$, let m_{wz} be an element of M denoting the information passed from w to z. The *information received by* w is thus the vector $m_w = (m_{zw})$, where z is in W^* and $z \neq w$, and the *information transmitted by* w is the vector $m^w = (m_{wz})$, where z is in W^* and $z \neq w$. We suppose that m_{wz} is a function M^{wz} of d_w, that is,

$$m_{wz} = M^{wz}(d_w),$$

for all w in W and $z \neq w$ in W^*. Each M^{wz} is assumed to satisfy certain undescribed admissibility criteria. Information transmitted by the director is taken as given. The vector of functions indicating the information transmitted by w is abbreviated by

$$m^w = M^w(d_w),$$

where $M^w(d_w)$ is the vector $(M^{wz}(d_w))$ the components of which vary over $z \neq w$ in W^*. Similarly, the information received by w is shortened to

$$m_w = M_w(d_{(w)}),$$

where

$$M_w(d_{(w)}) = (M^{1w}(d_1), \ldots, M^{w-1w}(d_{w-1}), M^{w+1w}(d_{w+1}), \ldots, M^{nw}(d_n), m_{*w}),$$

and m_{*w} is the information transmitted to w from the director.

Worker w's utility function now is specified as

$$p_w = P_w(d_w, Y_w(d_w), G_w(d_w), V^w(d_{k_1}, \ldots, d_{k_w}), M_w(d_{(w)})),$$

where $d_{k_1}, \ldots, d_{k_w}$ and $d_{(w)}$ are determined by workers other than w. We assume that given $d_{k_1}, \ldots, d_{k_w}$ and $d_{(w)}$, worker w chooses d_w so as to maximize P_w over D_w subject to the constraint that the chosen a_w component of d_w lies in the set R_w^* of restrictions imposed by his superiors. Note that the definition of D_w ensures that the chosen r^w components of d_w are z-admissible for every subordinate z of w.

In spite of the lack of quantifiability of d_w, conditions on D_w and P_w sufficient to guarantee the existence of a constrained maximizer of P_w are known (Katzner, 1976). These are assumed here without further discussion. However, since some parameters in each worker's utility function are the result of the decisions of others (namely $d_{k_1}, \ldots, d_{k_w}$ and $d_{(w)}$), we are still not assured that a solution exists when all workers maximize utility simultaneously. Thus, it is necessary to investigate the internal consistency of the model as a whole. The first step is to show that it is not underspecified. Let β_w be the cardinality of $\underline{S}_w$, and let γ_w be the cardinality of C_w. Then a breakdown of the number of variables is as shown in Table 1.

TABLE 1

Variable	Number
a_w	n
q	1
R_{wz}	$\sum_w \beta_w$
m_{wz}	n^2
p_w	n
y_w	n
g_w	n
v_{wz}	$\sum_w (\gamma_w{}^2 - \gamma_w)$

Thus, there are a total of

$$n^2 + 4n + 1 + \sum_w \beta_w + \sum_w (\gamma_w{}^2 - \gamma_w)$$

variables.[4] The equations line up as shown in Table 2.

TABLE 2

Equation	Number
$q = f(a)$	1
$p_w = P_w(d_w, \alpha_w)$	n
$y_w = Y_w(d_w)$	n
$g_w = G_w(d_w)$	n
$v_{wz} = V_{wz}(d_z)$	$\sum_w (\gamma_w{}^2 - \gamma_w)$
$m_{wz} = M^{wz}(d_w)$	n^2

Thus, there are $n^2 + 3n + 1 + \sum_w (\gamma_w{}^2 - \gamma_w)$ equations, or a deficit of

$$n + \sum_w \beta_w$$

equations with respect to the unknowns. But each worker chooses d_w to maximize P_w, thus specifying $(\beta_w + 1)$ variables as functions of parameters in the utility function. Hence the maximization process determines an additional

$$\sum_w (\beta_w + 1) = \sum_w \beta_w + n$$

equations, thereby accounting for the deficit.

Therefore the model is exactly specified. The next step is to obtain solutions. For it could happen that some equations are derivable from others, or even if all equations are independent, there still may be no vector of variable values satisfying all equations simultaneously. Fortunately, further conditions on the equations of the model (beyond those already required) are known which, without relying on quantification, ensure the existence of solutions (Katzner, 1973, 1976). These, too, are assumed. Additional restrictions could be imposed to obtain uniqueness. However, the latter are not necessary for subsequent argument and consequently are not postulated.

The last step is to ensure that all components of solutions of the equations are consistent with those requirements of the model not expressed in equation form. Consider a vector $d = (d_1, \ldots, d_n)$ in D which is not necessarily a solution. Then d may also be written as $d = (a, r)$ where $a = (a_1, \ldots, a_n)$ and $r = (r^1, \ldots, r^n)$. Now each r^w consists of a vector of rule-sets R_{zw} chosen by w. We say that *d is admissible* whenever

$$R_w^* \neq \phi,$$

for $w = 1, \ldots, n$, where here R_w^* is defined as it was earlier except that the rule-sets which make it up now have been chosen by superiors and the director. In other words, d is admissible as long as the choices of rules leave each worker with at least one act in his act set to choose from. We call *d feasible* provided that d is admissible and a_w is in the R_w^* chosen by the superiors of w, for each w. That is, d is feasible if each worker actually chooses from decisions remaining in his act set after all rules are imposed. Although feasibility depends on the director's rules R_*, the incentive functions $Y_w(d_w)$, indeed, on all parameters and functions of the model, in what follows we only identify for emphasis those parameters and functions which at the time seem to be most relevant. It is clear that there can be feasible points d in D which are not solutions. But for the model not to be vacuous, it is necessary to assume, as we do here, that feasible solutions exist.

To simplify rather difficult arguments below, only a truncated version of the above model is employed in the remainder of this paper. With one exception to be noted later, all communication variables, and all value orientation and premise functions hereafter, are discarded. Thus, utility functions reduce to

$$p_w = P_w(d_w, Y_w(d_w)),$$

for each w in W. It is assumed that if $Y_w(d_w)$ is an incentive function satisfying the admissibility constraints alluded to (but not specifically described) earlier, then so does the incentive function $Y_w(d_w) - \epsilon$ for all sufficiently small real numbers $\epsilon > 0$. Furthermore, as a function of two variables, each $P_w(d_w, Y_w)$ is taken to be continuous on its domain.[5]

Profits, π, are defined by

$$\pi = q - \sum_w y_w,$$

or, in functional form, as

$$\pi(d) = f(d) - \sum_w Y_w(d_w),$$

where $d = (d_1, \ldots, d_n)$ and output price is set at unity. Costs associated with the implementation of rules are assumed to be zero. Finally, throughout subsequent discussion, proofs of the theorems are relegated to an appendix.

Conditions for Pareto optimality

We now proceed to investigate conditions under which profit maximization leads to Pareto optimality.

A collection of incentive functions $\{Y_w(d_w) : w \text{ is in } W\}$ is an *incentive system*. The incentive system $\{Y_w(d_w)\}$ is *efficient* with respect to the director's rules R_* whenever there is no other system $\{Y'_w(d_w)\}$ such that with d feasible given $\{Y_w(d_w)\}$ and R_*, and d' feasible given $\{Y'_w(d_w)\}$ and any R'_*,

$$P_w(d'_w, Y'_w(d'_w)) \geqslant P_w(d_w, Y_w(d_w)),$$

for every w in W,

$$P_w(d'_w, Y'_w(d'_w)) > P_w(d_w, Y_w(d_w)),$$

for at least one w in W, and

$$f(d') - \sum_w Y'_w(d'_w) \geqslant f(d) - \sum_w Y_w(d_w).$$

In other words, efficient systems have the property that at any feasible d they cannot be modified so as to increase profits without lowering the utility of at least one worker. Efficiency is defined with respect to R_* because the latter, in part, determines which decisions in D are feasible. The same incentive system could be efficient under one R_* but not under another.

Let B be a subset of D. A decision d in B is *Pareto-optimal over B* if d is feasible for some R_* and incentive system $\{Y_w(d_w)\}$, and there is no other d' in B, feasible for some R'_*, such that for all w in W,

$$P_w(d'_w, Y_w(d'_w)) \geqslant P_w(d_w, Y_w(d_w)),$$

where

$$P_w(d'_w, Y_w(d'_w)) > P_w(d_w, Y_w(d_w)),$$

for at least one w, and

$$f(d') - \sum_w Y_w(d'_w) \geqslant f(d) - \sum_w Y_w(d_w).$$

Thus, at a Pareto-optimum d, no feasible reorganization of production can make one worker better off (and no one else worse off) without lowering profits. Recall that with $d = (a, r)$ and $d' = (a', r')$, only when $a' \neq a$ does $f(d') \neq f(d)$. If there were a feasible d' in B satisfying the above inequalities (so that d could not be Pareto-optimal), then d' would be called *Pareto superior* to d in B. When d is Pareto optimal over D, it is referred to as simply *Pareto optimal.*

Let $D^* = \{d = (a, r): d$ is in D and $R_* = \{a\}\}$, that is, D^* is the collection of decisions constrained by the director choosing the acts of each worker. Our first result asserts that if the director chooses each worker's act, and if the incentive system is efficient, then any feasible solution is Pareto optimal. Roughly speaking, this makes precise the conditions ensuring optimality in the authoritarian portion of the Coase-Simon model described earlier. Recall that in their approach the capitalist chose the specific task each worker was to perform.

Theorem 1. Let $d^0 = (a^0, r^0)$ in D^* be a feasible solution for $R^0_* = \{ a^0 \}$ and the incentive system $\{ Y_w(d_w) \}$ employed by the director. If $\{ Y_w(d_w) \}$ is efficient with respect to R^0_*, then d^0 is Pareto optimal over D^*.

Note that although d^0 may be Pareto optimal over D^*, it need not be Pareto optimal over the larger set D.

Even without the director choosing the acts of each worker, it is still possible to have Pareto-optimal solutions. An incentive system $\{ Y_w(d_w) \}$ is said to be *act-stable* on D if for each $d = (a, r)$ in D, feasible given $\{ Y_w(d_w) \}$ and some R_*, there is an $\epsilon > 0$ and an r' such that $d' = (a, r')$ is feasible given some R'_* and the modified incentive system

$$\{ Y_w(d_w) - \epsilon : w \text{ is in } W \} .$$

Alternatively put, the act component of a feasible decision remains the component of some feasible decision in the face of slight variations in incentives. Neither d nor d' are necessarily solutions.

Theorem 2. If the incentive system $\{ Y_w(d_w) \}$ employed by the director is act-stable and efficient with respect to some R_*, then any solution in D, feasible given R_* and $\{ Y_w(d_w) \}$, is Pareto optimal.

As we know, at any feasible solution d^0, efficient incentives cannot be modified so as to obtain a new feasible decision d yielding increased profits without, at d lowering the utility of at least one worker. Thus, it is not surprising that efficient incentives lead to Pareto optimality. But Theorems 1 and 2 indicate that for the argument to go through, additional conditions are needed. These are required to ensure the feasibility of decisions being compared to d^0. This feasibility is achieved through the restriction that the director choose each worker's act in Theorem 1, and through act-stability in Theorem 2.

A decision d^0 in $B \subseteq D$ *maximizes profit over B* given $\{ Y_w(d_w) \}$ whenever

$$f(d^0) - \sum_w Y_w(d^0_w) \geqslant f(d) - \sum_w Y_w(d_w),$$

for all d in B. When $B = D$, we say simply that d^0 maximizes profit. If d^0 is profit maximizing over B and if d^0 is also one of the feasible solutions given $\{Y_w(d_w)\}$ to which Theorem 2 (or Theorem 1) applies, then d^0 is Pareto optimal. There are, however, further special circumstances in which profit maximizing solutions are Pareto optimal. Several of these are now considered in turn.

In the first case to be considered, workers are motivated exclusively by monetary incentives, and as long as these incentives are chosen 'properly' by the director, optimality prevails.

We say w in W is *incentive motivated* if for any $d^0 = (d_1^0, \ldots, d_n^0)$ and $d' = (d_1', \ldots, d_n')$ in D and any incentive function $Y_w(d_w)$ such that d^0 is feasible given $Y_w(d_w)$ and some R_*^0, and d' is feasible given $Y_w(d_w)$ and some R_*' if

$$Y_w(d_w') \geqslant Y_w(d_w^0),$$

then

$$P_w(d_w', Y_w(d_w')) \geqslant P_w(d_w^0, Y_w(d_w^0)).$$

Thus, an incentive motivated worker cares about decisions only in so far as they affect his income.

An incentive system $\{Y_w(d_w)\}$ is *profit-efficient* whenever $f(d') > f(d)$ implies

$$f(d') - \sum_w Y_w(d_w') > f(d) - \sum_w Y_w(d_w),$$

for all $d = (d_1, \ldots, d_n)$ and $d' = (d_1', \ldots, d_n)$ in D such that d and d' are feasible with respect to $\{Y_w(d_w)\}$ and some (not necessarily the same) R_*. In other words, profit efficiency means the incentive system is such that an increase in output is always accompanied by an increase in profit. With profit-efficient incentives, maximum profit can only occur at feasible decisions where output is maximal.

Theorem 3. Let $\{Y_w(d_w)\}$ be profit-efficient. If all workers are incentive motivated, then any profit maximizing solution, feasible given $\{Y_w(d_w)\}$ and some R_*, is Pareto optimal.

Further situations in which we would expect profit maximization to yield Pareto optimality arise when workers' preferences are constituted so that, of their own free will, workers choose decisions which conform perfectly to the needs of the director or to the premises and goals of their superiors. To formalize these ideas requires the specification of ordering relations on decisions and rules.

Consider any worker w in W. Let d_w be distinct from d'_w in D_w. When

$$f(d_1, \ldots, d_{w-1}, d'_w, d_{w+1}, \ldots, d_n) > f(d_1, \ldots, d_{w-1}, d_w, d_{w+1}, \ldots, d_n),$$

for all d_z in D_z such that $z \neq w$ and both $(d_1, \ldots, d_{w-1}, d'_w, d_{w+1}, \ldots, d_n)$ and $(d_1, \ldots, d_{w-1}, d_w, d_{w+1}, \ldots, d_n)$ are feasible, then we say d'_w *dominates* d_w and write $d'_w > d_w$. Here it is not necessary to single out for emphasis specific functions and parameters with respect to which feasibility holds. Dominance thus requires output to rise upon substitution of d'_w for d_w in d, regardless of the values of the remaining components of d. We write $d'_w = d_w$ if under the above conditions output remains unchanged, and $d'_w \geqslant d_w$ if either $d'_w > d_w$ or $d'_w = d_w$. Clearly dominance ($>$) on D_w is irreflexive, asymmetric and transitive.

Theorem 4. Let $d^0 = (d^0_1, \ldots, d^0_n)$ and $d' = (d'_1, \ldots, d'_n)$ be in D. If $d'_w \geqslant d^0_w$ for all w in W, then $f(d') \geqslant f(d^0)$. If, in addition, $d'_w > d^0_w$ for at least one w in W then $f(d') > f(d^0)$.

The definition of dominance among rule sets is more complicated. For any w, let $\mathcal{R}_w$ be the collection of all admissible intersections R_w of rule-sets imposed by the superiors of w. Consider first a worker w in W who has no subordinates. We say R'_w dominates R_w provided that R'_w and R_w are in $\mathcal{R}_w$, $R'_w \subset R_w$, and for any d'_w in R'_w and d_w in $R_w - R'_w$, we have $d'_w > d_w$. Confusion will not arise by using the same symbol '$>$' to denote both dominance on $\mathcal{R}_w$ and dominance on D_w. Write $R'_w \geqslant R_w$ when $d'_w \geqslant d_w$, and $R'_w = R_w$ when $d'_w = d_w$. If w has subordinates, dominance on $\mathcal{R}_w$ is defined only after dominance on $\mathcal{R}_z$ is defined for every z in $\underline{S}_w$. In this case, R'_w is said to dominate R_w if, in addition to the above conditions, $R'_{zw} > R_{zw}$ for all z in $\underline{S}_w$, where R'_{zw} (and R_{zw}) is the rule-set imposed by w on z in decision d' (and, respectively, d).[6] Again, $R'_w \geqslant R_w$ when both $d'_w \geqslant d_w$ and $R'_{zw} \geqslant R_{zw}$ for all z in $\underline{S}_w$, and $R'_w = R_w$ when both $d'_w = d_w$ and $R'_{zw} = R_{zw}$ for all z in $\underline{S}_w$. Thus, $>$ is defined recursively over $\mathcal{R}_w$ for every w in W.

For each w, dominance of rule-sets ($>$) on $\mathcal{R}_w$ is clearly irreflexive and asymmetric since dominance on D_w has these properties. To see that $>$ on $\mathcal{R}_w$ is also transitive, it suffices to consider only the circumstances in which w has no subordinates. Suppose $R''_w > R'_w$

$>R_w$. Then, $R''_w \subset R'_w \subset R_w$. Hence, $R''_w \subset R_w$. Let d''_w be in R''_w and d_w be in $R_w - R''_w$. Now either d_w is in R'_w or it is in $R_w - R'_w$. In the former case $d''_w > d_w$ since $R''_w > R'_w$. In the latter choose any d'_w in $R'_w - R''_w$. Then $d''_w > d'_w > d_w$ because $R''_w > R'_w > R_w$. Since $>$ is transitive on D_w, we have $d''_w > d_w$. Therefore $>$ is transitive on $\mathcal{R}_w$.

The last dominance relation is defined on D_w. Let d'_w and d_w be in D_w. If $d'_w > d_w$ and $R'_{zw} > R_{zw}$ for all z in $\underline{S}_w$ where R'_{zw} and R_{zw} are components of d'_w and d_w, respectively, we write $d'_w \circledgt d_w$ and say that d'_w *strongly dominates* d_w. Both $\circledgeq$ and $\circledequal$ are defined in the obvious way, and $\circledgt$ is clearly irreflexive, asymmetric and transitive. Note that an alternative way to define $>$ on $\mathcal{R}_w$ when w has subordinates is that $R'_w > R_w$ if and only if $R'_w \subset R_w$ and for any d'_w in R'_w and d_w in $R_w - R'_w$ we have $d'_w \circledgt d_w$.

We say that a worker, w, *internalizes the values of the firm* whenever $d'_w \circledgeq d_w$ implies

$$P_w(d'_w, Y_w(d'_w)) \geqslant P_w(d_w, Y_w(d_w)),$$

for all incentive functions $Y_w(d_w)$ and all d'_w and d_w which are respective components of decisions d and d' in D, feasible given some (not necessarily the same) $\{Y_w(d_w)\}$ and R_*.

Theorem 5. Let $\{Y_w(d_w)\}$ be profit-efficient. If all workers internalize the values of the firm, then any profit maximizing solution, feasible given $\{Y_w(d_w)\}$ and some R_*, is Pareto optimal.

At this point it is worth enlarging our truncated model by reinstating the premise functions $G_w(d_w)$ introduced in the first section to illustrate how the above analysis can be applied in a more general setting. We continue to ignore value orientations and message transmissions. Utility functions are therefore written as

$$p_w = P_w(d_w, Y_w(d_w), G_w(d_w)),$$

for each w. Earlier definitions are revised accordingly. Thus, the notion of Pareto optimality remains unchanged except that utility functions now are written as indicated here and it is emphasized that decisions are feasible with respect to three items (instead of two), namely, an incentive system $\{Y_w(d_w)\}$, a system of premise functions $\{G_w(d_w)\}$, and the director's rule-sets R_*. On the other hand, internalization of the values of the firm requires not only the more general utility function, but also must be strengthened so that the statement

$d'_w \textcircled{\geqslant} d_w$ implies that $P_w(d'_w, Y_w(d'_w), G_w(d'_w)) \geqslant P_w(d_w, Y_w(d_w), G_w(d_w))$ now holds for all premise functions, G_w, in addition to everything else. Incentive motivation is treated analogously to internalization of the values of the firm by generalizing utility functions and extending the definition to hold for all premise functions. The only change necessitated in the definitions of incentive-efficiency, act-stability, profit-efficiency, and the orderings among decisions and rule-sets is the substitution of the revised emphasis in the notion of feasibility. Obvious modifications of the theorems and their proofs correspond.

Parallel to the concept of incentive motivation, worker w is called *vertically influenced* provided that for any incentive function $Y_w(d_w)$ and premise function $G_w(d_w)$, if $G_w(d'_w) \geqslant G_w(d_w)$, then

$$P_w(d'_w, Y_w(d'_w), G_w(d'_w)) \geqslant P_w(d_w, Y_w(d_w), G_w(d_w)),$$

for all d'_w and d_w which are respective components of decisions d and d' in D, where the latter are feasible given some (not necessarily the same) $\{ Y_w(d_w) \}$, $\{ G_w(d_w) \}$ and R_*. In addition, G_w is referred to as *non-decreasing with respect to* $\textcircled{\geqslant}$ on D_w when $d'_w \textcircled{\geqslant} d_w$ implies $G_w(d'_w) \geqslant G_w(d_w)$, for all d'_w and d_w subject to the above feasibility restriction.

Theorem 6. Let $\{ Y_w(d_w) \}$ be profit efficient and $\{ G_w(d_w) \}$ non-decreasing with respect to $\textcircled{\geqslant}$ for each G_w. If all workers are vertically influenced, then any profit maximizing solution, feasible given $\{ Y_w(d_w) \}$, $\{ G_w(d_w) \}$ and some R_*, is Pareto optimal.

These theorems provide several illustrations of the circumstances in which profit maximization gives rise to Pareto optimality. In each case the conditions demanded are quite restrictive. For a variety of reasons optimality cannot be expected to obtain in general. In the first place, if (as is likely to be the case) the director does not know the preferences of his workers, then he is unable to select efficient incentives. He can still make sure incentives are profit efficient, but his workers may be neither incentive-motivated nor vertically influenced. They also may not internalize the values of the firm. Reinstating value orientations and message transmissions magnifies the possibility of non-optimal solutions considerably. In general, then, there may be no internal mechanism within the firm which guarantees that the process of profit maximization combined with utility maximization subject to rule constraints will produce a Pareto-optimal solution. Of course the process may still yield solutions which are Pareto superior to other 'attainable' modes of work organization, but this question can be resolved only through a more detailed analysis than that given above.

Our story, however, does not end here. Beyond the efficient allocation of human resources, the director of the firm surely is interested in the means by which profits can be increased. The next section examines some of the issues involved.

Conditions for profitability

What are the attributes of a good worker? Economic theory has been traditionally quite indisposed to broach this question. Indeed, were profit maximization Pareto optimal, the problem would reduce to one of the technical conditions of production; as such, it would not be an 'economic' issue per se. But we have seen that, in general, this is not the case. Hence, an answer is needed in order to have a theory of the labor market proper, as well as to evaluate alternative economic institutions and social policies (Bowles and Gintis, 1976).

In our model worker attributes can affect profitability through (a) his possession of skills (i.e. the nature of A_w); (b) his preferences and hence choices among decisions; (c) his susceptibility to being motivated by incentives; (d) the way he imposes rules on his subordinates; (e) the nature of premises he presents to his subordinates; (f) the weight he places on the premises of his superior; (g) his value-orientations of his co-workers; (h) the way he receives and transmits information; and so on. Several of these possibilities are examined now in the context of our truncated model described at the end of the first section and explored extensively in the second section.

Consider any worker w with act set $A_w \Subset A$. Let $\bar{A}_w \Subset A$ be a second act set such that $A_w \subset \bar{A}_w$, and write $d_w = (a_w, r^w)$ and $\bar{d}_w = (\bar{a}_w, \bar{r}^w)$ when, respectively, a_w is in A_w and $\bar{a}^w$ is in $\bar{A}_w - A_w$. If $\bar{d}^w \oslash d_w$ for all such $\bar{d}^w$ and d_w in D_w, and if $\bar{A}^w$ is substituted for A_w, then we say that w has *become more skilled.* Thus, increasing skills means that potential output rises. But there is no guarantee that w will use his new skills (i.e. choose an act from $\bar{A}^w - A_w$) and that jealous co-workers will not attempt to subvert them so that output can, in fact, rise. The firm is *receptive to new skills if* w if in arriving at a new feasible solution after w has become more skilled and $\bar{A}^w$ has been substituted for A_w, the constrained set out of which w chooses his acts always contains at least one element of $\bar{A}^w - A_w$. Sufficient conditions under which more skills increase the value of the worker to the firm are as follows.

Theorem 7. Let $\{ Y_w(d_w) \}$ be profit-efficient. Suppose w internalizes the values of the firm and the firm is receptive to new skills of w. Given a feasible solution d, if w becomes more skilled and, at the same time, no other worker $z \neq w$ alters his chosen act, then profits are greater at the new feasible solution $\bar{d}$.

The restriction concerning internalization of the values of the firm in Theorem 7 can be replaced by incentive motivation provided that the incentive function chosen by the director for w exhibits an additional property. The incentive function $Y_w(d_w)$ is referred to as *non-decreasing with respect to* $\geqslant$ on D_w whenever $d'_w \geqslant d_w$ implies $Y_w(d'_w) \geqslant Y_w(d_w)$ for all d'_w and d_w in D_w.

Theorem 8. Let $\{ Y_w(d_w) \}$ be profit-efficient. Suppose w is incentive motivated, $Y_w(d_w)$ is non-decreasing with respect to $\geqslant$ on D_w, and the firm is receptive to new skills of w. Given a feasible solution d, if w becomes more skilled and, at the same time, no other worker $z \neq w$ alters his chosen act, then profits are greater at the new feasible solution $\bar{d}$.

Yet a third set of sufficient conditions can be expressed with the aid of premise functions in the context of the slightly enlarged model discussed at the end of the second section.

Theorem 9. Let $\{ Y_w(d_w) \}$ be profit-efficient. Suppose w is vertically influenced, $G_w(d_w)$ is non-decreasing with respect to $\geqslant$ on D_w, and the firm is receptive to new skills of w. Given a feasible solution d, if w becomes more skilled and, at the same time, no other worker $z \neq w$ alters his chosen act, then profits are greater at the new feasible solution $\bar{d}$.

These theorems codify the sense in which workers with more skill are preferred by the director to those with less. The reader should note that the conditions under which the propositions are true are not always met, and are certainly not trivial.

Discarding premise functions once again, we now formulate a proposition describing circumstances under which certain worker utility functions are more valuable to the firm than others. Let $P_w(d_w, Y_w(d_w))$ and $Q_w(d_w, Y_w(d_w))$ be two utility functions defined on D_w for a worker w in W. Let $\hat{d}_w$ be chosen under P_w, and $\bar{d}_w$ under Q_w. We say

P_w *dominates* Q_w and write $P_w > Q_w$ if for any incentive function $Y_w(d_w)$ and all $\hat{d}_w$ and $\bar{d}_w$ in D_w, we have $\hat{d}_w > \bar{d}_w$.

Theorem 10. Let $\{Y_w(d_w)\}$ be profit-efficient, $\hat{d}$ a feasible solution given utility functions P_z for every z in W, and $\bar{d}$ a non-profit-maximizing feasible solution given utility functions Q_w for some worker w, and P_z for $z \neq w$. If $P_w > Q_w$ and the chosen act of each $z \neq w$ is the same for both $\hat{d}$ and $\bar{d}$, then profits are greater at $\hat{d}$ than at $\bar{d}$.

The above theorem illustrates one of the major ways in which the employer-employee relation differs from a true market relationship. In a true market exchange the participants are concerned only with the properties of the entities exchanged, and not with the personal attributes of each other (Arrow and Hahn, 1971: 23). Indeed, this observation is the crux of the purported 'performance-orientation' of a capitalist economy which abjures all ascriptive and particularist valuations (Parsons, 1951; Friedman, 1962). Yet we see that the employer cares very much about the preference structures of his employee, and not only about their skills.[7]

Our last proposition relates increased incentive motivation on the part of workers to greater profitability for the firm. Consider any worker w and two utility functions $P_w(d_w, Y_w(d_w))$ and $Q_w(d_w, Y_w(d_w))$ on D_w. Again, suppose $\hat{d}_w$ is chosen under P_w and $\bar{d}_w$ under Q_w. If for all incentive functions $Y_w(d_w)$,

$$Y_w(\hat{d}_w) > Y_w(\bar{d}_w),$$

then we say w is *more highly motivated by incentives* under P_w than under Q_w.

Theorem 11. Let $\{Y_w(d_w)\}$ be profit-efficient, $\hat{d}$ a feasible solution given utility functions P_z for every z in W, and $\bar{d}$ a non-profit-maximizing feasible solution given utility functions Q_w for some worker w and P_z for $z \neq w$. If w is more highly motivated by incentives under P_w than under Q_w, if $Y_w(d_w)$ is non-decreasing with respect to $\geqslant$ on D_w, and if the chosen act of each $z \neq w$ is the same for both $\hat{d}$ and $\bar{d}$, then profits are greater at $\hat{d}$ than at $\bar{d}$.

Conclusion

The fundamental observation emerging from the preceding analysis is that except under highly restrictive conditions, the pursuit of profit maximization by the firm may not allocate internal human activity Pareto optimally. The reason for this has to do with the manner in which we view the production process. In neoclassical theory, once technology and preferences are given, all that matters are the 'neoclassical quantities', i.e. the number of labor hours flowing through markets in conjunction with quantities of non-labor inputs and outputs consumed by the worker. Optimality follows from the constraints of competition and the postulates of rationality (maximization). But in our approach, even if labor hours and other neoclassical quantities could be determined independently, the worker would still have to choose acts, rules, value orientations, premises and messages in order to carry out the responsibilities of his job. At the same time he would also be subject to other rules, value orientations, premises, messages and incentives thrust upon him. Now since incentives are defined over worker decisions, acts and rule-sets may be viewed as 'market-type' elements. After all, the director can reward certain acts and rules over others and, as we have seen, in certain cases workers respond to these incentives as the director would like them to. Thus, it is possible to speak of the 'demand and supply' of acts and rule-sets in much the same way as one speaks of the demand and supply of labor hours. However, even with rationality remaining the guiding hand of human behavior, it is clear that premises, value orientations and messages do not flow through markets. Nor are they constrained by the institutional mechanism of competition. Rather, in our model they serve as the basis for the formation of social relations among people which are crucial to the production process. Thus, there is no reason to expect that the allocation of human activity within the firm would lead to Pareto optimality – even if it manages to maximize profits.

In a larger sense, the only proper conclusion to this study is a plea for further research. While our model is quite complex, we have shown it to be amenable to rigorous analytical investigation. Our major propositions barely scratch the surface in understanding the complex interaction of acts, rules, incentive systems, preference structures, and patterns of influence involving values, premises and information. At least three important problems stand out. First, the model needs to be integrated into a more expansive framework in which wage rates and labor market conditions bear on internal decisions and structures. Ideally one would also want to include interaction with consumers, other firms, labor unions, and the government. Secondly, a general model of organizational structure ought to be developed of which hierarchical organization is but one form. This model should be capable of determining, on the basis of profitability or efficiency, the precise conditions under which the hierarchical form will be chosen. Thirdly, the situation arising when workers do not necessarily obey the rules imposed by their superiors requires investigation.

The last of these issues deserves a final word. Organizational experience indicates that the costs of enforcing rules imposed by superiors rises rapidly as the number of violators increases. An individual who does not follow rules can be threatened or dismissed, but mass violations based on collusion between superiors and subordinates, and among co-workers, can swiftly destroy the downward transmission of rules, and render inoperative certain necessary transmissions of information, value orientations and premises. The solidarity of a worker coalition depends on such things as the commonality of interests, the benefits accruing to a worker upon withdrawal from it, and whatever penalties the coalition can impose on deviant members. On the other hand, the capitalist can discourage coalition-formation by fragmenting work-groups, increasing the 'social distance' between superiors and subordinates, and routing important decision-making power through higher levels to minimize the degree of control a group of workers may exercise over a co-worker.

To integrate these insights into our model requires that our analysis of interpersonal behavior be enlarged to include game-theoretic and bargaining elements. The difficulties associated with such an approach are well-known. The benefits, however, should prove substantial.

Appendix

Proof of Theorem 1

Let $d^0 = (a^0, r^0)$ be a feasible solution in D^* for R^0_* and $\{Y_W(d_W)\}$. If d^0 were not Pareto optimal over D^*, then there would be a feasible $d' = (a', r',)$ in D^* where $R'_* = \{a'\}$ and

$$P_w(d'_w, Y_w(d'_w)) \geqslant P_w(d^0_w, Y_w(d^0_w)), \tag{1}$$

for each w in W,

$$P_z(d'_z, Y_z(d'_z)) > P_z(d^0_z, Y_z(d^0_z)), \tag{2}$$

for some z in W, and

$$f(d') - \sum_w Y_w(d'_w) \geqslant f(d^0) - \sum_w Y_w(d^0). \tag{3}$$

Define the incentive function

$$Y'_z(d_z) = \begin{cases} Y_z(d_z), & \text{if } d_z \neq d'_z, \\ Y_z(d_z) - \epsilon, & \text{if } d_z = d'_z, \end{cases}$$

for some $\epsilon > 0$, and consider the incentive system $\{ Y'_w(d_w) \}$ obtained as

$$Y'_w(d_w) = \begin{cases} Y_w(d_w), & \text{if } w \neq z, \\ Y'_w(d_w), & \text{if } w = z. \end{cases}$$

This is permissible according to the assumptions listed at the end of the first section. Since $R'_* = \{a'\}$, d' is also feasible with $\{Y'_w(d_w)\}$. Hence from (1),

$$P_w(d'_w, Y'_w(d'_w)) \geqslant P_w(d^0_w, Y_w(d^0_w)), \tag{4}$$

for each w in W. With ϵ sufficiently small, the continuity of preferences and (2) imply

$$P_z(d'_z, Y'_z(d'_z)) > P_z(d^0_z, Y_w(d^0_z)). \tag{5}$$

Lastly, from (3),

$$f(d') - \sum_w Y'_w(d'_w) > f(d^0) - \sum_w Y_w(d^0). \tag{6}$$

But (4)-(6) contradict the efficiency of $\{Y_w(d_w)\}$ with respect to R^0_*.

Q.E.D.

Proof of Theorem 2

The proof is the same as that of Theorem 1 except that both feasibility under the modified incentive system and the fact that $f(d')$ does not change when the incentive system is modified, now follow from act-stability.

Q.E.D.

Proof of Theorem 3

Let d^0 be a profit maximizing solution which is feasible with respect to $\{Y_w(d_w)\}$ and R_*. Then

$$f(d^0) - \sum_w Y_w(d^0) \geqslant f(d) - \sum_w Y_w(d_w)$$

for all d in D. If $d^0 = (d_1^0, \ldots, d_n^0)$ were not Pareto optimal, then there would be a $d' = (d_1', \ldots, d_n')$ in D, feasible given $\{Y_w(d_w)\}$ and some R_*' such that,

$$P_w(d_w', Y_w(d_w')) \geqslant P_w(d^0, Y_w(d_w^0)), \tag{7}$$

for each w in W,

$$P_z(d_z', Y_z(d_z')) > P_z(d_z^0, Y_z(d_z^0)), \tag{8}$$

for some z in W, and

$$f(d') - \sum_w Y_w(d_w') = f(d^0) - \sum_w Y_w(d_w^0). \tag{9}$$

Note that (9) cannot be an inequality since d^0 is profit maximizing. Now from (7) and (8), since all workers are incentive motivated,

$$\sum_w Y_w(d_w') > \sum_w Y_w(d_w^0). \tag{10}$$

Combining (9) and (10),

$$f(d') > f(d^0). \tag{11}$$

Applying profit-efficiency to (11),

$$f(d') - \sum_w Y_w(d'_w) > f(d^0) - \sum_w Y_w(d^0_w),$$

contrary to (9).

Q.E.D.

Proof of Theorem 4

Consider the sequence of vectors:

$$\begin{aligned} b^0 &= d^0, \\ b^1 &= (d'_1, d^0_2, \ldots, d^0_n), \\ b^2 &= (d'_1, d'_2, d^0_3, \ldots, d^0_n), \\ &\ \ \vdots \\ b^{n-1} &= (d'_1, \ldots, d'_{n-1}, d^0_n), \\ b^n &= d'. \end{aligned}$$

When $d'_w \geqslant d^0_w$ for all w,

$$f(b^0) \leqslant f(b^1) \leqslant \ldots \leqslant f(b^n), \tag{12}$$

so that $f(d^0) \leqslant f(d')$. If $d'_w > d^0_w$ for some w, then the corresponding inequality in (12) is strict. Hence, in the latter case, $f(d^0) < f(d')$.

Q.E.D.

Proof of Theorem 5

Let d^0 be a profit maximizing solution which is feasible with respect to $\{ Y_w(d_w) \}$ and R_*. Then profit efficiency implies

$$f(d^0) > f(d), \tag{13}$$

for all feasible d in D distinct from d^0. If $d = (d^0_1, \ldots, d^0_n)$ were not Pareto optimal, then there would be a $d' = (d'_1, \ldots, d'_n)$ in D, feasible given $\{Y_w(d_w)\}$ and some R'_* such that

$$P_w(d'_w, Y_w(d'_w)) \geqslant P_w(d^0_w, Y_w(d^0_w)), \tag{14}$$

for each w in W,

$$P_z(d'_z, Y_z(d'_z)) > P_z(d^0_z, Y_z(d^0_z)), \tag{15}$$

for some z in W, and

$$f(d') - \sum_w Y_w(d'_w) \geqslant f(d^0) - \sum_w Y_w(d^0_w).$$

Since each worker internalizes the values of the firm, (14) and (15) imply $d'_w \circledgeq d^0_w$ for all w, and $d'_z \circledgt d^0_z$. Hence, from Theorem 4 and the definitions of $\circledgeq$ and $\circledgt$,

$$f(d') > f(d^0). \tag{16}$$

But (13) applies to all feasible decisions, including d'. This contradicts (16).

Q.E.D.

Proof of Theorem 6

The proof is similar to that of Theorem 5.

Q.E.D.

Proof of Theorem 7

Write $d = (d_1, \ldots, d_n)$ and $\bar{d} = (\bar{d}_1, \ldots, \bar{d}_n)$, where d and $\bar{d}$ are the feasible solutions appearing in the statement of the theorem. Set $d_z = (a_z, r^z)$ and $\bar{d}_z = (\bar{a}_z, \bar{r}^z)$ for every z in W.

Since the firm is receptive to w's new skills, upon becoming more skilled and substituting $\bar{A}_w$ for A_w, w will always be able to choose at least one decision $\hat{d}_w = (\hat{a}_w, \hat{r}^w)$ such that $\hat{a}_w$ is in $\bar{A}_w - A_w$. But because w has become more skilled, $\hat{d}_w > \tilde{d}_w$, where $\tilde{d}_w = (\tilde{a}_w, \tilde{r}^w)$ is any decision with $\tilde{a}_w$ in A_w and the appropriate feasibility constraints are satisfied. Now w also internalizes the values of the firm so

$$P_w(\hat{d}_w, Y_w(\hat{d}_w)) \geqslant P_w(\tilde{d}_w, Y_w(\tilde{d}_w)).$$

Therefore, $\hat{d}_w$ will always be chosen over $\tilde{d}_w$. The same must also be true of the respective components $\bar{d}_w$ and d_w of the feasible solutions $\bar{d}$ and d. Hence, $\bar{d}_w \oslash d_w$, from which we have $\bar{d}_w > d_w$. Since we have assumed a_z and $\bar{a}_z$ are identical for each $z \neq w$, it follows that $\bar{d}_z = d_z$ for $z \neq w$. By Theorem 4, $f(\bar{d}) > f(d)$. Profit efficiency now implies that profits are greater at $\bar{d}$.

Q.E.D.

Proof of Theorem 8

The proof is similar to that of Theorem 7 with the role of internalization of the values of the firm now being played by the hypotheses of incentive motivation and the non-decreasing property of $Y_w(d_w)$.

Q.E.D.

Proof of Theorem 9

The proof is similar to that of Theorem 7 with the role of internalization of the values of the firm now being played by the hypotheses of vertical influence and the non-decreasing property of $G_w(d_w)$.

Q.E.D.

Proof of Theorem 10

Write $\hat{d} = (\hat{d}_1, \ldots, \hat{d}_n)$, and $\bar{d} = (\bar{d}_1, \ldots, \bar{d}_n)$, where $\hat{d}$ and $\bar{d}$ are the feasible solutions appearing in the statement of the theorem. Let $\hat{d}_z = (\hat{a}_z, \hat{r}^z)$ and $\bar{d}_z = (\bar{a}_z, \bar{r}^z)$ for all z in W.

Now, since it is assumed that $P_w > Q_w$ and that $\hat{a}_z$ and $\bar{a}_z$ are identical for $z \neq w$, we have $\hat{d}_w > \bar{d}_w$, and $\hat{d}_z = \bar{d}_z$ for all z in W distinct from w. By Theorem 4, $f(\hat{d}) > f(\bar{d})$, so from profit efficiency, profits are greater at $\hat{d}$.

Q.E.D.

Proof of Theorem 11

The proof is the same as that of Theorem 8 except here $\hat{d}_w > \bar{d}_w$ follows from the facts that w is more highly motivated by incentives under P_w than under Q_w, and $Y_w(d_w)$ is non-decreasing with respect to $\geqslant$.

Q.E.D.

Notes

1. Two notable exceptions are Coase (1937) and Simon (1957b) discussed below.
2. All of this draws heavily on Gintis (1976).
3. We have abstracted from non-human production inputs in order to simplify subsequent argument.
4. There are n^2 variables m_{zw} since each of n workers sends out a message to each of $n-1$ workers and one additional message to the director. The director's message to each worker is taken as given.
5. It is possible to define continuity in the absence of measurement (Katzner, 1973, 1976).
6. In terms of earlier notation, $d_w = (a_w, r^w)$ and $r^w = (R_{1w}, \ldots, R_{\ell_w w})$ where ℓ_w denotes the number of elements in S_w.
7. This point has also been documented empirically (Bowles and Gintis, 1976: ch. 5).

References

ARROW, K. J. and F. H. HAHN (1971) *General Competitive Analysis.* San Francisco: Holden-Day.

BARNARD, C. I. (1966) *The Functions of the Executive.* Cambridge, Mass.: Harvard University Press.

BOWLES, S. and H. GINTIS (1976) *Schooling in Capitalist America: Educational Reform and the Contradictions of Economic Life.* New York: Basic Books.

COASE, R. (1937) 'The Nature of the Firm', *Economica* 4 (November).

FERGUSON, C. E. (1971) *The Neoclassical Theory of Production.* Cambridge: Cambridge University Press.

FRIEDMAN, M. (1962) *Capitalism and Freedom.* Chicago: University of Chicago Press.

GINTIS, H. (1972) 'Consumer Behavior and the Concept of Sovereignty', *American Economic Review* 62 (May).

––, (1976) 'The Nature of the Labor Exchange and the Theory of Capitalist Production', *Review of Radical Political Economics* 8 (Summer).

HURWICZ, L. (1960) 'Optimality and Informational Efficiency in Resource Allocation Processes', in: K. J. ARROW, S. KARLIN and P. SUPPES (eds.), *Mathematical Methods in the Social Sciences 1959.* Stanford: Stanford University Press.

KATZNER, D. W. (1973) 'On the Analysis of Systems Containing Non-Quantifiable Elements', *Kybernetes* 2 (July).

––, (1976) 'Analysis Without Measurement', mimeo. Amherst: Department of Economics, University of Massachusetts.

PARSONS, T. (1951) *The Social System.* New York: Free Press.

SAMUELSON, P. A. (1947) *Foundations of Economic Analysis.* Cambridge, Mass.: Harvard University Press.

SIMON, H. A. (1957a) *Administrative Behavior.* New York: Free Press.

––, (1957b) *Models of Man.* New York: Wiley.

• Comment

David Marsden

University of Sussex, Brighton, UK

It is not necessary to believe in the existence of rigid disciplinary boundaries to see that there are difficult problems involved in interpreting the significance of research findings which bear on the phenomena one is studying, but which originate in a different discipline to one's own. Of course it is always possible to comb the research of another science for findings which support one's own particular theory, but this is hardly sufficient and requires such faith in the research methods of one's own science that agreement with them is a sufficient criterion for the selection or rejection of some other science's results. One of the main problems is that to take acount of such findings usually requires some reformulation of the accepted presuppositions of one's own discipline.

In many respects this is what Gintis and Katzner's contribution sets out to do and partially achieves. Rather than try to show why the hierarchical structure of the division of labour in the firm is optimal once a certain size has been reached, and deny the authoritarian nature of relationships as do Alchian and Demsetz,[1] Gintis and Katzner are attempting to build a model in which different types of relationships are possible, and among which hierarchical and authoritarian relationships are only one case. However, allowing for the possibility of authoritarian relationships means that it is the link between Pareto optimality and profit maximization which has to give way. Implicit in Alchian and Demsetz's argument that the structure of the firm is based on free consent (subject of course to certain material constraints) is a denial of the importance of the kind of diversity of relations within companies which recent comparative research has been bringing to light. In contrast, Gintis and Katzner's model provides a framework into which such diversity can be at least partly introduced, but it also illustrates the kind of adaptation to economic theory that is necessary for this to be possible.

The main innovation introduced by Gintis and Katzner is to specify a job structure, and the relations binding this, to relativize the concept of incentives and to allow for the influence that workers' values, attitudes to authority and collective norms can have upon productivity. This is done by the inclusion of a premise function and value orientations in the worker's utility function. The premise function is introduced to allow for the goals guiding a worker's decisions, and which can be influenced by a worker's superior to support his authority and to ensure that the 'right' kind of decisions are taken in his absence, and the worker's value orientations are included to allow for the influence of his own values and of the decisions of his fellow workers upon his own choices.

My main problem with the article lies in the extent to which the firm's 'job structure', and the various components of the utility function (the 'incentive function', the 'premise function', and the 'value orientations') should be analysed separately.[2]

A growing amount of research based on comparisons of the internal structure of industrial enterprises and of workplace relations suggests that such factors as the authority structure, the division of labour, the system of incentives, the value of orientations of the workforce, and the goals for which management seek to inspire support, rather than imposing separate sets of constraints on the decisions that can be made by individual workers, interact with each other in what Dore,[3] comparing a British and a Japanese enterprise, called an 'employment system', or in what Maurice, Sellier and Silvestre,[4] comparing French and German enterprises, have called different 'models' of the enterprise. To give a clearer idea of the nature of this interaction, I shall sketch a brief outline of the principal findings of these two pieces of research. Before doing so, I should warn that my account of their findings is restricted to those which I believe most important in the present context, and that the researchers themselves may well wish to stress other aspects of their work.

Dore's research was based on a comparison of factories in two enterprises, one British and the other Japanese, both of which were in the same sector of engineering and both of which were fairly representative of large firms in manufacturing industry. At the close of his study, Dore suggested that the differences could be characterized in terms of a 'market' and an 'organization-oriented' employment system.

Perhaps the strongest difference between the two lies in the relationship between the 'job strcture', skill, and the nature of the incentive system. In the British 'market-oriented' system the 'job set' appears to be more structured and reallocation of workers between jobs, and of tasks between jobs, is less easy than in the Japanese 'organization-oriented' system. This is partly because of the difference in the relationship between a worker and his skill. In the market-oriented system it is his individual property (symbolised by his craft papers, and his ownership of many of his tools), the results of his investment, and it is up to him to get the best price he can. In the organization-oriented system skills are much more closely tied to the organization. Reallocation is also less easy because of the widespread importance of shopfloor bargaining over the pricing of individual tasks, and over the extent to which unforeseen changes, or new tasks, constitute part of the job a man is already being paid for, or additional tasks requiring extra payment. In a word, the regulation of job content is itself an object of bargaining. This contrasts with the wider use of group incentives, and of age and merit ratings in Japan, together with a more flexible job structure. Thus 'job structure' and the incentive system can act upon each other.

The two systems are also characterized by different value orientations as consciousness of class differences between workers and management is much stronger. This, too, is related to the ownership of skill and the job structure in that the worker expects to make his living by plying his skill rather than by seeking promotion within the company. The smaller amount of promotion from manual grades means that there is less chance that class inequalities in access to the education system will be made up for later in life. This is not to deny inequalities in Japanese educational system, nor the importance of an employee's first job with a company in determining his future career prospects, but the greater importance of internal mobility does lessen the social cleavage between different levels in the organizational hierarchy. There is also an interesting contrast between the use of exhortation in the Japanese enterprise, suggesting a much greater attempt by Japanese management to communicate the goals of the enterprise to the workers, compared with the greater reliance upon sanctions and individual rewards (i.e. on the 'incentive function') in the British one. The interaction involved here is that British management would probably find it hard to use exhortion given the greater social cleavage between themselves and the manual workforce, and the lesser importance of team relations in work.

The comparison of a sample of matched French and German enterprises, also in the manufacturing sector, recently completed at the LEST, also highlights the importance of the interaction between the job structure and the elements included in Gintis and Katzner's worker utility function. Of especial interest in this case is the interaction between the incentive function, the pay structure, and the premise function and value orientations.

Very briefly, the research team set out from the findings of an earlier comparison[5] of matched French and German enterprises that the French enterprises employed a higher proportion of technical and managerial staff than their German counterparts and that, contrary to what one would expect from standard labour market theory, they also paid them more in comparison to their manual labour force.

The starting point for their interaction model is the education system.[6] While the German system selects people at the beginning of each educational cycle, using the selection process as a way of orienting people into different streams, and notably the highly developed technical stream, the French system opens the doors widely, selecting during and at the end of each cycle. As a result, the French system produces a much higher proportion of people without any technical qualifications.

In Germany, the highly developed system of technical education, and the hierarchy of diplomas that can be obtained after the apprenticeship, mean both that employers are well provided with qualified manpower, and that manual workers have a fair degree of independence with respect to their employers. Another important point is that the foremen are linked to the culture of the manual labour force as their diploma stands at the top of the manual diploma hierarchy. In contrast, French employers have to make good the lack of qualified manpower by organizing their own training to a much greater extent. As a result technical training, and most post-apprenticeship training, is tailored to the individual employer's needs, creating an environment in which internal labour mobility is likely to develop. This leads to interesting differences between the job structure in the two countries. While the strength of the identity of manual skill in West Germany underlies the importance of skilled workers in the German unions, and to the formation of collective agreements whose wage categories are defined with respect to level of training, the weak identity of manual skill in the French enterprises has led employers to establish a hierarchy of work posts to each of which are allocated a set of tasks the individual employee is to perform. Training organized by the company is geared to the requirements of these posts. An interesting implication of this is that while the German enterprises had a dual job structure with a cleavage between the manual and non-manual workforce, the French ones had a more or less continuous job structure, allowing much more mobility between manual and non-manual grades.

The interaction between the job-structure and the incentive function is particularly interesting and quite different from that observable in the Britain-Japan comparison. It is argued that the greater independence of manual skill in the Federal Republic underlies the link between earnings and individual output (a function of effort and training), while the tying of skill to the company's job structure in France underlies the linking of pay to the hierarchical coefficient attached to the post. Further bonuses and individual incentive schemes appear to have compressed the differentials established in collective agreements in Germany, they do not appear to do so in France. It is thus argued that the pay structure in France plays an important role in reinforcing the particular form of hierarchical division of labour found there.

Insofar as the internal pay strucutre also affects workers' orientations, either by reinforcing the hierarchy, or by encouraging vertical rather than horizontal mobility, one can argue that their findings also suggest an interaction with the value orientation component of the utility function.

My doubts arise because these phenomena seem to interact structurally. By this I mean that they act upon each other, influencing each other's development and behaviour. Their nature is rather more fluid, and the lines separating them from each other are much less clear than the model allows, and it is open to question how far there are common lines of cleavage between things like job structure, incentive and premise function emerging from these studies which would corroborate the definitions of the basic components of Gintis and Katzner's model. However, these are only doubts and, having said all this, I do not think that it detracts from the very interesting conclusions Gintis and Katzner reach concerning the type of worker motivations that have to be assumed if profit maximization and Pareto optimality are to coincide.

Notes

1. A. A. Alchian and H. Demsetz, 'Production, information costs, and economic organization', *American Economic Review,* December 1972

2. Gintis and Katzner do not have much to say about the fourth component, information, so I shall not deal with it.

3. R. P. Dore, *British Factory – Japanese Factory: The Origins of National Diversity in Industrial Relations,* George Allen and Unwin, 1973.

4. M. Maurice, F. Sellier, J.-J. Silvestre, 'Production de la hiérarchie dans l'entreprise: recherche d'un effect sociétal: Allemagne-France, mimeo 821 pages, Laboratoire d'Économie et de Sociologie du Travail (CNRS), Aix-en-Provence, 1977.

5. J.-J. Silvestre: 'Industrial wage differentials: a two country comparison', International Labour Review, Vol. 110 no. 6, 1974.

6. The 'interactive' nature of the explanation comes out more fully when the LEST explain why the education systems are so different.

Notes on Contributors

Gary Becker is University Professor of Economics, University of Chicago, USA. He is the author of *The Economic Approach to Human Behavior* and *Human Capital.*

Jon Elster is Associate Professor of History at the University of Oslo. His publications include *Logic and Society* and *Ulysses and the Sirens* (forthcoming).

Herbert Gintis is Professor of Economics, University of Massachusetts at Amherst, USA, and is currently a member of the Institute for Advanced Study, Princeton, New Jersey. He is the co-author, with Samuel Bowles, of *Schooling in Capitalist America.* He is a member of the editorial boards of the *Review of Radical Political Economy* and the *Socialist Review.*

Philippe d'Iribarne is Maitre de Recherche at the Centre National de la Recherche Scientifique (CNRS) and Directeur of the Centre de Recherche sur le Bien-Etre (CEREBE). He is the author of *La Science et le Prince, La Politique de Bonheur* and *Le Gaspillage et le Désir.*

Donald W. Katzner is Professor and Chairman, Department of Economics, in the University of Massachusetts at Amherst, USA. He is the author of *Static Demand Theory.*

Bertrand Lemennicier is Chargé de Recherche at the Centre de Recherche pour l'Etude et l'Observation des Conditions de Vie (CREDOC), and Maitre Assistant at the Université of Paris Dauphine.

Jacques Lesourne is Professor of Economics at the Conservatoire National des Arts et Métiers (CNAM), Paris. His publications in English include *Cost-benefit Analysis and Economic Theory* and *A Theory of the Individual for Economic Analysis*; in French, he has published *Les Systèmes du Destin.*

Louis Lévy-Garboua is Professor of Economics at the University of Paris-Nord, is on the research staff at the Centre de Recherche pour l'Etude et l'Observation des Conditions de Vie (CREDOC), and Director of the research program on 'Sociological Economics' granted by the Centre National de la Recherche Scientifique (CNRS). His other recent publication, co-edited with Jean-Claude Eicher, is *Economique de l'Education* (forthcoming).

Robert Michael is Associate Professor of Economics at Stanford University, USA, and is Director of the National Bureau of Economic Research, Palo Alto Office.

Gordon Tullock is University Distinguished Professor at Virginia Polytechnic Institute and State University, and is Editor of *Public Choice.* His recent publications include *Economics: A Way of Understanding Social Order* and *The New World of Economics: Explorations into the Human Experience*, both with Richard B. McKenzie.